Philadelphia
Freedoms

Philadelphia Freedoms

Black American Trauma, Memory, and Culture after King

Michael Awkward

TEMPLE UNIVERSITY PRESS PHILADELPHIA

For Patsy "Tank" Yaeger:
dazzling thinker,
wonderful friend

TEMPLE UNIVERSITY PRESS
Philadelphia, Pennsylvania 19122
www.temple.edu/tempress

Library of Congress Cataloging-in-Publication Data

Awkward, Michael.
    Philadelphia freedoms : black American trauma, memory, and
culture after King / Michael Awkward.
        pages cm
    Includes bibliographical references and index.
    ISBN 978-1-4399-0708-5 (cloth : alk. paper) —
ISBN 978-1-4399-0709-2 (pbk. : alk. paper) —
ISBN 978-1-4399-0710-8 (e-book)   1. American fiction—African
American authors—History and criticism.   2. African Americans—
Intellectual life.   3. Collective memory in literature.   4. Psychic
trauma in literature.   I. Title.
    PS153.N5A947 2013
    810.9′896073—dc23
                                                              2013016621

♾ The paper used in this publication meets the requirements of the
American National Standard for Information Sciences—Permanence
of Paper for Printed Library Materials, ANSI Z39.48-1992

Printed in the United States of America

2 4 6 8 9 7 5 3 1

Contents

Preface   vii

Acknowledgments   xiii

Introduction: Keeping the Past in Lively Memory after King:
The Traumatic Implications of Black American Oppression   1

1   "Philadelphia Did Not Burn": *Quelling Riots and Deferring Hoop
Dreams in the Age of the Militant Black Athlete*   23

2   Haunted Longings: *Nostalgic Black Musical Formulations
of Masculinity and the Patriarchal Family*   68

3   A "Genuinely Afro-American Narrative": Sarah Phillips
and the Politics of Black Textual Authenticity   108

4   Screening the (Beloved) Novel: *On Oprah Winfrey
and the Protocols of Adaptation*   159

Conclusion: No Longer at Home?   213

Notes   221

References   229

Index   241

Preface

The City of Brotherly Love serves as a rich, but often inhospitable, dreamscape for *Philadelphia Freedoms*. This study investigates four moments, drawn from the twentieth century's last decades, that demonstrate the continuing costs of the United States' denial to blacks of constitutionally guaranteed freedoms that were composed in, and are consonant with, the founding ethos of its First City. While reflecting major sociopolitical, cultural, and economic changes that were brought about in large part as a consequence of the efforts of Martin Luther King, Jr., these moments indicate that, at times, black American psychic investment in the rituals, ideologies, and institutions that bolster feelings of national citizenship are limited at best.

In each of these instances, ontological challenges associated with black American collective memory—the impulse to repress or keep alive its harshest aspects, the inability to disentangle personal misfortunes and racial traumas—arise at points of acute awareness of both the seductive promises of constitutionally guaranteed freedoms and the anguish that informs our experiences as a result of their lengthy denial. King, a major or implicit presence in the texts and events I have chosen to represent post–civil rights era dilemmas associated with Philadelphia, used deeply American forms of social agitation to draw attention to the inseparability of national rhetoric and racial agony. Fully committed to and enthralled by the nation's sustaining ideals, King exposed the depth and breadth of black suffering in hopes of pressuring elected and unelected officials alike to put an end to racist regional and national laws, policies, and practices, positioning himself, in the process, as the twentieth century's preeminent U.S. intimate stranger. Indeed, his forms of exacting patriotism and civil disobedience were both widely embraced by factions within the black community, including in Philadelphia,[1] and frequently challenged by figures from across ideological and racial divides who were skeptical about the effectiveness of his nonviolent tactics.

I began researching this book in fall 1996, soon after I finished *Scenes of Instruction*, a memoir that examines the enduring impact of my South Philly origins, including during my time as a graduate student at the University of Pennsylvania. Despite a vague but long-standing desire to return home as I was writing the memoir, I was ensconced in the academic and parenting cultures of Ann Arbor and had stopped seriously considering the possibility five years earlier when I turned down a job offer to return to Penn as a faculty member. But when the possibility was proposed again in 1995 and included a tenure-track job for my then-wife, I recklessly jumped at the opportunity and was devastated when the humanities dean informed me in May 1996 that the Personnel Committee of the School of Arts and Sciences faculty had voted against offering me the position, which he and other administrators had insisted verbally and in writing was forthcoming.

Overwhelmed by what felt like personal betrayal—I was, after all, an up-from-poverty native Philadelphian with a Penn Ph.D., an earlier job offer, and measurable professional success—and unsure how else to respond, I accepted the university's face-saving offer of a perk-filled visiting professorship. During that year, I read *Daily Pennsylvanian* articles that blandly reported the shocking departures of the dean of Arts and Sciences, ostensibly to update a twenty-year-old textbook, and of the provost simply because he was a candidate for college presidencies to which he ultimately was not named. These and numerous other astonishing events were too peculiar and painful to process during the first months of a traumatic homecoming, as I buttressed myself by beginning research on what I took to calling "my Philly book," which I conceived largely to legitimize my unwelcomed presence. The sweet romance of home finally dissipated after decades of school-, work-, and family-related sojourning, I resolved that if I survived this shame-filled period—the shame exacerbated by the sense of entrapment I felt when I was offered a full professorship at the end of that first year—I would never again be a resident of Philadelphia.

I first left the city in September 1973, a shy fourteen-year-old scholarship boy bound for a mysterious white New England boarding school. In truth, however, my journeying began years earlier, albeit within the boundaries of the vast city, when I was an inquisitive preteen deeply enamored of Independence Park, a history-saturated threshold dividing South Philly and Center City. During these journeys, I sought telling connections between urban dangers, the park's national treasures, and Center City's stark juxtapositions of junk jewelry and sun-sparkled diamonds. Despite the hold Philly maintained on me in part because of such juxtapositions, in the decades between my initial departure and my calamitous midlife return, I had grown to feel uneasy in my hometown. Having been compelled to reimagine myself in a bastion of rural whiteness that Boston's WILD R&B radio signal barely reached, the Philadelphia locations that had previously rooted me—the Italian Market, the shopping district in Center City, the playground where I had learned the intricacies of urban basketball and black masculinity—all came to feel disturbingly peculiar.

These touchstones, and the physical and metaphoric routes I had established as a child, felt inadequate to the demands of my new reality. With the prospects of a middle-class life readily available to me as a consequence of my prep school and, later, elite college matriculations, I remained acutely aware of myself, particularly when I journeyed home, as a poor black boy transgressing a series of discernible boundaries. Traveling through Independence Park when I returned home during vacations from academic cauldrons where I learned about the Civil War, I wondered why its well-scripted spokespersons hardly mentioned slavery. Still, I was thrilled to be walking on grounds trod by the Founding Fathers, whose achievements elevated the park to a stature equivalent to that of the pyramids, King Arthur's Round Table, and the Batcave.

Since I initially confronted it as an eleventh grader overwhelmed by the ferocity of the New England winter, I have been fascinated by Robert Frost's assertion in "The Death of the Hired Man" (1969) that home is a place of vexing obligation "where, when you have to go there, they have to take you in." Certainly, I have learned that if home is, indeed, debt-laden, the treatment received by those who return to it may be inhospitable enough to make their stay intensely painful and marked by animosity, fear, and self-doubt. I had worked diligently to transcend my impoverished origins via, among other things, a deep immersion in black American literature and the scholarship it has generated, but I was deemed troublingly deficient by the very institution where I had learned of its urgency and liberating possibilities. Having returned home and to Penn, I failed to wear the mask, disentangle inside and outside, and live duplicitously with my head in the lion's mouth, and as a consequence, I felt more bewildered as an Ivy League professor than I had as an insufficiently audacious South Philly ghetto child. Certainly, I lacked the insurrectionist gumption of inspiring black Philadelphians of my youth: Cecil Moore, whose protests forced Girard College, a well-funded educational haven for fatherless white boys, to admit blacks; Falaka Fattah, longtime head of the House of Umoja, who fought to eliminate black gang violence and other antisocial youth ills; radio station WDAS's Georgie Woods, the man with the goods to speak out on his daily show against segregation and the Vietnam War; Reverend Leon Sullivan, founder of the acclaimed job training program Opportunities Industrialization Centers; and the high school kids brave enough to face the wrath of Frank Rizzo's repressive policemen as they marched to the Board of Education Building to demand curricular change.

Eventually, after seven years of appreciable personal, professional, financial, and psychic damage, I was able, finally, to leave Penn, if not Philadelphia. Beginning in 2003, I commuted weekly for four years between Philly and Atlanta's Emory University and, finally, southeastern Michigan, until my older child went off to college and his sister joined me in Ann Arbor. Slowly, I began to recover my equilibrium and, during three sanity-recovering years at Emory, completed a book on R&B cover songs. And in the summer of 2007, a year after returning to the University of Michigan, overjoyed that the end of my eleven-year Philly fiasco was imminent, I wrote maniacally, exhilaratingly, about the "nappy-headed ho" controversy.

Even as I was writing about soul covers and Don Imus's faux pas, however, my abandoned Philly book nagged at me. Hoping to prove—primarily to myself—that my psychic wounds had begun to heal, and persuaded by emergent examinations within black American literary and cultural studies of the interconnectivity of traumatic individual and collective memory, including Hershini Bhana Young's idea that "the black body is . . . always collective as it remembers both its ghosts and that which has traumatically marked it as Other" (2005, 6), I realized that the real and fictive events that I had mulled over seem inextricable from my own blues journey home and, hence, might best be explicated via notions of black American collective trauma.

Still, I am not interested here in emphasizing connections between my own investments, choices, joys, and pain and those that I analyze extensively in the following pages. I do preface the chapters with brief recollections, which I believe suggest the interdependence of self and group, of individual and collective memory. These recollections, like the texts and events I offer to represent black American negotiations in the post–civil rights era of integrated institutions such as higher education, popular music, and professional sports, are necessarily fragmentary and incomplete. I hope that, along with the analyses of First City–centered texts and events that make up the bulk of this study, these autobiographical asides shed light on the dilemmas with which black Americans have continued to struggle, despite and because of the efforts of King and a variety of courageous people to actualize the nation's inspiriting principles—principles that were devised by flawed, idealistic men whose ghosts bump up against bruised, battered, stone-legged black Americans as they continue to roam the still-exhilarating streets of Philadelphia.[2]

Acknowledgments

I thank family members, friends, students, and colleagues at Michigan, Penn, and Emory who encouraged me to sharpen my thinking about memory, history, Martin Luther King, Jr., 76er history, James Brown, Philly Soul, R&B fathers, black American literary tradition, MOVE, Oprah, and the costs of remembered trauma. I resist the temptation to name all of these individuals, in part because I want to highlight the contributors who assisted me during the crucial final stages of what I hope is a fully realized, if still imperfect, exploration of the challenges of black American freedom.

My children, Cam, Leah, and Shan, chided me—at times gently and always lovingly—to finish so that I could stop torturing them with my excuses for not meeting self-imposed deadlines. The faith in my fortitude and abilities exhibited by my wife, LaSonia, is deeply heartening, and I hope that this book offers at least minimal evidence that that faith is justified. Three emerging scholars with ties to the University of Michigan, Meg Ahern, Paul Farber, and Jina Kim, provided immeasurable assistance in crucial ways: Meg by forcing me to continue to think about the ever-expanding boundaries of interdisciplinary trauma studies, Jina by uncovering sources that had fallen victim to my failing memory and poor citation practices, and Paul by providing me with a wealth of secondary material that helped buttress my claims. Last, I single out my daughter, Leah Awkward-Rich, who helped me put together the book's index; Rebecca Logan, who led me masterfully through the daunting process of final revision; and the staff of Temple University Press, especially Janet Francendese, whose patience, excitement, and brilliant stewardship helped me see this project through to its completion.

Introduction

Keeping the Past in Lively Memory after King

The Traumatic Implications of Black American Oppression

As part of his efforts to nationalize his largely Southern campaign of nonviolent resistance, and despite the objections of Philadelphia's civil rights leaders, Martin Luther King, Jr. lent his support in 1965 to the efforts to integrate Girard College. The boarding school, as prescribed in the will of its benefactor, served fatherless white boys exclusively until 1968. (Courtesy of the Philadelphia Evening Bulletin Collection, Special Collections Research Center, Temple University Libraries, Philadelphia, PA.)

I n an illuminating discussion of the origins of the field that was originally termed Afro-American or black studies, Julius Lester reminds us that the nascent enterprise

> was not invited into the curricula of colleges and universities because it was thought to have something new and vital to offer the humanistic body of knowledge. . . . It fought its way in through demonstrations in the sixties and seventies. Black studies was born because a man named [Martin Luther] King was assassinated. (Quoted in Cole 2004, 22)

The field of black studies originated in the rhetorically and physically confrontational late 1960s; its driving concern has been black American anguish stemming from the incontrovertible fact that "a race of people [was] brought into this country . . . to be slaves [and] . . . begins in a group experience of suffering and agony, of struggle and survival" (Lester, quoted in Cole 2004, 24). Having risen from ashes strewn across the United States during riotous black inner-city responses to King's assassination and increasingly ineffectual Great Society initiatives, black studies, an outgrowth of an urge for mainstream institutional respect, recognition, and representation, has been associated with the most radical accounts of the black American condition. As a result, King's generative place within a field created in response to his death is often overlooked, even when scholars explore issues that propelled King's agitation for black American freedom, which he explained in masterfully delivered speeches and well-crafted articles and books that illuminate his religious, philosophical, political, and sociocultural beliefs.

Perspectives such as Lester's[1] compel us to consider if and how the views of King, whom August Meier insists operated "not only as an organ of communication with the Establishment and majority white public opinion, but as something of a bridge between the activist and more traditional or 'conservative' civil rights groups" (1992, 218), are embodied in the field's investigative emphases and institutional practices. Such investigations are possible despite the fact that, as Fabio Rojas asserts in *From Black Power to Black Studies*, students and professors working to establish centers of black scholarship viewed their efforts as sharp departures from King's integrationist endeavors:

> The push for black studies revolved around black intellectuals, student groups, and the debates within the civil rights movement concerning black power and cultural nationalism. Viewing the civil rights movement as a limited and underwhelming effort, nationalists

adopted a more radical position, demanding the creation of institutions specifically dedicated to serving the African American community. (2007, 5)

Notwithstanding the urgency of such demands, the programs that were ultimately the most impactful—those with longevity, records of significant scholarly productivity, and a modicum of institutional power—"serve[d] the entire university" of which they were a part, offering "courses taken by both black and white students" taught by faculty using methodological assumptions that propelled disciplines such as history, sociology, English, art, and political science, many of whom produced analyses that engaged the most sophisticated findings of these disciplines. The entity that Rojas designates as "academic black studies," then, is, in actuality, a field with "extremely porous boundaries" (2007, 100).

In ways that demonstrate his analytical acuity and political practicality, King vividly describes urban riots as wrenching expressions of black pain. Recognizing that fire-this-time machinations undermined his negotiating ability on behalf of the black American freedom struggle, King calculated the political costs of rioting and vengeance-driven forms of black militancy. Ultimately, he concludes, racial violence and its threat were illogical, ineffectual, and counterproductive:

> A violent revolution on the part of American blacks would find no sympathy and support from the white population and very little from the majority of the Negroes themselves. This is no time for romantic illusions and empty philosophical debates about freedom. This is the time for action. What is needed is a strategy for change, a tactical program that will bring the Negro into the mainstream of American life as quickly as possible. So far, this has only been offered by the nonviolent movement. (1986f, 249)

Condemning rioting both tactically and philosophically, King deems the isolationist stance of the younger blacks unlikely to increase their sociopolitical, economic, or cultural power in a white-dominated United States. While recognizing Black Power as an invigorating "reaction to the psychological indoctrination that led to the creation of the perfect slave" (1986g, 580), he considers Black Power "a nihilistic philosophy" premised on the belief "that American society is so hopelessly corrupt and enmeshed in evil that there is no possibility of salvation from within" (580). Its adherents, in King's view, were convinced "of the inability of the Negro to win and . . . the infinitude of the ghetto" (584–585). Recognizing that lifting "the Negro out of the economic depression caused by centuries of deprivation" (586) requires more than frustration-fueled bravado, he implores blacks to join his disciplined mass force that had already secured significant black American sociopolitical and economic progress.

King's writings test his commitments against influential scholarly, religious, and sociopolitical arguments. These writings, which social historian David Steigerwald insists "blended the spirit of the preacher with the thoughtful, reasoned analysis of the scholar," reveal the efforts of an intellectual who "returned to his roots with a Ph.D. from an illustrious program at a major northern university steeped in the major theological doctrines of his day and well schooled in Western philosophy" (1995, 41). King measured his ideas of social advancement against sometimes diametrically opposed perspectives, including the era's preeminent theorist of black identity, Frantz Fanon. Recognizing the civil rights leader as a scholar of the psychodynamics of American race relations encourages us to consider his ruminations as serious commentary on formulations that were being deemed more persuasive and usable assessments of black American racial pain than King's by figures whose insights would go on to propel black studies.

In "Where Do We Go From Here?" King disputes the claims of Fanon, whose *The Wretched of the Earth* offers a blueprint for U.S. "proponents of Black Power who argued passionately about the validity of violence and riots." Rejecting Fanon's assertion "that violence is a psychologically healthy and tactically sound method for the oppressed," King claims that black rioters manifest "a desire for self-destruction, a suicidal longing," and insists that "nowhere have the riots won any concrete improvement such as have the organized protest demonstration" (1986g, 591). And in the following formulation of black Americans' peculiar challenges, he questions the efficacy of both Fanon's view of cathartic violence and Black Power's embrace of sociopolitical marginality:

> The Negro's greatest dilemma is that in order to be healthy he must accept his ambivalence. The Negro is the child of two cultures—Africa and America. The problem is that in the search for wholeness all too many Negroes seek to embrace only one side of their natures. Some, seeking to reject their heritage, are ashamed of their color, ashamed of black art and music, and determine what is beautiful and good by the standards of white society. They end up frustrated and without cultural roots. Others seek to reject everything American and to identify totally with Africa, even to the point of wearing

African clothes. But this approach leads also to frustration because the American Negro is not an African. The old Hegelian synthesis still offers the best answer to many of life's dilemmas. The American Negro is neither totally African nor totally Western. He is Afro-American, a true hybrid, a combination of two cultures. (1986g, 588)

King situates black ontological ambivalence within Hegelian dialectics, echoing what Rojas identifies as the "only . . . nearly undisputed canonical" text in black studies (Rojas 2007, 201), W.E.B. Du Bois's *The Souls of Black Folk*, in his contention that black U.S. identity is essentially interstitial, an amalgam of African and American ideals. Identifying the black American psyche as fundamentally bifurcated—"an American, a Negro; two souls, two thoughts, two unreconciled strivings; two warring ideals in one dark body" (Du Bois 1989, 45)—Du Bois's much-discussed theory of double consciousness emphasizes synthesis:

The history of the American Negro is the history of . . . this longing . . . to merge his double self into a better and truer self. In this merging he wishes neither of the older selves to be lost. He would not Africanize America, for America has too much to teach the world and Africa. He would not bleach his Negro soul in a flood of white Americanism, for he knows that Negro blood has a message for the world. He simply wishes to make it possible for a man to be both a Negro and an American, without being cursed and spit upon by his fellows, without having the doors of Opportunity closed roughly in his face. (45–46)

The black self figured here, the victim of an internal war, is fearful of being "torn asunder" (46) by the psychic strife that results from living in a democratic nation whose doors remain "closed roughly." According to King, however, who urged his followers to accede to being—in Du Bois's words—"cursed and spit upon" to dramatize racial hatred, black American integration (in at least two senses of the word) is possible only when we locate "that creative minority of the concerned from the ofttimes apathetic [white] majority, and together mov[e] . . . toward that colorless power that we all need for security and justice" (1986g, 589).

In light of these formulations, which emphasize the warring impulses endemic to being both what King calls "heirs of a past of rope, fire and murder" and inheritors of "the destiny of America" (1986g, 588), I propose "traumatized black subjectivity" as a way to conceptualize post–civil rights performances of identity that reflect both the complexities of the black American present and its relationship to the "past of rope, fire and murder." This concept encourages attentiveness to a pain-filled history, certainly, as well as to the largely still-deferred American Dream despite its availability to a supremely talented, industrious, or exceptionally lucky few. More than four decades after King's death, our era is marked, on the one hand, by unprecedented access to the most mainstream institutions and, on the other, by the bewildering celebration by hip-hop culture of what King terms "the infinitude of the ghetto." Our conditions and struggles have morphed to such an extent that few of us may still believe, as King did, that awareness of the sources and nature of black pain could compel "the whole of American society [to] take . . . a new turn toward greater economic [and other forms of] justice" (1986g, 586). Other factors are now at work than those that were apparent when King expressed these views, some of which can be investigated fruitfully in the context of notions of racial trauma.

I reference trauma here because of my sense that black American identities were and continue to be formed in response to what Lester termed, in a passage cited at the beginning of this Introduction, a "group experience of suffering and agony, of struggle and survival." I employ extant theories of trauma to examine black American identity as a cultural formation, analyzing black American conditions and behaviors as part of already rich conversations about such concepts as memory, space, class, gender, race, and nation. Trauma studies have flourished during the last two decades, even if scholars have been generally inattentive to black American suffering. Indeed, the psychic upheavals resulting from slavery and Jim Crow are parenthetical asides and afterthoughts in works such as *Trauma and Recovery*, where Judith Herman waits until the afterword to address "the legacy of [U.S.] slavery" (1992, 243). Nonetheless, her insights can be used to enhance our discussions of black American suffering and the implications of its historical denial. For example, when Herman insists that "without some form of public acknowledgment and restitution, all social relationships remain contaminated by the corrupt dynamics of denial and secrecy" (243), she confirms the perspectives of reparations advocates concerning the benefits of seeking atonement for the national government's sanctioning of slavery and Jim Crow. Additionally, her reading of reactions to the Rodney King verdict[2] indicates how and why unhealed black American trauma manifests itself as and through violence:

> The unhealed racial divisions of our country create an ongoing potential for violence. The worst civil disturbance of the past few years, the Los Angeles riots, were provoked by the failure of the justice

system to hold armed white police officers accountable for the severe beating of an unarmed man. Within the African-American community, it was widely understood that such abuses were political crimes, carried out as part of a systematic pattern of racial oppression. The issue at trial was whether the larger society would condone the most flagrant of these human rights abuses. The responsibility to bear witness fell to the jury in the criminal trial. In their refusal to see the crime that was documented before their eyes, we can recognize the familiar defenses of denial, distancing, and dissociation [that often accompany traumatic events]. . . . [And] it was this betrayal, not simply the violence of the police, that unleashed a communal outbreak of murderous rage. (243–244)

Herman's analysis of "prolonged, repeated trauma" (74) and her association of this condition with "forms of tyranny" suffered by "hostages, political prisoners, battered women, and slaves," all of whom "remarked upon the captor's . . . desire for total control over another person" (75, 76), encourages fruitful consideration of black American pain alongside, for example, the Holocaust and 9/11.

Both the hesitation of trauma scholars to engage black American pain and the potential benefits of its investigation are evident in an interview included in *Writing History, Writing Trauma* by Dominick LaCapra, a noted theorist of Holocaust historiography. Concerned about the avoidance by trauma scholars of the subject of U.S. racism, his Israel interrogator, Amos Goldberg, asks LaCapra to address whether "the overemphasis on the Holocaust in the popular culture, the politics, and the economics of America is some kind of denial of the traumas with which America is directly involved" (2001, 171). After acknowledging that "traumas (such as that of the African Americans and the Native Americans) are still relevant there, and America may be blinded to its present by emphasizing the traumas of others in the past" (171), LaCapra says of U.S. trauma studies' race problem:

Contemporary problems related to the heritage of slavery and the treatment of American Indians can . . . be obscured by a focus on the Holocaust. . . . [W]hy, on the Mall in Washington, [do] we have a Holocaust museum but no museum dedicated to slavery or to the American Indians[?] After all, they were our victims, and we were part of the force that tried to combat those who victimized the Jews in Europe. . . . The obvious answer is that people do indeed attempt to obscure or displace certain problems by focusing on other problems.

> This can happen; the point is to recognize it and try to resist it.
> (171–172)

Given the magnitude of the Holocaust, rather than condemn the field's Eurocentric biases—a tactic that black studies used to its advantage, especially in its institutional infancy—we would do well to heed LaCapra's advice "to avoid a displacement of competitive victimology onto competitive theory," (2001, 174) as he characterizes the possible recriminations of such a critique. Hoping to apply largely Holocaust-based formulations of trauma in a black studies context, I seek what "is significant for research into other areas, including . . . issues such as slavery" (174). Recognizing that while plantations and death camps were quite different sites of subjugation, trauma studies has the potential to assist black studies, in part because "slavery, like the Holocaust . . . , presents . . . problems of traumatization, severe oppression, a divided heritage, the question of a founding trauma, [and] the forging of identities in the present" (174). In the following section, I consider the fruitfulness of the formulations of trauma studies for an investigation of black American collective pain.

Judith Herman characterizes traumatic events as "extraordinary" in that

> they overwhelm the ordinary human adaptations to life. . . . They confront human beings with the extremities of helplessness and terror, and evoke the responses of catastrophe. . . . [T]he common denominator of psychological trauma is a feeling of "intense fear, helplessness, loss of control, and threat of annihilation." (1992, 33)

Because "traumatic symptoms have a tendency to become disconnected from their source and to take on a life of their own," they create in its sufferers a type of "fragmentation, tear[ing] apart a complex system of self-protection that normally functions in an integrated fashion" (Herman 1992, 34). Even "after the danger is past," Herman writes,

> traumatized people . . . cannot resume the normal course of their lives, for the trauma repeatedly interrupts. It is as if time stops at the moment of trauma. The traumatic moment becomes encoded in an abnormal form of memory, which breaks spontaneously into consciousness, both as flashbacks during waking states and as traumatic nightmares during sleep. Small, seemingly insignificant reminders can also evoke these memories, which often return with all the vividness and emotional force of the original event. Thus, even normally

safe environments may come to feel dangerous, for the survivor can never be assured that she will not encounter some reminder of the trauma. (37)

How might we extrapolate from Judith Herman's formulations an understanding of black Americans' attempts to grapple with their ancestors' mistreatment and their own sense of an incompatibility between their national and racial heritages? Our efforts can be enhanced by LaCapra's discussion of traumatic memory, which forces its sufferers to feel that "when the past is uncontrollably relived . . . , there were no difference between it and the present. Whether or not the past is reenacted or repeated in its precise literality, one feels as if one were back there reliving the event, and the distance between here and there, then and now, collapses" (2001, 89). Explorations of the role played by traumatizing events in the constitution of black American identities may enrich black studies in ways that are similar to Herman's efforts vis-à-vis the diagnosis and treatment of sexually and psychologically abused women and LaCapra's interrogation of "the problem of historical understanding" (1994, 1). Such emphases may enable us to examine more cogently "the Negro's greatest dilemma": constituting black American identity in response to the slow-changing face of racial oppression and nagging feeling that black Americans are constantly reliving the nightmarish conditions and irrepressible pain that marked slavery and Jim Crow.

Because contemporary black American identities were forged in response to psychic, physical, and spiritual pain associated with slavery and Jim Crow, overidentification with the victims of these regimes may be unavoidable, and psychic distance a luxury of the naïve and the strategically misinformed. LaCapra supplies a grammar of traumatic responses in the context of which the politics and performances of post–civil rights black identities can be evaluated. Indeed, the protagonists of the chapters that follow understand post–civil rights era challenges (and, hence, themselves) as inextricably bound—in their own estimations or in those of people who shaped their social, cultural, and political existence—to murderous antebellum and Jim Crow dilemmas.

In *Philadelphia Freedoms*, I position one particular traumatic incident—King's assassination—as compelling generations of black Americans to feel as if we are "back there reliving the event," as if "the distance between here and there, then and now, collapses." A violent repudiation of the nation's evolving racial politics and policies, King's assassination caused black American cultural trauma whose familiarity—the white cultural logic of slavery, Jim Crow, and countless acts of white brutality; its perpetrators' obvious intention to halt hard-won racial reformation—situates post–civil rights black American identities as inherently interstitial. These identities are already formed and perpetually in process: between the status of "surrogate victim" of racial barbarity and the distanced observer of its still-evident deformations, compelled to remember (and, sometimes, to see recent events as motivated by the very evil that produced our centuries-long dehumanization), yet striving to prevent active remembrance from sullying our access to contemporary freedoms.

The phenomenon's most extensive exploration to date, Ron Eyerman's *Cultural Trauma: Slavery and the Formation of African American Identity*, argues that "the formation of an African American identity" is connected directly to post-emancipation reactions to slavery as a "primal scene." For Eyerman, cultural trauma "refers to a dramatic loss of identity and meaning, a tear in the social fabric, affecting a group of people that has achieved some degree of cohesion. In this sense, the trauma need not necessarily be felt by everyone in a community or experienced directly by any or all" (2001, 1, 2). Further, he insists that "trauma links past to present through representations and imagination," suggesting that events like King's assassination often are not experienced directly, but "through newspapers, radio, or television" and conversations concerning social identities. Since black American identity is forged via "'a meaning struggle,' a grappling with an event [or events], identifying the 'nature of the pain, the nature of the victim and the attribution of responsibility'" (3), cultural trauma must be seen as a psychosocial "process that aims to reconstitute or reconfigure a collective identity through collective representation" (4).

Rather than emphasize agency in post-emancipation engagements of the trauma of slavery, I am interested in the apparent inescapability of cultural trauma by subsequent generations, who remain vulnerable, because of their "overidentification" with the anguish of ancestors that they encounter through representations, to a phenomenon that LaCapra terms "retraumatization." Concerned, like Eyerman, with trauma's "social dimension," Kai Erikson, an authority on the social consequences of catastrophic events, insists that the phenomenon "be understood as resulting from a constellation of life experiences as well as from a discrete happening, from a persisting condition as well as from an acute event" (1994, 185). American slavery and Jim Crow were not "discrete happening[s]" but clusters of experiences whose complexity, duration, and inescapability helped shape black American behaviors, presuppositions, and attitudes. These oppressive institutions, then, created "assemblies of traumatized persons" who shared with one another and their prodigy "a mood, an ethos—a group culture" that made them feel as if they "were invited to gather in a quarter set aside for the disfranchised, a ghetto for the unattached" (185, 186).

The attributes of traumatized communities—numbness, estrangement, detachment, ghetto habitation, and marginalization—are manifested by large numbers of black Americans, whose despondency and rage create intergenerational "ghetto[es] for the unattached" that become what Erikson calls "a cushion for pain, . . . a context for intimacy, [and a] . . . repository for binding traditions" (1994, 188).[3] Bound by a language and experience of trauma—and by modes of behavior and reasoning forged over time from scraps of African and American cultural practices—membership in "corrosive communities" is in large part determined by our responses to painful events that have placed them on the "fault lines" "divid[ing] the people affected by the event from the people spared. . . . Those not touched try to distance themselves from those touched, almost as if they are escaping something spoiled, something contaminated, something polluted" (189). To see black American culture as corrosive is to recognize race as a site of biological—as well as social, political, religious, economic, and cultural—warfare. The frustrations experienced by black Americans consequently work their way "so thoroughly into the grain of the affected community that they . . . dominate its imagery and its sense of self, [and] govern the way its members relate to one another." The shared experience of the ongoing trauma of blackness constitutes "a source of kinship," creating, in Erikson's words, "social climates, communal moods, that come to dominate a group's spirit" (190). The manifestations by black Americans of such a spirit are what I refer to here as "traumatized black subjectivity."

As Maurice Halbwachs insists, "There exists a collective memory and social frameworks for memory; it is to the degree that our individual thought places itself in these frameworks and participates in this memory that it is capable of recollection" (1992, 38). In describing the process of remembering, Halbwachs suggests that certain categories of modern people

> are free to choose from the past the period into which we wish to immerse ourselves. Whereas in our present society we occupy a definite position and are subject to the constraints that go with it, memory gives us the illusion of living in the midst of groups which do not imprison us, which impose themselves on us only so far and so long as we accept them. (50)[4]

Invariably, however, to be a self-conscious black American is to confront the weight of prejudices used to justify physical, spiritual, and psychological violence against one's people, to experience confinement as a persistent historical reality, and to understand that there is no previous period in U.S. history in which we can immerse ourselves to escape a collective subjugation. Hence, many black Americans of the post–civil rights era find themselves perpetually in the thralls of "postmemory," a term coined by Marianne Hirsch to describe "the relationship of children of survivors of cultural or collective trauma to the experiences of their parents, experiences that they 'remember' only as the stories and images with which they grew up, but that are so powerful, so monumental, as to constitute memories in their own right" (1999, 8). Bereft of comparatively significant personal or generational stories, "those who grow up dominated by narratives that preceded their birth" (8) recognize their own belatedness, often experiencing their own lives—demonstrably less besieged than those of their predecessors—as nearly as structurally inhibited, as well as physically and psychically perilous, as those of their forebears. Certainly, black Americans plagued by postmemory do not feel, as Halbwachs suggests, that "the most painful aspects of yesterday's society are forgotten because constraints are felt only so long as they operate and because, by definition, a past constraint has ceased to be operative" (1992, 51). (Indeed, black Americans are anything but immune to dilemmas implicit in King's notion of hybridity, as they are always cognizant of—and perhaps, as our responses to the beating of Rodney King and the death of Trayvon Martin suggest, still traumatized by—the painful presence of the starkly brutal racial past.) What LaCapra describes as the process of working through the traumatic past rarely is fully completed by black Americans, for whom the jagged grain of history remains unsmoothed.

Precisely because of its aggressively social nature, black Americans are unable to manipulate memory as freely as Halbwachs claims modern citizens are generally capable. Specifically, he argues that

> the various groups that compose society are capable at every moment of reconstructing the past. But . . . they most frequently distort that past in the act of reconstructing it. . . . [S]ociety can live only if there is a sufficient unity of outlooks among the individuals and groups comprising it. The multiplicity and diversity of human groups result from an increase in needs as well as from the intellectual and organizational faculties of the society. . . . [S]ociety tends to erase from its memory all that might separate individuals, or that might distance groups from each other. (1992, 182–183)

Emphasizing the impulse to distort and forget aspects of the past that do not jibe with a group's self-definition, Halbwachs describes society as an organism bent on its own survival whose bidding we do because we crave the benefits that accrue from our association with it—the security of belonging, a tangible historical place, ontological presence, and allies—even if that choice requires the radical reconstruction and distortion of the past. Belonging requires, in part, a disremembering of and disregard for differences, enabling people to satisfy the society's "need for continuity" by forging a cohesive whole out of "the multiplicity and diversity of human groups" (183).

However, constructing the past as a site of expansive racial pain is essential to efforts to forge an aggrieved black community, a collectivity that requires a reckoning with their implications for our contemporary place in the larger U.S. bent on seeing that pain reduced to sheer irrelevance. Hence, at times, it is deeply disconcerting for black Americans to participate in a national culture that aggressively downplays the significance of slavery and Jim Crow precisely because these epochs—and the lingering pain they signify—"distance groups from each other." As a consequence, many blacks struggling with the psychic strife of postmemory are compelled to ponder: How precisely do we embrace *both* metanarratives of U.S. exceptionalism—its compelling stories of democratic self-making, its glorious discourse of unparalleled opportunity, its seductive rhetoric of manifest destiny—*and* countermemories emphasizing our people's baleful treatment on its hallowed shores? What, for blacks, are the psychic benefits of American citizenship? How do we take pride in subversive tea party revolts, Jeffersonian rhetorical flights, and U.S. democracy's celebrated victories when our story had to be erased and our pain—our very humanity—discounted and denied in the service of national unity? To forge a sense of national belonging, must we strategically forget, misremember, or reinvent the past as we wish it had been?

A profound sense of traumatized subjectivity limits black Americans' ability to forget our historical degradation and to rely, as Halbwachs suggests is possible, on "reason or intelligence that chooses among the store of recollections, eliminates some of them, and arranges the others according to an order conforming with our ideas of the moment" (Halbwachs 1992, 183). Indeed, black Americans' "ideas of the moment" seem never to stray far from the subject of our historical oppression, and we resent our still-marginal place in a nation bent on "eras[ing] from its memory all that might . . . distance groups from each other," particularly those "ancient representations"—slave ships and heavy chains; Harriet Tubman's underground journeys to and from Southern killing fields; whipped, raped, charred, castrated, and lynched bodies; Emmett Till's shocking funereal face;[5] flesh-piercing fire hoses and ferocious dogs; Rodney King's surreptitiously filmed lynching—that "assume collective form" (Halbwachs 1992, 183) and, hence, help define the contours of contemporary black American identities.

One representative effort to forge national consent by condemning attempts to think through the contemporary implications of "ancient representations" is Arthur Schlesinger's 1992 book, *The Disuniting of America*. Worried that the United States is in danger of becoming "not a nation of individuals at all but a nation of groups" and that ethnicity is seen as "the defining experience for most Americans," Schlesinger insists that such thinking "reverses the historic theory of America as one people—the theory that has thus far managed to keep American society whole" (16). Trumpeting the notion of *E pluribus unum* as one of the nation's singular accomplishments, he nonetheless acknowledges racism as "the glaring contradiction of American ideals and the still crippling disease of American life" (14). Despite his awareness of racism's "crippling" effects, Schlesinger professes to being taken aback by the "cult of ethnicity [that] has arisen . . . [to] denounce the idea of a melting pot, to challenge the concept of 'one people,' and to protect, promote, and perpetuate separate ethnic and racial communities" (15).

Bemoaning our failure following the civil rights movement to forge what Halbwachs calls "a sufficient unity of outlooks" among the staggering "multiplicity and diversity of human groups" (1992, 183), Schlesinger insists that the United States has been weakened by ethnic groups who fail to see making sense of and taking pride in cultural and historical differences as psychically healthy alternatives to the strategic forgetfulness demanded of the dispossessed by the nation's forces of conservation. According to the famed historian, developing national pride is essential for black Americans who need to embrace the "American creed": "the cluster of ideas, institutions, and habit" that all U.S. citizens share, including "the ideals of the essential dignity and equality of all human beings, of inalienable rights to freedom, justice, and opportunity" (1992, 27). Developing faith in this creed is a challenge for the dispossessed, Schlesinger admits, largely because the nation's "noble ideals had been pronounced as if for all Americans, yet in practice they applied only to white people" (38). But because he privileges the rhetoric of national unity over a consideration of the psychological impact of racially motivated scorn and violent rebuke, he insists that all of its citizens must establish psychic allegiance to the United States and unquestioned faith in its creed, or risk being denied "the means of improvement and achievement and . . . the opportunities of national life" (94).

Schlesinger's perspectives notwithstanding, is it possible to imagine self-respecting notions of black American identity that wholeheartedly embrace narratives of national allegiance, given that the United States' governing ideal, "we the people," explicitly excludes those blacks for whom the indignities of slavery and Jim Crow continue to resonate? Such questions haunt the lives of self-aware black residents of history-saturated sites of national commemoration such as Philadelphia. Both longtime Philadelphians and visitors of African descent to the First City continually bump up against the legacies of Jefferson, Franklin, Washington, and numerous other white men who forged the nation's still-invigorating concept of freedom in response to oppressive British colonial rule while insisting that black men and women remain enslaved. The hybrid nature of black American identity as King describes it requires that we luxuriate in the nation's accomplishments and abhor the United States' baleful treatment of our forebears simultaneously. Hence, a profoundly disconcerting sense of national belonging is experienced with alarming regularity by black Philadelphians confronting the nation's investment in both New World freedom and old-fashioned slavery.

Prompted by historian Gary Nash's sumptuous study of contested memories of Philadelphia's history, I position myself alongside "individuals and groups outside of the circle of cultural arbiters try[ing] to gain a claim on the past by resisting 'official' truth and telling different stories" (2002, 12). Insisting that "people have seen their history through a variety of different lenses—depending on . . . what experiences, ideas, and values they bring to the act of looking back" (12)—Nash encourages interpretations of the past that "see the world clearly in both short and long perspectives." Such interpretations enable readers

> to see the past as it was experienced differently by Philadelphians of various stations in life; to see how our understanding of bygone eras depends partly on what historical materials were collected, preserved, and exhibited; to look at artifacts, documents, and paintings from different angles of vision. (13)

Nash's notion of bifocal investigation, inspired by one of favorite son Ben Franklin's First City accomplishments, resonates with Du Bois's theory that black Americans are gifted with "second sight in this American world" of stark racial marginalization and "unreconciled strivings" (Du Bois 1989, 45). Because black Philadelphians and other U.S. citizens struggle to embrace "short and long perspectives" on white hegemony, the central concern of black American history is the nation's persistent thwarting of blacks' efforts to satisfy what Du Bois calls "this longing . . . to merge his double self into a better and truer self" (45) and King describes as a pain-filled attempt to "accept his ambivalence" (1986g, 588). Up to and including King's messianic efforts, the push for access to "the doors of Opportunity" whose entrance would enable blacks to be "both a Negro and an American" led to us "being cursed and spit upon by his [and her] fellows" both literally and metaphorically. Largely because of King, racially motivated acts of cursing and spitting on blacks came to be seen as the aberrant behavior of white racists. But the memory of the state-sanctioning of broken bones, shattered lives, gashed psyches, and murder lingers, informing blacks' often-conflicted ideas of our national place.

Influential blacks have referenced Philadelphia's symbolic significance in highlighting constitutional commitments to freedom that still had not been extended to their people. Note, for example, Frederick Douglass's 1870 proclamation in Philadelphia following the passage of the Fifteenth Amendment, which guaranteed that black Americans would enjoy the same constitutional rights as whites: "I am no longer a black man . . . but a citizen." However, instead of joining Douglass in the celebration of this legislation, some whites launched "a sickening attack on the day's festive procession," transforming this moment of celebration into another painful episode in "black Philadelphians' long historical travail—their Philadelphia history" of having to "face . . . violence when they claimed equal right to public spaces" (Nash 2002, 259). Nearly two decades later, Douglass insisted that while they wanted to put "the nightmare of life in chains . . . behind them," "colored people of this country are bound to keep the past in lively memory till justice shall be done them" (quoted in Nash 2002, 313). Douglass's later remarks suggest the "lively" bifocal nature of black Philadelphian memory, which enables the discernment of "contradictions, ambiguities, and paradoxes" that "now streak" "the Philadelphia story" (319).

If the histories of fabled locations such as Philadelphia are always strategic inventions, we would do well, in this era of expansive possibility, to embrace the challenges inherent in the observation that history is befuddling in its incompleteness. If we can never know or tell the whole truth about the past, we can certainly be honest about, and make keen intellectual use of, the predilections that inspire our choices of which erased or marginalized events to highlight from our self-consciously demarcated vantage points. And we can acknowledge that efforts to highlight underexplored dimensions of metropolitan and national events are motivated by a desire to remake the past in an image that is amenable to a view of history as contested terrain.

Philadelphia Freedoms, which takes as its subject an eclectic mix of events and texts from each of the last four decades of the twentieth century, explores contestations over the meanings of black identity that occurred at a time when freedom seemed finally to be discernible on—to borrow a phrase from Andrea Lee's *Sarah Phillips*—"the endlessly beckoning horizon" ([1984] 1993, 15). Mirroring the messiness of traumatic cultural memory, on the one hand, and, on the other, the continued urgency felt by black Philadelphians in particular and black Americans generally "to keep the past in lively memory till justice shall be done," I acknowledge the veracity of Halbwachs's claim that we are

> incapable of mentally reproducing all the events in their detail, the diverse parts of the tale in proportion to the whole, and the whole series of traits, indications, descriptions, propositions, and reflections that progressively inscribe a figure or a landscape in the mind of the reader, which allow him to penetrate to the heart of the matter. (1992, 46)

Cognizant at such moments that "a gap continues to exist between the vague recollection of today and the impression . . . which we know was vivid, precise, and strong," we also cannot fully "recall the mental state in which we found ourselves" when we first encountered books, films, and songs. Hoping "to relive the memory," eventually we come to understand that what remains from past encounters are decontextualized parts, textual scraps, imagistic snatches and flashes, to which we can bring coherence only by "forc[ing] them to enter into the framework of the present" (Halbwachs 1992, 46).

Because it is informed by such perspectives, what I offer in the following pages is decidedly not a history of black Philadelphia in the post–civil rights era. Rather, it is an investigation of carefully selected episodes and flashes of pages, lines, and visual memory that I take to be representative of efforts to shape, broaden, or challenge the contours of black American identities in the wake of our first encounters with full citizenship on U.S. shores. Unlike Douglass, who offered stirring First City notions of a raceless American manhood, scores of blacks have responded to their unprecedented access to U.S. educational, business, cultural, and political institutions by emphasizing what Henry Louis Gates, Jr. has called our "signifying . . . black difference" (1988, xxii). That choice, while confounding and ill-advised according to figures like Schlesinger, indicates, at the very least, that Du Bois's concept of double consciousness and King's notion of hybridity continue to signify the status of black Americans as perpetual outsiders if assimilation—at least psychic occupation of the national center—requires a devaluation of aspects of a culture constructed to protect its adherents from the pain of racial discrimination.

Philadelphia Freedoms does not seek to install an inherently psychoanalytical concept, "traumatized black subjectivity," as the point of departure and primary object of black studies. It does, however, pursue illuminating connections between this concept and presuppositions that inform scholarship in this expansive field. Specifically, it brings together findings from a variety of modes of black critical inquiry in an effort to construct broadly persuasive examinations of texts and cultural events connected to Philadelphia, and to topics such as place, class, memory, and gender that have enlivened humanistic discourses over the past two decades and, in turn, have the potential to inspire even more cogent work. The City of Brotherly Love serves as a beacon of hope because of its exalted place in the nation's history, even if, for blacks, it has not always proven to be a site—in Doreen Massey's words—of "stability, oneness, and security" and its meanings are formed "by the juxtaposition and co-presence there of particular sets of social interrelations, and by the effects which that juxtaposition and co-presence produce" (1994, 168–169).

As a native South Philadelphian in exile, as it were, I am compelled by what Lucy Lippard has identified as "the lure of the local." According to Lippard, this lure

> is the pull of place that operated on each of us, exposing our politics and our spiritual legacies. It is the geographical component of the psychological need to belong somewhere, one antidote to a prevailing alienation. The lure of the local is that undertone to modern life that connects it to the past we know so little and the future we are aimlessly concocting. (1997, 7)

"A place called home" by the nation and its citizens, Philadelphia signifies democratic possibility and, for me, unconditional familial affection. However, it is also, for black Americans—and nostalgic black sons and daughters like me—a terrain of sometimes shockingly undemocratic treatment; Philadelphia has caused pronounced levels of racial insecurity precisely because blacks' mistreatment has occurred mere blocks from locations where exalted national promises were composed and will echo in perpetuity. The city's status as home and not-home, as a dreamscape of liberty forever deferred, informs our responses to the symbols, episodes, and recollected fragments that others have held to be uncompromisingly dear before and after the civil rights movement.

The First City's name derives from *philia*, a Greek word signifying the promotion of well-being when assisting or befriending others. Philadelphia certainly has not always lived up to its name in its treatment of black Americans. In this study, I explore precisely how that history of non-*philia* behavior resonates in response to efforts to describe or perform post–civil rights black identities in circumstances where Philadelphia's character is central. Because of its place in the nation's zeitgeist, the First City is a critical site of traumatized black subjectivity, a sense of racial being that, to reference the influential theorist of trauma Cathy Caruth, can be described as the "peculiar and sometimes uncanny way in which catastrophic events seem to repeat themselves for those [blacks] who have passed through them." Often, "these repetitions . . . appear as the possession of some people by a sort of fate, a series of painful events to which they are subjected, and which seem to be entirely outside their wish or control" (Caruth 1996, 2). The texts and events I have chosen to represent both Philadelphia as a fraught site and black subjectivity as a form of traumatic possession encode the pain of belonging and not-belonging simultaneously, of freedom promised but conditional at best and always under threat. They communicate the provisional nature of post–civil rights freedom as well as black Americans' struggle to achieve a secure grasp on its constitutional promise. Seemingly random and unrelated, these moments contain within them both the roots of black American terror and, implicitly, like all narratives of trauma, the means to effect its transcendence.

Like Samuel Otter's *Philadelphia Stories*, which focuses on people for whom "Philadelphia was the place where, in concentrated form, a peculiarly American experiment was being conducted" (2010, 8), this study examines texts and events where the promise of American freedom is placed alongside the First City's status as a site of black American oppression. Hence, it grapples with the United States' dogged refusal to actualize the rhetoric of brotherhood, religious tolerance, and representative government that originated in Philadelphia, pondering what it has meant to traverse such a sacred national place after the successes of the King-led civil rights movement, where the term *place*, which Tim Cresswell insists "has been rejuvenated by the humanistic and radical reactions to spatial analysis," signifies "a meaningful location" (1996, 13, 7).

For black Americans Philadelphia has been a location that has meant—among numerous other things—freedom's haunting denial, along with the emergence of the strife of double consciousness caused by the tension it has produced between the comforts of place and the threat of space. As a symbolic location, then, Philadelphia means provisional freedom and conditional brotherhood, compelling its black citizens both to revere its discourse of democratic freedoms and to recognize that these freedoms may be denied to them at any point. According to Yi-Fu Tuan, "Long residence enables us to know a place intimately, yet its image may lack sharpness unless we can also see it from the outside and reflect upon our experience" (1977, 18). The self-conscious black Philadelphian is at points overwhelmed by experiential and spatial bifurcation that positions him or her as an intimate stranger in a location that is both peaceful and wild, place and space, cause and effect, pause and movement.

In 1970, Arthur L. Smith—now known as Temple University's maverick Africologist, Molefi Asante—claimed in the inaugural "Editor's Message" of the *Journal of Black Studies* that the inherently "interdisciplinary" field was "born with so much pain and anguish." He implored scholars to produce work that is sufficiently "dynamic, innovative, and creative" to "add . . . to the factual, analytical, and evaluative" understanding of black life and its representations (Arthur Smith 1970, 3). Scholars have met Smith's challenge by utilizing a range of theories and methodological approaches in an effort to understand the devastating psychic, economic, cultural, and spiritual consequences of racial oppression. Adding the formulations of trauma studies and theories of space and place to our analytical arsenal can further enrich our discussions of post–civil rights manifestations and representations of the "pain and anguish" of U.S. hybridity as well as the meanings of symbolic locations such as Philadelphia.

At the very least, trauma studies can assist our efforts to demonstrate the conceptual depth, breadth, and weight of the concept of double consciousness, the field's core formulation. If, as Cathy Caruth argues, truly compelling examinations of traumatic stories require that analysts marshal an array of ways "of knowing and of acting" (1995, ix), we can fruitfully examine the residue of slavery and of black Americans' displacement in projects addressing traumatic black subjectivity as a state of strange national intimacy arrived at following our nominal achievement of civil, legislative, and political freedom.

Drawing heavily on former Philadelphia 76er Chet Walker's exploration of its racially charged causes and traumatic implications, Chapter 1 considers the decision to begin the 1967–1968 National Basketball Association semifinal series between the 76ers and the Boston Celtics on the day after King's April 4, 1968, assassination. I examine this choice in its local context, which includes the institution of repressive law enforcement measures devised to ensure that major riots did not erupt in Philadelphia in the aftermath of King's murder. Also, I analyze it in the light of national debates about how to respond respectfully to the civil rights leader's death and whether black athletes should boycott the 1968 Olympics to draw attention to the United States'

racial inequalities. Finally, I situate this decision alongside the intrigue surrounding James Brown's celebrated performance in the Boston Garden on
the same night.

Chapter 2 examines rhythm-and-blues songs from the 1970s exploring
black fatherhood specifically and black masculinity more generally, including the O'Jays' "Family Reunion," the 1975 release by the successful Philadelphia International Records group. These songs are considered in the context
of major social, political, and artistic developments that led some commentators to see the decade as marked by a significant fragmenting of the black
body politic. The O'Jays' song, which critiques social movements of the 1960s
such as women's liberation, describes what it sees as the devastating impact
of this progressive movement on black families. Essentially confirming the
findings of the 1965 Moynihan Report, which tied black American socioeconomic progress to the race's capacity to replicate a patriarchal white family structure, the song insists that patriarchy is both divinely sanctioned and
"the solution to the world's problems." In light of this report, as well as literary texts and other songs that emphasize the contours of a traumatized black
manhood in particular and role of the black father especially, this and other
songs' nostalgia for patriarchy is more easily comprehended.

Chapter 3 offers a reading of Andrea Lee's 1984 novel, *Sarah Phillips*,
whose focus is the conflicts experienced by a young black female Philadelphia Main Line resident whose parents expose her to both the fruits and the
psychic challenges of post–civil rights integration. When the novel is read in
the context of, among other works, William Julius Wilson's groundbreaking
work *The Declining Significance of Race*, its marginalization by black feminist critics and by theorists of black literary production seems unjustified.
This chapter argues, in fact, that in its ambivalence about the meanings of
race and class, Lee's novel represents some of its period's central tensions,
including how we might understand the black American literary tradition. I
address what happens when performances of blackness are not passed down
from parent to child as cultural practices because members of elite classes are
unwilling to risk contamination by traumatizing blues possibilities, including rape, teenage pregnancy, and gangs.

The final chapter concentrates on the 1998 Philadelphia premiere of *Beloved*, which was filmed in and around the First City in the summer of 1997,
and seeks to explain its commercial and artistic failures. Considering it in
a variety of relevant contexts—including Oprah Winfrey's television, book
club, and magazine enterprises; contemporary films that investigate almost
unimaginable atrocities; and other works by director Jonathan Demme—
I argue that the film fails commercially because of the nation's aversion to

depictions of slavery and fails artistically because of its refusal to delve deeply enough into the horrors of that U.S.-peculiar institution to illuminate Sethe's decision to kill her child and, hence, to justify the film's excursion into the painful historical past.

Philadelphia Freedoms concludes with a brief discussion of two early twenty-first-century incidents, centered in the City of Brotherly Love, in which tensions between the traumatic nature of black American identities and the false idealism of national rhetoric are evident. These incidents are (1) the 2002 debate about the commemoration of George Washington's newly unearthed presidential residence, whose subterranean slave quarters complicates our image of the nation's truth-loving First Father, and (2) then–presidential candidate Barack Obama's 2008 speech on race, which was delivered at Philadelphia's Constitution Center. In the speech, Obama uses the city's glorious history of national self-creation to distinguish his patriotic visions of evolving race relations from the embittered views of his pastor, Philadelphia native Jeremiah Wright, whose jeremiads condemning U.S. domestic and foreign policies were used to challenge his parishioner's political and ideological—as well as racial—fitness to hold the nation's highest public office. As these twenty-first-century examples indicate, Philadelphia's symbolic meanings will continue to be examined in our conversations about the contours of black American identity. The First City's—my city's—complicity in the perpetuation of black suffering cannot always be drowned out by even the most melodious national rhetoric.

1

"Philadelphia Did Not Burn"

*Quelling Riots and Deferring Hoop Dreams in the Age
of the Militant Black Athlete*

*Philadelphia 76er Chet Walker shooting over Boston Celtics guard Sam Jones. Walker's
1995 memoir explores the psychic consequences of having been coerced to participate in
the opening game of the teams' 1968 playoff series on the day following Martin Luther
King, Jr.'s assassination.* (Photo by Focus on Sport/Getty Images.)

*T*he first event of national significance to have made an impact on me was the April 4, 1968, assassination of Martin Luther King, Jr. I was not wholly oblivious to other major events that occurred during the turbulent 1960s. I distinctly remember, for example, watching reports of President Kennedy's assassination along with my mother and her buddy, Naomi, in our second-floor rear apartment in a three-story row house on Ninth Street near Lombard. But at age four, I had only a vague conception of what a president was, so his murder was no match for the drama that immediately followed Miss Naomi's departure, when my mother exclaimed—to herself, mostly, but also to me and my younger sister, Debby, both of us too young to join our older siblings at McCall Elementary School—that she had been robbed. Kennedy's assassination was hardly noteworthy—besides, apparently famous people I had barely heard of got murdered with regularity during the decade[1]—compared to the news that my mother's negligence and her friend's larcenous act would affect what and how much I would get to eat for the next two weeks.

King's death, though, was deeply meaningful, not only because I was twice as old when it occurred than I was in November 1963, but because his aural, visual, and spiritual presence in my household exceeded that of every other public figure, including Ray Charles, my mother's favorite singer. I did not understand the importance of King's message of racial equality because of any experience I had had in our economically and racially integrated neighborhood. Rather, I had listened attentively to my mother's stories about the unconscionable prejudice she confronted as a schoolgirl in nearby Darby; to news of bombings and beatings narrated with frightening solemnity by Chet Huntley and David Brinkley; to the red-faced frustrations of Bull Connor, George Wallace, and their ilk; and to stern, empathetic white teachers overseeing a sometimes combustible mixture of upper-middle-class WASP and Jewish kids and impoverished blacks who were in the process of being displaced from run-down but structurally sound Society Hill houses and, hence, from an excellent public school a quarter of a mile from the nation's most hallowed grounds. By September 1967, when I entered third grade, I understood that blacks were considered inferior to whites, all of whom seemed to have more money and power than all of the black people I knew. But I knew nothing of slavery, and I had virtually no comprehension of the devastating effects of Jim Crow on the psyches of my people beyond the expressed need for the Southern battles King waged and my mom's lamentations about her hometown's segregated movie theater.

But every Saturday morning, I heard King's "I Have a Dream" speech. My mother played it, I think, because of its unequivocal indictment of racism and faith that whites would acknowledge the nation's responsibility for the fact that "one hundred years" after Lincoln's "momentous decree . . . , the Negro is still sadly crippled by the manacles of segregation and the chains of discrimination" (1986b, 217). Also, she loved King's learned, black Southern preacher's voice and that this speech is one of the supreme cultural performances anyone had ever recorded. Uncertain if she also played the speech for her children's edification, I knew that its themes mirrored lessons she taught us about how to be good black people: keep your promises (his discussion of America's defaulting on its promissory note is brilliant); be well spoken; be cognizant of racism; and strive always to fulfill both your potential and your obligations to others, particularly members of the race.

The speech also struck an especially strong chord in me, a flatland-bound city kid, evoking scenic heights from which King implored the United States to let freedom ring: both mundanely referenced Southern mountains (Stone in Georgia and Lookout in Tennessee) and rhetorically embellished non-Southern ones ("the prodigious hilltops of New Hampshire," "the curvaceous slopes of California" [1986b, 219]). As a child attending an integrated elementary school and the sensitive son of a father who had left the family he had produced with my mother for the one he had previously made with his wife, I was enthralled by the fact that a well-spoken black man had incorporated into his ideal vision of America "little black boys and black girls" whom he believed were destined to "live in a nation where they will not be judged by the color of their skin but by the content of their character" (219). He fought tirelessly for adults, certainly, but also for his children—two girls, two boys, just like my siblings and me—and I knew that, unlike my father, he was fighting for me, too. Brilliant, verbally gifted, morally courageous, highly principled, and paternalistic, King seemed more deeply patriotic and dedicated to the service of others than I could ever imagine or hope to be. To a young, precociously cynical, not-easily-impressed fatherless boy, he was not merely admirable but unimaginably heroic.

His assassination is this book's primal scene because I believe it both enabled and stifled much of the nation's consideration of the legacy of American racism and inaugurated the possibility of a post–civil rights black identity. But this choice is also deeply personal. When King was murdered, I was in Thomas Jefferson Hospital in Center City for surgery on my legally blind, strabismus-afflicted lazy right eye. I learned about the assassination two days after it had occurred, sitting in a Yellow Cab headed toward home and feeling unbelievably nauseated. My good eye was patched per orders of my doctor, a last-gasp effort to force my cosmetically corrected eye to function more normally. Within seconds of hearing the news I convinced myself that King's death and my operation were intertwined events and that, had I not gone to the hospital, he would not have been assassinated.[2] Enthralled, even then, by narrative continuity, I knew that it could not have been mere coincidence that I lay anesthetized, *bloody, and, after my operation, floating in and out of consciousness in a hospital bearing the name of the author of the Declaration of Independence, as King, a deep admirer of that document, was shot and rushed to a Memphis hospital, where he pronounced dead. However silly my illusions of grandeur now seem, what has stuck with me, from that moment, was the sense of obligation I bore to this man who had sacrificed so much for me, my people, and the mountainous nation he helped me to envision.*

During our sometimes embittered efforts to comprehend our simultaneously more secure and more perilous place, black Americans recognize that this assassination did not cause the throbbing racial wound still evident on our collective body. Indeed, King himself often acknowledged that wound's existence, noting in "I Have a Dream," for example, that "millions of Negro slaves . . . had been seared in the flames of withering injustice" and that their descendants—"still languish[ing] . . . in the corners of American society and . . . in exile"—remained "sadly crippled by the manacles of segregation and the chains of discrimination" (1986b, 217). His tireless campaign for justice and his death point the way to useful answers for a long-traumatized people striving to heal as we seek to understand what it now means to be black and American. How, precisely, should the history of black American suffering affect our relationship to the nation and to our fellow citizens? What are the obligations of privileged blacks to struggling members of the race? Can black families thrive in a nation in which their people have been imperiled, maimed, and murdered with impunity, and who, perhaps in response to their baleful treatment, make sometimes injudicious choices that hamper our ability to prosper economically, scholastically, and otherwise? Can we resolve our internal differences amicably enough to work together for the betterment of the race? Can we ever agree on what forms "the betterment of the race" should take?

Discovering satisfactory answers for these and other questions after King's death means not only acknowledging the deleterious conditions under which black American identities have been shaped but coming to terms with trauma as a defining racial condition. The challenge of describing what it has meant to live with the threat of psychological, physical, and spiritual violence is made even more daunting by our insistence on countering claims that we suffer from genetic or culturally determined inferiority with increasingly dubious descriptions of an indomitable black American strength, creativity, and adaptability. Of course, choosing between polarized interpretations of black Americans as total victims and as soulful survivors is a dubious activity at best. For his part, King insisted that we acknowledge both our pain and our strength, as well as the lessons to be found in both our tragic history and sacred national texts authored largely in Philadelphia that contain the possibilities for tragedy's transcendence and transformation. In the estimation of many, his faith in America's capacity to become truly "a great nation," its greatness attached inexorably to the success of our freedom struggles, was and is hopelessly naïve. For others, his pursuit of inalienable rights, his appeal to nonviolence, and his cogent explorations of the troubled and troubling black American condition produced not only U.S. history's most successful example of civil rights agitation but an intellectually expansive and practicable vision of how most effectively to make the necessarily painful journey still from the despised margins to the complicated center of the American experience.

In Philadelphia and elsewhere, public figures—including athletes, politicians, and entertainers—grappled with discernible discomfort with the implications of King's assassination in the riotous hours, weeks, and months following this traumatic event. These figures' representations of their own pain and sense of obligation, to themselves, their people, and their nation, evince the dangerous nature of the freedoms black Americans experienced in the post-civil rights era—freedoms that King's efforts helped engender.

———

King's death produced "a unique display of nationwide racial unity" as African Americans took rage and grief to urban streets, fashioning major riots in over sixty cities that culminated in over forty deaths and twenty thousand arrests, some of which took place on television.

—Amy Bass, *Not the Triumph but the Struggle*

Disorder did not erupt as a result of a single "triggering" or "precipitating" incident. Instead, it was generated out of an increasingly disturbed social atmosphere, in which typically a series of tension-heightening incidents over a period of weeks or months became linked in the minds of many in the Negro community with a reservoir of underlying grievances. At some point in the mounting tension, a further incident—in itself often routine or trivial—became the breaking point and the tension spilled over into violence.

—United States National Advisory Committee on
Civil Disorders, *Report of the National
Advisory Committee on Civil Disorders*

Fog rolled through the streets of Philadelphia that afternoon, bringing traffic almost to a halt and hiding the signs of the

> sporadic rioting the city had endured. In the middle of the after-
> noon, [Wilt] Chamberlain had called the 76ers general manager,
> Jack Ramsay, to say he didn't want to play, but Ramsay pointed out
> that tickets had been sold, all the players had a contractual obliga-
> tion to play, and if the game was canceled the crowd could turn
> ugly. Later in the afternoon, Chamberlain received a call from
> [Bill] Russell saying the Celtics had decided to play, and the two
> men agreed that it would be a bad idea to risk angering the fans.
>
> —John Taylor, *The Rivalry*

> The Boston-Philadelphia rivalry always meant more to me
> than just a basketball battlefield. Much of what I learned about
> American history as a schoolboy in Benton Harbor was bound
> up with the images of these two cities. To me Philadelphia meant
> the Liberty Bell and the cradle of freedom, Ben Franklin and In-
> dependence Hall, where the Declaration had been signed that set
> Americans free. The Philadelphia I knew in the mid-1960s also
> was home to Frank Rizzo, the city's racist police chief and future
> mayor, who was, to black people, like some nightmare sheriff
> who'd followed them from Mississippi or Alabama.
>
> —**Chet Walker and Chris Messenger**, *Long Time Coming*

I n a striking account of the Olympic boycott movement and its aftermath, Amy Bass cites comments offered in November 1967 by two-hundred-meter sprint champion Tommie Smith concerning steps he was willing to take to improve the plight of blacks:

> "I am not willing to sacrifice my manhood and the basic dignity of
> my people to participate in the Games," he said. "And I am quite will-
> ing not only to give up participation in the Games but my life if nec-
> essary if it means that it will open a door or channel by which the
> oppression and injustice suffered by my people in America can be
> alleviated." (2002, 90–91)

Smith's remarks were referenced in March of the following year in a *Saturday Evening Post* article by Harry Edwards of the Olympic Project for Human Rights (OPHR) titled "Why Negroes Should Boycott Whitey's Olympics," where they were prefaced by the OPHR leader's discussion of the movement's "simple" motive:

For 36 of the 72 years that the modern Olympics have been staged, American Negroes have contributed greatly to U.S. victories. And while they were winning medals, they were also being hailed before the world as symbols of American equality—an equality that has never existed. We are putting Washington and the world on notice that they can no longer count on the successors of Jesse Owens, [decathlete] Rafer Johnson and [sprinter] Bob Hayes to join in a fun-and-games fete propagandized as the epitome of equal rights, so long as we are refused these rights in white society. (1968, 6)

Like the sit-ins and marches designed to end Southern segregation that preceded it, then, discussion of a possible Olympic boycott drew national and world attention to the persistent forms of racism in the United States and, hence, pressured whites to cease denying black Americans their constitutionally guaranteed freedoms. But because this discussion occurred during a period of "pronounced generational and ideological differences between the Southern Christian Leadership Conference (SCLC) and the Student Non-Violent Coordinating Committee (SNCC), [which] would further splinter *the* civil rights movement," accompanying SCLC-style nonviolent protests and rhetorically measured formulations of America's failed promises were heated comments about nation building, social responsibility, racial treason, and the ideological and practical implications of the mesmerizing rallying cry, "Black Power." As Bass asserts, "The seemingly unified national spectacles of civil rights that had dominated the first half of the decade were over, to be replaced by localized actions such as the Black Panthers' community programs" (2002, 4–5).

This chapter, which is concerned with commemoration, grief, and riot prevention in the wake of King's assassination, assesses fascinating manifestations, drawn from the arenas of professional basketball and soul music, of the impact that "national spectacles" can indeed have on "localized actions." The event on which I focus primarily—the decision of the National Basketball Association's premier teams, the Philadelphia 76ers and the Boston Celtics, not to postpone the opening game of their playoff series on the evening following King's assassination—is particularly compelling because of the rhetoric of boycott connected to the approaching Olympics. By choosing to play this game on the scheduled date in Philadelphia, the city most closely associated with constitutive national texts whose principles King referenced continuously in his campaign for black American freedom, these franchises demonstrated a chilling indifference to the meanings of the civil rights leader's efforts and his violent death for the nation as a whole and their black players in particular. As members of weak players' unions and, hence, subject to the sometimes tyrannical edicts of owners with little sensitivity to such concerns as pensions, equitable distribution of revenue, and black social advancement, even widely recognized figures such as the Celtics' Bill Russell and his fabled rival, the 76ers' Wilt Chamberlain, were unable to call attention to the shortsightedness of management practices in their sport in as dramatic a fashion as the amateurs threatening an Olympic boycott. However, as even their conflicted responses to being asked to perform on the night following King's murder indicate, these athletes had been heavily influenced by efforts to mobilize Americans generally in the service of black social progress.

According to sports historian David Wiggins, black athletes during this era, like others who were subjected to racial discrimination, struggled with the psychic costs associated with being both black and American. Wiggins argues that they were

> compelled . . . to live split existences. On the one hand, black athletes were proud of their race for its forbearance and ability to survive, and fought against the negative images of black inferiority. At the same time, black athletes aspired to success in American sport which necessitated that they adhere to values upheld in the dominant society. (1997, 133)

This tension between racial pride and mainstream success is particularly apparent in the ultimate recognition of Olympic-caliber athletes following a year of boycott threats that "the price to pay for non-participation was simply too high." Having been taught "to be humble, tolerant, and respectful of power," black American male track and field stars were encouraged by Edwards, a former junior college discus thrower who had become a sociology professor at San Jose State, where several top-notch sprinters were enrolled, "to be outspoken, defiant, and disrespectful of authority" (Wiggins 1997, 148). Confronted by the prospects of losing both "a chance to compete against the best athletes in the world" and their "ticket to a brighter future and a more rewarding way of life," Smith, four-hundred-meter star Lee Evans, long jumper Bob Beamon, and others voted overwhelmingly to participate in the Olympics. Instead of boycotting, they resolved to voice their concerns during the Games via public acts that called attention to U.S. discriminatory practices (Bass 2002, 149, 226).

From the vantage point of both Wiggins and Edwards, even the best remembered of these acts of protest, the Black Power salute performed by two-hundred-meter standouts Smith and John Carlos as "The Star Spangled Banner" played to celebrate their medal-winning performances, was a tepid compromise. Despite the militant rhetoric that resonated throughout the United States in the run-up to the Olympics, ultimately the boycott organizers

> could not manufacture a comprehensive harmony. While Tommie Smith and John Carlos, once in Mexico, would solidify the notion in the midst of intensifying political fragmentation through their individual actions, their actions were not the empowering symbol that Harry Edwards had originally envisioned and were not the challenge he wanted to pose to the existing power structures of the Olympics and beyond. Rather than rally a concentrated identity around a symbolic move *at* the Olympics, Edwards maintained his objective to produce a solidified stance in absentia. However, as he and his cohort found, it can be all but impossible to make a diverse body into one and translate ideological political values into effective political action. (Bass 2002, 190–191)

Looked at in light of Du Bois's notion of irreconcilable strivings, OPHR's attempts to compel athletes cognizant of the brevity of their athletic careers to exhibit "concentrated identity" and "comprehensive harmony" were doomed to fail. However, Smith and Carlos's Olympic gesture, which stands alongside Muhammad Ali's repudiation of military service as U.S. sport's most widely remembered antiestablishment act of the era, was intended to aid the reconstitution of a physically, economically, and psychically oppressed race as a vibrant, empowered, and potentially cohesive community. According to Bass, Carlos and Smith

> created a moment of resistance and confrontation with dominant and existing forms of racial identity. They borrowed pervasive and normative conceptions of the nation and substituted new representations by replacing the dominant image of the American flag with a black-gloved fist. In front of a global audience of approximately four hundred million people, the duo used their moment to denounce racism in the United States, creating a cultural strategy effective in its attempt to change or shift the "dispositions of power." . . . Their protest, then, exemplified a collective transformation from "Negro" athlete to "black" athlete, one that mediated various internal identities of political consciousness and enunciated a new cohesiveness to the protest's expansive audience. (2002, 239)

These nationalistic words and symbols compelled the country to recognize that many of its elite black athletes had rejected the Jesse Owens–Joe Louis model of gentlemanly public decorum. As we have seen, Smith proclaimed that he was ready to die to advance the cause of black social equality. Similarly, Evans argued that "there is need for anything that brings about unity among Black people and points up the fact that successful Blacks maintain their ties with the Black community" (Bass 2002, 205). And in an OPHR booklet that Martin Luther King, Jr. advised him to produce, Edwards asserted that "we must no longer allow this country . . . to use a few 'Negroes' to point out to the world how much progress she has made in solving her racial problems when the oppression of Afro-Americans in this country is greater than it ever was." Edwards goes so far as to proclaim that "any black person who allows himself to be used in the above manner is not only a chump—because he allows himself to be used against his own interest—but he is a traitor to his race . . . and most importantly, a traitor to his country because he allows racist whites the luxury of resting assured that those black people in the ghettos are there because that is where they belong or want to be" (Bass 2002, 206–207). Such proclamations forced "the politically defined athlete"

> to decide whether to "sacrifice" the opportunity to compete while under "tremendous pressure . . . by Black activists." Indeed, one of the most central goals "for this new generation of black athlete is the sense of obligation to the black community," [sportswriter Robert] Lipsyte contended. "Competing . . . might seem hypocritical to those who believe that this country has offered black Americans only 'tricks and tokenism.'" (96)

If it is possible to see the choice of these athletes not "to 'sacrifice' the opportunity to compete" out of a "sense of obligation to the black community" as a capitulation to American aspirations that had been given luminous voice and compelling rhetorical form by King, how might we read "localized actions" that followed in the wake of "national spectacles" of virulent reactions to his death?

In the rest of this chapter, I examine the decisions to hold two events that had been scheduled for the evening following King's April 4, 1968, murder: the opening game of the National Basketball Association (NBA) Eastern Conference championship series in Philadelphia featuring the 76ers and the Celtics and a James Brown concert in the Boston Garden, the Celtics' home arena. Beyond the incalculable debt the nation owed King for successfully challenging Southern racism, a number of factors might have encouraged officials to postpone the game in particular, including rioting in scores of American cities and national debate about a possible boycott of the Olympics. Given, among other considerations, King's inspirational accomplishments and enduring—if, at the time of his death, highly contested—place as the nation's foremost civil rights leader, the fact that neither the game nor the concert was rescheduled speaks volumes about the premium that was being placed on preserving order and suppressing dissent at the end of the 1960s, as Richard Nixon's election seven months later would attest.

In the wake of the September 11, 2001, terrorist attacks, as the nation considered when it would be appropriate to resume scheduled athletic activities, *Daily News Live*, a local television show involving beat reporters and columnists of Philadelphia's tabloid newspaper's heralded sports section, featured a lengthy discussion of how various social and political events had affected sports. Under the heading "Sports Cancellations: Reactions of Various Sports to Historic Events," the show's graphics department listed D-Day, which prompted professional baseball to cancel its exhibition schedule; John Kennedy's assassination, to which college administrators responded by canceling their slate of football contests, in contrast to the National Football League (NFL), which played its full Sunday schedule of games despite newly installed President Lyndon Johnson's decree that the nation had entered a period of official mourning; and the attempted assassination of Ronald Reagan on March 30, 1981, the day of the National Collegiate Athletic Association (NCAA) basketball title game—which was neither canceled nor postponed—between North Carolina and eventual winner Indiana in Philadelphia's Spectrum, the home of the 76ers, the city's professional basketball team, which had opened before the start of the 1967–1968 season.

Given the innumerable crises and occasions of mourning Americans faced during the twentieth century, it was perhaps inevitable that the show's list would be incomplete. However, considering its momentous local import and the riotous responses it engendered throughout the United States, the absence of King's assassination from both the list and the panelists' appropriately subdued discussion was unfortunate. Interestingly, reactions to this cataclysmic event confirm the perspectives of scholars such as Jeremy MacClancy, who insists that "sport does not merely 'reveal' underlying social values . . . [but] is a major mode of their expression" (1996, 4), and Amy Bass, who argues that "as a part of the expansive relationship between popular culture and nationalism, sport provides a contradictory terrain upon which a multitude of questions and claims of identity—race, gender, ethnicity, class, sexuality—are constructed and contested, challenged and yet sustained" (2002, 3).

Indeed, the intersection of the terrains of sports and race as they were constituted both locally and nationally during early April 1968 most concerns me here. Collectively, the myriad responses engendered by King's assassination suggest how a besieged racial community, a symbolically resonant city, and an aggrieved nation confronted by questions concerning its status as the world's model democracy all absorb both threats to and confirmation of their organizing principles and terms of order.

The varied reactions of Philadelphia professional sports teams and their rivals to King's death belie Jules Witcover's assertion in *The Year the Dream Died: Revisiting 1968 in America* that it engendered respectful reflection both locally and nationally:

> A nation that by now had been well schooled in the protocols of political assassinations showed the proper sensitivity to the circumstances—unlike the spectacle in the wake of President Kennedy's death in 1963, when the National Football League played its scheduled games on the same Sunday the nation was mourning its loss. The April 8 opening of the major league baseball schedule was postponed, as were the Stanley Cup professional hockey and the National Basketball Association playoffs. (1997, 159)

In fact, however, the date of the season-opening game between the Phillies and the Los Angeles Dodgers, the franchise heralded for integrating the sport by installing Jackie Robinson as its second baseman more than two decades earlier,[3] was changed only after its management, which had been told that the Philadelphia team would forfeit the game rather than "play the Dodger Stadium opener as scheduled because of the interment of civil rights leader earlier that day, relented . . . and agreed to postpone" (A. Lewis 1968, 26). It is impossible to know precisely what inspired the California franchise to change its position. But whatever inspired it, its capitulation, along with the principled stance of the Phillies officials and the rest of the teams in the league, reflected a recognition on their part of the political implications of sports, the significance of the civil rights leader's accomplishments, and their social responsibility to refrain from suggesting that rigid capitulation to an easily revised schedule was of greater importance than acknowledging the wellspring of grief caused by King's assassination.

By contrast, the management and players of the NBA—which was well on its way to offering a stylistically "spontaneous and inventive" product dominated by blacks who "played increasingly above the rim and with a . . . luminous athleticism" (Pomerantz 1993, 123)—failed to manifest a keen awareness of "the protocols of political assassination." League officials, along with the management and players of the 76ers and the Celtics, decided not to postpone the opening game of their playoff series. While baseball was poised to begin its regular season when King was killed, the 76ers had already completed an eighty-two game schedule and the first round of the playoffs and were slated to play their archrivals for the Eastern Conference Championship.

The series pitted the aging Celtics, led by defensive stalwart Russell, the league's quintessential winner and its first black coach, against the Philadelphia native Chamberlain–led 76ers, whose championship team of the previous season is considered by many experts to be "the best collection of brain, blood, bones and sinew [ever] to grace the courts of the NBA" (Bruton 1986, D1). The Celtics' best scorers were John Havlicek, Bailey Howell, and Sam Jones, while the 76ers featured, in perennial All-Star Hal Greer and the injured Billy Cunningham, two performers who, along with their center (and Celtic rivals Russell, Havlicek, and Jones), would be named among the league's fifty greatest players during the 1996 celebration of the NBA's fiftieth anniversary.[4] The series was highly anticipated because of the rivalry between Russell, the revolutionary defensive force, and the reformed scoring machine Chamberlain, whose newfound commitment to teamwork had compelled him during the 1967–1968 season to become the only center ever to lead the league in assists, and because the 76ers had ended the Celtics' remarkable run of eight consecutive championships during the previous postseason. Certainly, such a matchup promised to enhance the profile of a league struggling to establish itself in a nation dominated by Major League Baseball and the National Football League, and in the first year of battling the American Basketball Association (ABA).[5] Whatever its motivation, the NBA ignored a host of issues—negative reactions less than five years earlier to the NFL's decision to play its scheduled games as the nation mourned the loss of a beloved president; riots engulfing numerous American cities, which inspired Philadelphia's mayor, James Tate, and its police commissioner, Frank Rizzo, to institute a limited state of emergency that made the sale of alcohol and public assemblies of more than twelve people illegal; and the reservations of many of the players—decreeing that the Eastern Conference finals series would commence as scheduled on the evening of April 5, 1968.

Philadelphia had defeated the Knicks in the previous series, inspiring *Daily News* sportswriter Jack Kiser to insist, in an article titled "76er 'Corpse' Is Alive!," that "with Billy Cunningham out with a broken wrist and two others hobbled with serious leg injuries," the team, "bruised and battered and all but buried by the experts" who had expected the younger, healthier New York squad to defeat the defeating champions (1968b, 61), was playing well. Thus, the playoff series story line, replete with images of compromised bodies, death, and reincarnation, was set: Could the injured 76ers continue their push to become a dynasty, or would the aging Celtics, having lost the division title to their Philadelphia rivals for a third consecutive year, reassert themselves as the sport's preeminent team?

Three brief items appearing in the *Daily News* before and after King's murder indicate the provisional nature of the April 5 date and the tepid or boldly insensitive nature of the response of league officials in its aftermath.

1. Four days before the playoffs between the 76ers and Celtics began, it was reported that if both of the teams won their initial best-of-seven series in six games, they would begin their own series on April 7—three days *after* King's assassination ("East Final Fri." 1968).

2. The scope of King's loss was registered by religious leaders including Billy Graham and Pope Paul VI; politicians from countries such as Canada, Great Britain, India, and Denmark; and newspapers throughout Western Europe, where memorial services began on the day of his assassination. "Church and other leaders likened [the impact of King's murder to] . . . the assassination of President John F. Kennedy and Mohandas K. Gandhi, the leaders [*sic*] of India's non-violent struggle for freedom" ("'Tragic' Death of Dr. King" 1968, 4).

3. A United Press International report announced that "player representatives agreed unanimously to play an exhibition All-Star Game in New York's Singer Bowl August 14 as a tribute to King" and a benefit for his Southern Christian Leadership Conference ("NBA to Play Game as King Memorial" 1968, 30).

The schedule's obvious fluidity and the ability of league officials, hours after King's death, to secure both a location and player support for an August exhibition game suggest that the NBA had sufficient time and awareness of the import of the assassination to have postponed the playoff semifinals. Compelled to wait until April 10 to resume the playoffs by President Johnson's mandating of a day of mourning for King on Monday, April 8, the day before his funeral, one argument league officials could have made was that postponing Game 1 would have greatly enhanced the series' continuity.

The consequences of the choice to begin the series as scheduled were assessed in numerous journalistic, historical, and autobiographical accounts of the game. For example, in a book about their 1966–1967 championship season, Wayne Lynch insists that while "the 76ers weren't sure they wanted to play," "the Celtics had made a firm decision after meeting with [general manager Red] Auerbach and [coach Bill] Russell . . . to take the court"; in Lynch's view, "the 76ers' indecision about playing followed them onto the basketball court" (2002, 207), contributing to their losing 127–118. Similarly, Roland Lazenby insists in *The NBA Finals* that "the atmosphere was dead in Philadelphia because of" King's assassination and that "the tragedy cast a pall over the whole series" (1996, 130). And in a summary of the semifinals for *Sports Illustrated*, Frank Deford, who speaks of "the ultimate effect of the murder of Martin Luther King" on the 76er-Celtic opening game as "imponderable," notes that "neither [Russell nor Chamberlain] really wanted to play" (1968, 39).

The renowned Philadelphia sportswriter Jack Kiser, writing just moments after the game's completion, offered the most succinct assessment: "It was a bad night to play a basketball game, period" (1968a, 30). He goes on to insist that "a great majority of the players certainly didn't want to play. They felt strongly that this was no time for playing a game—that it should have been postponed out of respect of assassin victim Dr. Martin Luther King." Kiser includes responses to the decision by three of the game's hesitant combatants. A "numb" Chamberlain, who "couldn't get up mentally for this game" and "couldn't play my best," says that "if we had been given a free choice, we wouldn't have played. We feel the club owners should have postponed it, but most of the players thought we might be doing more harm than good by refusing to play." Also concerned about the reactions of fans, Russell claims to have felt "that if people came out expecting to see a game . . . , not seeing one . . . would increase the danger of something happening." Lastly, the 76ers' Wally Jones, "sick and stunned" by the news of King's death, reminded sportswriters that when he was in college at nearby Villanova University, officials had canceled a scheduled game in response to President Kennedy's assassination. Comparing his post-assassination experiences in Philadelphia, Jones notes that his college team "didn't play a basketball game then and I don't think we should have played one tonight" (Kiser 1968a, 30).

Unlike Jones, who puts the unfortunate decision in an appropriate local context, Russell and Chamberlain in particular offer remarks that exploit the rhetoric of riotous racial dissent, implying that "harm" or "danger" might have resulted from an announcement, as the stands were filling up, that the game was being postponed out of respect for King's memory. As Charles Kaiser suggests in *1968 in America*, televised images of rioting in Watts, Harlem, Detroit, and Newark had compelled the United States to "degenerate . . . into an immense armed camp" in which "55 percent of all whites and 32 percent of all blacks kept guns in their homes—and 51 percent of these gun owners said that they would use them in a race riot" (1988, 23–24). According to David Steigerwald, who sees 1960s riots as a reaction to "accumulated general grievances—racial, economic, political, the urban crisis in its totality," their "single most important, frequent, and notorious spark was local police action" in areas where "the [white] police neither protected nor served the black community." On such occasions, Steigerwald contends, white police presence was seen as an "intrusion of authority" precipitating responses that many blacks perceived "not as riots but as 'revolts,' self-conscious outbreaks of violence with clear political ends" (1995, 212–213).[6] In a nation whose citizens increasingly see themselves as occupants of an "armed camp," then, urban rioting was instigated almost exclusively by groups of black Americans replying spontaneously to perceived or actual white police malfeasance.

Consequently, the stated concern of 76er and Celtic team representatives and of black players that the overwhelmingly white fans would riot in or outside the Spectrum seems unfounded, unless they were imagining whites attacking blacks, as during the pro-slavery riot that took place in Philadelphia in 1834 when the homes of nearly fifty blacks were destroyed. Interestingly, the obfuscations that mark their explanations—Chamberlain's statement that not playing would "do . . . more harm than good," and Russell's claim that acting in accord with his stated preferences to postpone the game would "increase the danger of something happening"—appear intended solely to placate white fans, if not white sportswriters, whose columns the following day chided the NBA for its disrespectful response to King's assassination.

One player whose opinions Kiser did not record was 76er starting forward Chet Walker, who, despite scoring thirty-one points in the game, appears to have been more negatively affected by King's assassination and the teams' decision to play than the fabled centers or even native Philadelphian Jones. As his 1995 autobiography, *Long Time Coming: A Black Athlete's Coming-of-Age in America*, indicates, Walker told one of Kiser's rivals, a *Philadelphia Inquirer* reporter:

> I would like to have seen the Eastern Division championship games postponed, especially the first one. I said, "I've been in a state of shock. I didn't sleep last night. Usually, before a Boston game, I get myself up for the game, but when I heard that Dr. King had been shot, I forgot all about the game. It just didn't seem important to me anymore." (Walker and Messenger 1995, 201)

Walker depicts his participation in this game as the most traumatizing of a series of events during which he was called on to perform against his better judgment while risking his psychological, physical, and racial health. He had endured, and continued to perform admirably as a Bradley University star in the late 1950s and early 1960s despite, Jim Crow accommodations, vitriolic racist taunts, and a gambler-initiated drugging that left him with permanent kidney damage. Just before his first NBA All-Star game appearance in 1964, he had an experience that "forced me to recognize how little freedom or control NBA players had." Hours before the game, veterans threatened to boycott the annual exhibition because NBA owners refused "to recognize a players association that could bargain on such issues as contracts, playing conditions, and a pension plan." Because they had no collective bargaining agreement and, hence, "no right to strike" to improve their conditions, the players' lawyer urged the All-Stars to threaten to boycott one of the league's showcase events. Walker writes that less than a half hour before the scheduled tip-off, as "Boston Garden began to fill up," the commissioner "promised us that if we agreed to play the game, a pension fund would be initiated" (Walker and Messenger 1995, 152–153).

Walker offers no direct comparison between the threatened All-Star game boycott—which he considers the "shaky start" of "the strongest players' group in sports" that ended the heretofore "subservient relation of players to management" (Walker and Messenger 1995, 154)—and his post-assassination experience. Still, it is difficult to ignore their disconcerting similarities and startling differences. As I have suggested, he often faced deplorable conditions despite and because of his athletic gifts. During Walker's first extended college trip, for example, the opponents' "band marched out playing 'Dixie,' and we came out on the court surrounded by a sea of waving Confederate flags, which almost made me sick to my stomach" (78). The "nightmare" continued after the game when he and the team's other two black players were refused service in a Chinese restaurant; "hungry and depressed," he "knew if we did [protest] that Bradley University might accuse us of being troublemakers" (78–79). A sensitive nineteen-year-old Mississippi native whose family had moved to Michigan when he was in elementary school, Walker endured "endless maneuvering just to eat and sleep somewhere" and fans throwing "lit cigarette butts . . . at us and scream[ing], 'Nigger,'" cognizant that any prideful response on his part could endanger his scholarship and mark him as a troublemaker rather than one of racial trouble's easily accessible victims.

Evidence of the precariousness of Walker's situation includes his coach's castigation of him at halftime of a game during which the quality of his play had faltered in the face of racist insults. The coach "berated me, yelling, 'Don't quit on me, Chet,'" and questioned his star player's character:

> "All-American, my ass!"
>
> Well, there it was, the accusation that I didn't have what it took when the going got rough. He didn't care about the trauma of this trip to a nineteen-year-old kid. He just wanted to win, and I was supposed to help him. . . . My fleeting sense of equality was gone. (Walker and Messenger 1995, 80)

Walker was an early beneficiary (and victim) of a win-at-all-costs ethos compelling the integration of higher education—an ethos at odds with the nation's entrenched racist ideology—but he was lacking in self-confidence in part because, "like countless black kids before and after me, I'd been placed in a white society that seemed unnavigable" and where "my options were zero." Consequently, his "soul died a little each time a nightmare like that southern trip had to be lived through" (83), as he recognized that "if I publicly expressed my anger or desire, . . . they would destroy me" (82).

Walker's analysis of the motivations for such treatment, along with his commitment to availing himself of the opportunities that his athletic success afforded him, led him to embrace silent accommodation and passivity as his modus operandi. Reflecting on his "time in the public eye . . . from the mid-1950s to the mid-1970s," he offers the following perspective on the paradoxes informing his own notions and performance of black identity:

> I experienced a constant ebb and flow of confidence and fear of failure, of shyness and suspicion coupled with a need to be liked and to trust people. One minute I was an All-American basketball player as full of myself as a powerful young man could be. But the next minute, I was reduced to the nigger in the doorway. No amount of sports heroism in America could change that. Early on I understood this doubleness and that it would never truly change for me. (Walker and Messenger 1995, 82)

Indeed, the emotional costs of being both a confident All-American and a fearful "nigger in the doorway" are explored throughout this narrative, whose resolution occurs when a mature Walker, undervalued by the Chicago franchise for which he excelled after his trade from the 76ers following the 1968–1969 season, retires rather than accept a lucrative contract from a patronizing owner.

Interestingly, he achieved psychic integration only after a lengthy, psychologically liberating vacation in St. Croix, when he ruminates on the historical implications of the Bulls owner's claim that he "was 'legally the Bulls' property'":

> I sat there reflecting on the word property. I thought about my father, grandfather, and great-grandfather, and how they must have felt living in Mississippi where they were looked upon as property. Their experience had now become mine—the disgust at being in bondage and under the control of an owner. Making $200,000 a year, I knew I was a slave by perhaps no one's definition but my own. . . . Yet with Mr. [Arthur] Wirtz's claim to own me, I felt that two hundred years of my family's history in America had suddenly become real to me. Precisely because I was making that much money . . . , I was in a position to choose. I didn't have to . . . accept his claims of ownership. Until this moment, I had always been afraid to challenge the authority of white people in control over me. . . .
>
> I decided not to play. . . . Mr. Wirtz represented the person to whom I had to say no at this time in my life because I had to do it for all the times I'd been called "nigger," real or imagined, all the times I'd been turned away or judged in advance. There, in Mr. Wirtz's office . . . , all the negatives over the years gave me the push to say no! And when I did, I felt a powerful relief. The oppression I'd felt for years just rushed out of me. Every other time I'd figured out too late what to do for my own self-respect. But now I knew what to do, and I was ready. (Walker and Messenger 1995, 248–249)

Walker suffuses this episode with symbolic weight, signaling his refusal to continue to endure overt and subtle racist insults and to compromise his values as he felt compelled to do following King's murder. However individuated his experiences, clearly he situates them in the context of, and insists that they are enabled by, the civil rights and Black Power movements whose emphasis on nonviolent disobedience and militant self-assertion, respectively, constitute the behavioral parameters between which black Americans who came of age in the 1960s were compelled to choose. Having achieved the maturity, as well as the financial and emotional resources, to resist the lure of athletic acclaim, Walker's growing self-possession is evinced as he concludes his narrative by embracing his family history and resolving his double consciousness.

During Walker's time as a member of the 76ers, the "Civil Rights revolution" shared the stage with, and eventually gave way to, a more radical, more rhetorically vitriolic Black Power movement, some of whose Philadelphia representatives—including the Black Panthers and the Nation of Islam—sought Walker's support and membership. He resisted their entreaties, believing he "couldn't afford to become an active, visible part of a radical political organization," as his "insecurities about what I had achieved and the tenuous nature of my place in society wouldn't allow me to risk everything in a public forum" (Walker and Messenger 1995, 192). And because he was deeply concerned about the possible consequences of public risk, he believed that joining a radical black organization and leading a movement to get the game postponed were beyond his capacities. Such behavior would have felt especially dangerous for him at a time when, in an effort to quell the threat of urban violence, police commissioner Frank Rizzo, who believed that "the only thing these black power leaders understand . . . is force," "set himself up as the man willing to stop the flow of violence in America at Philadelphia's borders" (Paolantonio 1993, 85). Rizzo had earned the reputation as "the baddest cop on the force" during his time as a patrolman (84) and was later given "a 'free hand' in running the police department" by a Democratic mayor desperate to maintain the white ethnic working class vote (87). During Walker's years with the 76ers, for example, Rizzo authorized raids on the local chapter of SNCC, instructed his overwhelmingly white force to "get their black asses" when rambunctious high school students protested over the Eurocentric biases reflected in their curriculum, and purchased two military-style tanks to help ensure that riotous urban energies did not overtake Philadelphia. Certainly, the police commissioner was not above trying to embarrass prominent blacks such as Walker by disseminating information gleaned from the aforementioned raids of black organizations if he believed that doing so would help preserve to the city's state of relative quiescence.

While acknowledging moments of notable triumph, including winning the 1966–1967 NBA championship with the 76ers and emerging as a star player for the Chicago Bulls during the first half of the 1970s, Walker's memoir emphasizes an overriding sense of powerlessness. His portrayal of a racially circumscribed coming of age is generally consistent with descriptions of trauma, a debilitating psychic phenomenon that Cathy Caruth characterizes as "the possession of some people by a sort of fate . . . [that] seem[s] to be entirely outside their wish or control" (1996, 1–2). To speak of blackness as a condition akin to uncontrollable traumatic fate may appear extreme, even as it applies to Walker, who acknowledges being incapable of self-assertion in interracial settings for much of his life. But if, as Caruth argues, trauma is "a wound . . . upon the mind" causing a "breach in the . . . experience of time, self, and world," if it is, hence, "an event that . . . imposes itself again, repeatedly, in the nightmares and repetitive actions of the survivor" (3–4), then looking at Walker's narrative as a representation of a series of traumatic events helps us recognize the inseparability of the body and mind, the individual and (racial) group, the personal and communal within a psychically fraught national context.

If King's assassination was and is experienced by the black American collective body as a continuation of its traumatic historical experience and confirmation of its unceasing nature, as this study suggests, that tragic event must be seen as uncovering festering psychic wounds whose exposure—after a too-brief curative period for which King's efforts are partly responsible—served as a systemic shock to its fragmented consciousness and identity. Looked at from such a vantage point, it is understandable that Walker would represent King's death as symbolically both his own and his people's tragedy, and that one of his subsequent insights on the subject of life on the color line would concern differences among blacks that seasoned white observers are unwilling or unable to see. Watching a riotous expression of black rage, the media interprets that antisocial behavior as emblematic of "all black people," thereby in Walker's view "transform[ing] . . . black people into the problem. Here we were, victims mourning Dr. King's death, but in short order, we were seen as a threat to the very survival of the nation's order, an order that excluded us" (Walker and Messenger 1995, 202).

In representing himself and other blacks as victims, Walker emphasizes his sense of himself as a powerless outsider rather than his relatively secure place within a lucrative mainstream institution such as the NBA, the complexion of whose participants had grown significantly darker during the previous half-decade. All five of the 76ers' starters, for example, were black, as were the opposition's coach and six other members of the Celtics, along with eight of the league's top ten scorers, and nine of its top ten assist leaders (his teammates Wilt Chamberlain and Hal Greer appeared on both lists). Walker's attitude reflected the prevailing notions of his time—and ours—in which

> the black athlete serves as one of *the most visible integrated* racial subjects in modern society, seen in all facets of media, cheered by millions of fans, teamed with white counterparts, and, at least on the surface, accepted. Yet cultural encounters of identity surround the figure of the black athlete because of its undeniably crucial place within the American imagination, as the athletic playing field also subsists as a central realm where black masculinity and physicality are visually represented and reproduced. (Bass 2002, 3)

These types of encounters reinforced Walker's sense of his social marginality, nullifying many of the psychic benefits of his public visibility and relative wealth. Not having yet reached a point where he stops seeing himself through the eyes of whites, he views himself as solely a victim of vicious racist acts, or what Judith Herman terms a trauma survivor. Consequently, he sees the behavior of the media, as well as that of league and team officials, as insensitive to the variegated nature and collective suffering of a group constituted in part by its historic oppression. Hence, he responds to perceived and actual slights during his NBA career, including the choice not to postpone the beginning of the 76er-Celtic series, as if they are a repetition of the physical and psychic abuse he had undergone as a youth.

As I have indicated, Walker recognizes links between events in his life and those of his male elders, insisting—perhaps unpersuasively, he admits—that, like them, he had been a virtual slave "in bondage and under the control of an owner." Acknowledging both his place in a line of dispossessed Walker men who had been "looked upon as property" and athletic accomplishments that afforded him freedoms that they never enjoyed, he claims the right to self-definition and self-possession—enabled by civil rights struggles in which Walker was not actively involved and compromises he made to garner lucrative recompense—in his rejection of the team owner's characterization of him. He grants that there are tangible distinctions between antebellum, Jim Crow, and civil rights era manifestations of the status of black males as property, understanding, in the words of legal scholar Margaret Jane Radin, that the "meaning of the word 'property' can change over time" (1993, 123). Still, there is sufficient constancy in the word's employment by whites to reduce black men to their capacity as cotton-picking, rope-swinging, net-swishing agents of white material and psychological profit to justify his resistance to being so categorized and, hence, my own sense of his place in a line of traumatized Walker men.

Examining "the flexibility of memory," Bessel van der Kolk and Onno van der Hart identify two questions that are essential for survivors such as Walker to ask themselves: "How can one bring the traumatic experience to an end, when one feels completely unable and unwilling to resign oneself to the fact that one has been subjected to this horrendous event or series of events? How can one resign oneself to the unacceptable?" (1995, 178). In Walker's case, "traumatic experience" involves a series of events, the most historically resonant of which followed King's murder, when he felt he had been reduced to the status of a thoroughly manipulated pawn remunerated with the material and psychological benefits of basketball stardom. Still deeply affected by his inability "to stop a basketball game from being played on a night when black America was mourning and screaming in pain" following King's death, Walker eventually moves beyond "helpless rage" and passive acceptance by addressing individually and racially charged situations where he found himself "screaming in pain." According to van der Kolk and van der Hart, the termination of unremitting anguish and of a sense of helplessness is possible only when survivors can imagine "an alternative, less negative or even positive scenario" into which to fit the painful scenes they have not been able to incorporate into a manageable memory in the past.

> Many patients . . . are helped by imagining having all the power they want and applying it to the perpetrator. Memory is everything. Once flexibility is introduced, the traumatic memory starts losing its power over current experience. By imagining these alternative scenarios, many patients are able to soften the intrusive power of the original, unmitigated horror. (178)

Unlike these survivors, Walker is not resigned merely to "imagining having all the power" because, in his encounter with Wirtz, he takes sufficient control of a familiar, heretofore debilitating "scenario" to be able to divest a symbol of white hegemony of its omnipotence. He then exerts imaginative power over the experience that "still deeply affects me"—his passive response to King's assassination—by constructing a narrative that connects that event and his late-career interaction with the Bulls owner. By conquering his fear of white authority figures and controlling his yearning for American acceptance, Walker "soften[s] the intrusive power of the original, unmitigated horror."

Despite the experiential and financial differences between Walker and his forebears, his recovery is contingent on his acknowledgment that, like these men, he has been anchored to slave patterns, deleterious repetitive actions, and the stifling belief that he is destined to serve white hegemony. If his individual experiences and racial heritage can be characterized as elements of his traumatic past, Walker's achievement of "empowerment and reconnection," "the core experiences of recovery" (Herman 1992, 197), is, in fact, contingent on his understanding the social or communal dimensions of his individuated, privileged, race-inflected life. While he had been unable to organize his teammates (or, for that matter, his own thoughts) and to express dismay that the 76ers and Celtics were even considering playing a game when the preeminent civil rights leader had just been killed, and while he acknowledges hoping that a King-like figure would intervene and save him from another deeply compromising experience, by the end of his athletic career, he is able to act in concert with his own racial conscience.

Looking at the situation in light of notions of trauma, it is possible to suggest that Walker regards King's assassination and its aftermath—especially his responses thereto—as scenes from a recurring nightmare of circumscribed, infantilizing black male public action, as part of an enduring pattern of social and political repression in which he had been powerless to intercede. To be skilled enough to compete at the highest levels of his profession is clearly, for Walker, both a hard-earned blessing and a damning curse, for it exposes him to racially charged situations in which he has largely been unable to act with integrity, craving, as he does, both the physical and psychic freedoms that are the goal of civil rights activists and the economic and national perquisites offered by white-dominated institutions. Consider, for example, his responses to the news of King's assassination, whose description anticipates the sense of powerlessness he experiences as his team decided whether to play:

> When I woke up on Friday morning, I was stung to realize that I hadn't been dreaming, that Dr. King was really dead. I hung around my apartment, still absorbing the shock. No one connected with the 76ers called me about the game that night. I did call Hal Greer, but he knew as little as I did. On my way to the Spectrum that afternoon, a thick fog engulfed the streets, slowing traffic to a crawl. Marvin Gaye was singing on the radio about saving children, about who really cares enough to do so. I suppose that's what Dr. King was thinking about in Memphis when he took a hand in the garbage workers' strike. Save the children by allowing their families to put enough food on the table. (Walker and Messenger 1995, 197)

Earlier he tells us that he witnessed the negotiations that averted a boycott of the 1964 All-Star game, where he saw owners "bully their superstars"; learned to equate "oppression and ownership," whose "power constitutes itself not only in racial but also in economic terms"; and discovered that these rich Americans saw rebellious players as "wage earners [trying to] spoil our party" (153). Consequently, Walker's representation of his passivity in this case appears intended to indicate something other than his continuing naïveté. This passage contrasts his own immobility and sense of powerlessness—responses common to trauma survivors—with the inspiring acts of cultural heroes; depicting himself as a distraught, just-awoken child who is forced to "crawl" in "a thick fog," he remembers the legendary Marvin Gaye pleading with his listeners to protect defenseless children and King working to save striking garbage workers whose primary concern is feeding "the children." Had he been able to act as heroically as Gaye and King, instead of waiting for 76er officials to intercede, he might have called the team's five other black players and the Players' Association lawyer to solicit their assistance in postponing the game and hence served as an empowering example for future generations. But feeling "vague and purposeless, disconnected from everyone" as he arrived at the Spectrum, Walker fantasizes a collective response to the assassination that would have liberated him: "Wouldn't it be wonderful if nobody showed up tonight? No players, no fans. Just a spontaneous honoring of Dr. King. Each person deciding in his own heart to honor Dr. King's memory" (197).

Walker's nonconfrontational reaction replicates his responses to other encounters with the combustible combination of race and sports in the civil rights era. Having learned, as a product of the Deep South and of big-time athletics, that the basketball court was the only site where he could assert himself safely and gain a measure of retribution, he confines his fantasies of revenge strictly to the hardwood. Indeed, Walker presents himself as ill-equipped to participate in nonviolent, militant, and other acts of social resistance. Note, for instance, his reactions to comments concerning King by the player who would guard him during the series:

> I will never forget the Celtics' Bailey Howell, a white veteran from Mississippi State, asking, "Who was Martin Luther King? He wasn't president, you know? Why was he so important that we should cancel the game?"
>
> Dr. King wasn't president, but I felt that he was my voice and the voice of my people in this country. Dr. King had fought for me as a person, for my rights, my worth. He fought to bring humanity and dignity to me and to all people. When the majority of the Celtics and 76ers voted to go along with what the owners and fans wanted—to play this game—I went along and participated against my will in the game. But I wanted to take Bailey Howell to school and show him a thing or two. If I had chosen not to play, I would have been in violation of my contract and would have been stepping over the boundaries of my role. (Walker and Messenger 1995, 198)

Well aware of American racial boundaries, Walker limits his encoded reactions to attitudes such as Howell's solely to the court. In his reconstruction of his reactions, Walker emphasizes qualities that King possessed that he himself lacks ("voice," the courage and commitment to fight "for me . . . , my rights, my worth . . . , humanity and dignity"). Feeling yet again that he lacks a voice—his own or King's, which had spoken *for* him and "my people in this country"—he cannot describe the tremendous importance of King to a white opponent whom he characterizes as a thoughtless antagonist from the Deep South. And unlike a verbally proficient King, who refused to heed unjust laws and social proscriptions that reinforced white dominion, Walker finds himself unable to "violat[e] my contract" and "step . . . over the boundaries of my role."

His sense of powerlessness is further demonstrated in his reactions to the team vote, management's manipulations thereof, and his impulse to engage in symbolic action:

> We voted 7–2 to play, but I'm convinced if we'd met earlier in the day and voted then, the results might have been reversed. At about 2:30 P.M. Wilt had told general manager Jack Ramsay that he didn't want to play, and Ramsay had invoked contracts, fan safety, the city's volatile mood. . . . The owners . . . maneuvered us into an untenable position, holding off the vote until there was no choice as far as I was concerned. No one wanted another riot to break out if the game was canceled. I was trying to balance my social conscience with my job as a professional and the reality of thousands of people waiting for a game that night. It's true that you only have split seconds to make your choice in a situation like that, one that might stay with you for decades.
>
> During the national anthem . . . , I stood there with bowed head. . . . I wish I could have done something symbolic right then and there to signify both my freedom and the sorrow of other black people. Only a few months later, Tommie Smith and John Carlos would stun and anger America at the Mexico City Olympics when they stood, each with a black-gloved fist clenched and raised high, their heads bowed on the victory stand after the 200-meter race. I admired them for that. They found a beautiful and dignified way to express their anger and pride. I did not. (Walker and Messenger 1995, 199)

Failing to offer a symbolically resonant response, Walker cannot meet the challenges of this moment to honor the martyred King or, like Smith and Carlos, come up with a compelling means of individual and racial articulation. But in confining the militant rhetoric of 1968 Olympics simply to the symbol of the "black-gloved fist clenched and raised high," Walker ignores the discourse of black athletic militancy that preceded his own moment of inaction and, hence, contextualized the sprinters' gesture. Hence, he represents this gesture not as a compromise by black athletes who were unable to become self-sacrificing warriors but as an act of fully realized self-articulation.

Because he ignores these distinctions and fails to recognize himself as part of a larger community of similarly conflicted athletes, he offers the following remarks about citizenship, professionalism, and race as if they were merely a private, local conversation rather than a part of a voluminous national and international discourse:

> After our Friday loss, we [he and a friend who played for the Philadelphia Eagles] sat up most of the night watching television and staring sadly at pictures of the rioting from Washington, north Philadelphia, Detroit, and Chicago. So much footage of black rage. We kept going over old familiar ground. Why weren't we as professional athletes able to speak our minds about politics or race? Were athletes prohibited from being complete citizens? (Walker and Messenger 1995, 200)

The questions he raises concerning the responsibilities of black athletes to articulate their perspectives on American racial dynamics are precisely those that animated the Olympic boycott movement. All around him, black athletes were, indeed, speaking their minds, critiquing their nation, and insisting on full black American citizenship. The seemingly well-informed Walker found Malcolm X's "rhetoric . . . hypnotic" and admired "his ability to keep changing and growing," "was seriously considering adopting a Muslim name and perhaps participating in the movement," and "worked to elect Hubert Humphrey in his race against Richard Nixon" (1995, 190–191, 192). Hence, it is likely that he was aware of discussions of the proposed Olympic boycott before he witnessed Smith and Carlos's gesture. But like clear instances of traumatic memory lapses in *Long Time Coming*, his purported ignorance of the voluminous militant black athlete exclamations of the late 1960s has significant rhetorical and thematic benefits.

Earlier, I cited Walker's reference to hearing Gaye's "Save the Children" during his drive to the Spectrum on the afternoon following King's assassination. However, he could not have possibly heard this song during this drive, since *What's Going On*, the classic album on which the song appeared, was not released until May 1971, more than three years after King's death. But the historical accuracy of Walker's recollection is less significant than the song's purposeful presence in this scene. Specifically, he brings together the song, in which Gaye anguishes over the fact that adults, overwhelmed by their own despair, seem generally unconcerned about the fate of their neglected children, and the martyred leader's commitment to Memphis's garbage collectors, whose courageous strike Walker insists had been motivated by these men's desires to provide their offspring with adequate clothing, housing, and food. Feeling infantilized by his own inability to engage the politics of race or voice his concerns about the conditions of his own employment, he lacks the gumption of "heroic Freedom Riders in the South, who would get on a bus to integrate it, knowing their fate was to be beaten and dragged off to jail time after time" (Walker and Messenger 1995, 205). Having been encouraged by these activists to "think about how our own lives could matter" (205), at this crucial junction, Walker positions himself politically at the precise moment when images of nonviolent protest were giving way to Black Power symbolism as the dominant articulation of black resistance. Consequently, his transition from acquiescent company man to articulate, "emboldened" activist requires his revaluation of his painful experiences via reparative acts of the imagination for which he was unprepared in the confusing, traumatic, grief-filled hours following King's violent death.

A round the time that the 76ers and Celtics were on a Philadelphia basketball court struggling through what sportswriter Leonard Koppett called "the eeriest, most subdued sporting event I've ever seen" (quoted in Pomerantz 1993, 192), in the Celtics' home stadium, the Boston Garden, James Brown was also attempting to devise an appropriate response to King's murder. While commentators and several of the participants insist that the 76ers and Celtics dishonored King's memory by playing the game, both Brown and members of Boston's political leadership have been celebrated in, for example, the documentary film *The Night James Brown Saved Boston* (2009) and James Sullivan's book *The Hardest Working Man: How James Brown Saved the Soul of America* (2009) for going through with the scheduled concert, which purportedly helped quell possible rioting in the Massachusetts city's black communities.

The singer insists in his eponymous autobiography that the nickname "Soul Brother Number One meant I was the leader of the Afro-American movement for world dignity and integrity through music" (Brown and Tucker 1986, 173). Unlike Walker, who felt compelled by the demands of his profession to resist the lure of political movements, Brown saw himself as a cultural leader charged with the responsibility of contributing energetically to black efforts at sociopolitical advancement. While much of the discussion of race in basketball that emerged following the 1960s emphasizes black players' use of the game as a vehicle of cultural expression, its potential as a vehicle for communicating a discernible set of meaningful oppositional practices is limited by their general confinement to the realm of the purely symbolic such as facial hair, Afros, funky moves, gravity-defining dunks, and a less regimented style of play. Symbolic acts, like Smith and Carlos's Olympic gesture, often yield unintended interpretations, as Smith, who felt compelled to explain it and its accompanying wardrobe accessories, was well aware:

> The right glove that I wore on my right hand signified the power within black America. The left glove my teammate John Carlos wore on his left hand made an arch with my right hand and his left hand also to signify black unity. The scarf that was worn around my neck signified blackness. John Carlos and me wore socks, black socks, without shoes, to also signify our poverty. (Bass 2002, 240)

Because Smith and Carlos were engaged in symbolic behavior, these gestures necessarily inspired conflicting interpretations. Despite their stated intentions after the fact, perhaps because of the boycott threats that had preceded the Games, when they "bowed their heads and simultaneously raised a black-gloved fist" as "The Star-Spangled Banner" began to play, "the stadium crowd slowly but steadily booed and jeered in reaction" (Bass 2002, 240), certain that they had conspired to belittle the United States. So while Bass believes that observers witnessed "two American athletes powerfully display both their connection to and their criticism of the United States" (241), the condemnatory reactions of the stadium crowd indicated that it perceived only criticism.

In contrast to gestures such as Smith and Carlos's, rhythm-and-blues music of the period—much of which, like the proposed Olympic boycott, was inspired by the black freedom struggle—used familiar gospel, jazz, and blues sounds to speak directly of socioeconomic conditions and political dilemmas confronting many black Americans. In songs like Sam Cooke's "A Change Is Gonna Come," The Impressions' "This Is My Country," Nina Simone's "Young, Gifted, and Black," and, as I discuss in the next chapter, the O'Jays' "Family Reunion," artists offered social commentary of sometimes unsurpassed poignancy. Certainly, the introduction by black professional basketball players of gravity-defying dunks, no-look passes, smooth finger rolls, and behind-the-back, through-the-legs, ankle-breaking crossover dribbles and stop-on-a-dime hesitation moves was stylistically significant, opening a heretofore conservative league to a funky style of play that it had previously shunned. But beyond these stylistic and, hence, demographic changes, their ideological thrust and import were infinitely more difficult to discern than, say, examinations of black impoverishment and critiques of black urban conditions in the music of artists like Brown, Gaye, Curtis Mayfield, and the Temptations. According to Brown, for example, the directness of his message in songs like "Say It Loud—I'm Black and I'm Proud" and "I Don't Want Nobody to Give Me Nothing (Open Up the Door I'll Get It Myself)" helped to elevate him to the status of a black "leader" whose commitment to "speak out for my people" led Stokely Carmichael to label him "the one person who was most dangerous to his movement at the time because people would listen to me" (Brown and Tucker 1986, 178, 169).

Not surprisingly, then, Brown saw his scheduled performance as an appropriate way to pay tribute to King's memory, particularly if it contributed to controlling the riotous impulses festering in neighborhoods like Roxbury, Mattapan, and Dorchester. Brown's perspective was enabled by the fact that, unlike Walker, who felt compelled to see his racial identity and athletic career as fundamentally incompatible, he recognized that "soul music and the civil rights movement went hand in hand" (Brown and Tucker 1986, 173). In other words, Brown, the soul force who had established a rapport with political figures both black (King, Carmichael, Rap Brown) and white (Humphrey, Nixon), felt empowered artistically, economically, and politically by his participation in the American public sphere. An exemplar of soul, a cultural entity that, he argues, "was about the roots of black music, and . . . being proud of yourself and your people" (173), and an entertainer in decidedly political times, Brown saw his role as compelling other blacks toward a greater sense of self- and cultural appreciation and respect for American values and opportunities. It would appear that Brown viewed the 1960s as a historic moment when black American "doubleness" could indeed be resolved. The singer implored members of his race grieving over King's death to continue to develop the optimism, self-respect, and self-discipline that the slain civil rights leader had demanded of them and eventually came to see as the only means, short of a radical transformation of American society, of suppressing the explosive rage that had begun to manifest itself in the form of summer riots in black communities throughout the nation. In addition to urging "people to stay calm, [and] to honor Dr. King by being peaceful" in the cities in which his radio stations were located, Brown went "through with my [Boston Garden] concert" in order "to keep some people off the streets that night—the night everybody was predicting the worst rioting for—and to talk to them about the situation" (183).

If Brown was indeed responsible for helping suppress rioting in New England's largest city in the days following King's murder, the memory of his efforts and especially those of Mayor Kevin White's administration to foster racial harmony quickly faded during the next decade. During the 1970s, tensions exacerbated largely because a national recession and attempts to reform Boston's "unconstitutionally segregated" school system by using busing "to achieve a balanced mix of white and black students in the schools" led whites to feel as if they had "to defend the sanctity of their 'neighborhood schools' with every weapon at their command" (O'Connor 2001, 243). Just as federal judge W. Arthur Garrity, Jr. sought via his busing ruling to enforce antidiscrimination legislation when he ruled that "the Boston School Committee . . . had knowingly carried out a systematic program of segregation" (243), black civil rights leaders, athletes, and entertainers challenged legal rulings, social norms, and performance contracts that unfairly hindered their pursuit of racial equality.

The experiences of black athletes following the 1968 Olympics suggest that Chet Walker was correct to worry about how whites would respond to evidence of political engagement on his part. Because of the Black Power salute and other comparatively minor symbolic gestures, the track athletes who had considered boycotting the Olympics experienced what Bass calls "the negative upshot of political collectivity" (2002, 317). Upon their return to the United States, retribution was swift and widespread: professional football contracts offered before the Games were withdrawn; endorsement deals were lost; athletes who had been in good standing with the Reserve Officers' Training Corps (ROTC) before the Olympics were "declared unfit for Vietnam"; and to cite a specific example, Carlos was informed by his agent that "one guy told him that after what I did in Mexico City, . . . no businessman in his right mind would hire me" (Bass 2002, 316–317). Clearly, the repercussions for these athletes, some of whom did not "subscribe to the tenets of [U.S.] citizenship in a sanctioned way" (314), were great. They were exiled from the Olympic Village and denied the spoils of victory upon their return to the United States; the "glove situation" and the militancy of their boycott discussion cost them dearly. Whether hundred-meter champion Jim Hines is correct that Smith and Carlos's "gesture cost me a total of $2 million" (316), it is indisputable that that gesture had significant financial, social, and psychological ramifications for which few of them appeared truly prepared.

In Wayne Lynch's study of the 76ers' 1966–1967 title team, former 76er general manager Jack Ramsay is quoted from a 1999 interview acknowledging that "if it [King's assassination] would have happened today, you would have done something different" (2002, 207). What neither he nor any other commentator on this choice has adequately addressed is this: how and why, after more than a decade of nationally televised images of protests, after innumerable discussions of pervasive institutional racism, "the militant black athlete," and the proposed Olympic boycott, team officials placed black players in the position of competing in a basketball game hours after the civil rights leader's murder. In the case of the Celtics, however, team management included Bill Russell, whose position as player-coach necessitated that he be directly involved in making a host of the day-to-day decisions and who openly supported both Ali's decision to resist military induction and the proposed Olympic boycott. Virtually every profile of Russell describes him as outspoken, militant, and uncompromising. Given these characterizations of Russell, it may appear surprising that he did not demand that the opening game of the series be postponed. At the very least, his outspokenness and his position as a part of the Celtics' management team render it impossible to characterize the decision to play as strictly as a function of white management insensitivity. Unlike Walker, Russell fully embraced the demands of a militant era. As William Van Deburg notes, the Celtics star believed that "to shun accommodation and to enter into 'the arguments, the tensions, the slanders, the violence' of a competitive world order" was "a sign of both wisdom and racial loyalty. According to Russell, blacks could win respect only by fighting back" (1997, 115).

His generally combative racial views notwithstanding, the famously cantankerous Russell justified his team's decision to play in the hours following King's assassination on the grounds that he was concerned about the potentially riotous response to news of the game's cancellation by the overwhelmingly white Spectrum crowd. However, his choice to play through racial and national pain appears to have been motivated primarily by his oft-repeated insistence that "winning is the only thing I really cared about. . . . It's the most democratic thing in the world. You either win or lose" (Sachare 1997, 164). His dubious notion of a necessary correlation between victory and democracy notwithstanding, Russell's privileging of winning places his decision alongside those of the militant athletes who later competed in the 1968 Olympics despite U.S. racism. To boycott exhibition games in New York or, for that matter, Lexington, Kentucky, as Russell did earlier in his career because he and other black Celtic players were denied service by white-owned establishments, is certainly admirable. However, preseason exhibitions are not a part of the official NBA record, which documents only regular season and playoff wins and losses. Consequently, these glorified scrimmages were not games Russell felt his team needed to win at any cost.

For Russell to push for the postponement of a series that had the potential to vindicate him as a coach—it was under his stewardship during the previous year that the Celtics suffered their first playoff series loss in almost a decade—and reassert his dominance over Chamberlain, he would have had to suppress his compulsion to win at any cost, a compulsion that led a former teammate to describe him as "the foxiest, smartest, meanest player, psychologically, that ever played the game" (Sachare 1997, 164). A cerebral tactician, Russell may have reveled at the opportunity to gain an advantage over the 76ers by winning the first game of the series in his opponent's new South Philadelphia arena much more than he would have cherished an opportunity to pay ceremonial homage to King, whose 1963 March on Washington he had argued two years earlier was marked by "disunity . . . from the outset" and symbolically flawed ("they merely marched from the feet of one dead President to the feet of another") (Russell and McSweeny 1966, 205).

It is difficult to imagine, then, that Russell's concern about fans on the day after King's murder would have been anything other than inconsequential in comparison to his considerations of how he might increase his team's chances of winning the series. At the very least, this purported willingness to allow his choices to be dictated by a fear of "the danger of something happening" if the game was postponed suggests that, like Walker and Chamberlain, he was struggling with conflicted impulses. "A proud and defiant black man" who wanted to "prove to whites in Boston and elsewhere that blacks were just as capable as they were in positions of power" (Whalen 2004, 8), Russell apparently privileged his management role over his membership in a grieving race that was fighting to achieve socioeconomic and political power.

In the introductory chapter of *Dynasty's End*, which examines Russell's last NBA season, 1968–1969, Thomas Whalen explores the history of racial tensions in Boston, a city that, before the 1960s, had never had a substantial black population. Whalen notes that newly elected mayor Kevin White's efforts to control rioting in his city in the days following King's death included "consulting with black community leaders around the clock and holding back overly zealous white police officers who were chomping at the bit to use armed force" (2004, 7). White clearly recognized the fact that the infamous mid-1960s riots that preceded King's murder, as urban historian Jon C. Teaford notes, generally "began with a police incident" involving a black civilian who was perceived by black bystanders as the victim of "prejudice and brutality" on the part of overwhelmingly white law enforcement officers. Despite the migration of blacks to sprawling American cities like Philadelphia and Boston that whites were abandoning for the quiet and relative safety of the suburbs, metropolitan police forces had "remained overwhelmingly white and seemingly insensitive to the feelings of the black community," for whose members "the white cop controlling the ghetto was a symbol of subjugation that they were no longer willing to tolerate" (1993, 128–129). As a consequence, Boston's mayor was wise to proceed cautiously in preparing for black responses to King's murder. As Thomas O'Connor argues in his history of the city, White generally

> worked hard to keep things calm in the city's restive African-American community. . . . White became a frequent visitor in the black neighborhoods, strolling along the streets . . . , and establishing personal contacts with local black leaders. He increased the number of black policemen in the Roxbury area to counteract charges of police brutality, [and] made an effort to include black residents as full members of the Boston community. (2001, 214)

White apparently considered quite seriously the issues addressed in the Kerner Commission Report on urban violence, recognizing that the amelioration of blacks' sense of disenfranchisement was essential to his efforts to create a hospitable "New Boston" (O'Connor 2001, 240). Certainly, he understood the need to avoid the sort of draconian measures employed by his Philadelphia counterpart following riots in Detroit and Newark in 1967 involving Mayor Tate's issuance of a "series of emergency proclamations banning citizens from gathering in the streets in a group of twelve or more." Knowledgeable commentators considered Tate's decree to be precisely the sort of "sheer nonsense" that moved the City of Brotherly Love in the direction of becoming "a police state" (Paolantonio 1993, 88–89).

Given this response to riots in other cities that were precipitated by relatively mundane events, it was not surprising that, following King's murder, Tate and his police commissioner Frank Rizzo again "put a state of emergency in force, . . . closed bars and liquor stores and . . . outlawed large gatherings" (Paolantonio 1993, 96). On April 5, 1968, as

> thousands of blacks, angry and sullen about the loss of King, congregated on the long, rectangular lawn in front of Independence Hall . . . , Rizzo was ready. He had seventeen busloads of police officers hidden among the 18th and 19th century buildings in Philadelphia's historic section. Black leaders kept a lid on emotions. Block captains from North and West Philadelphia moved through the crowd. No one wanted a repeat of the bloodshed at the Board of Education building in November. And Rizzo was eager to avoid the public outrage over the police behavior at that demonstration.
>
> And, again, Philadelphia did not burn. (96–97)

Unlike rioters in other cities, who generally confined themselves to areas near their own homes, these blacks left their neighborhoods to assemble at "the birthplace of the American nation" (Weigley, Wainwright, and Wolf 1982, 394), where "the United States was created on July 4, 1776, when the Continental Congress voted for the final form of the Declaration of Independence" and "was perpetuated on September 17, 1787, when the Federal Convention competed its work on the Constitution" (National Park Service 2002, 1).

Although Rizzo's biographer does not make this point explicitly, given the engagement by grieving black Philadelphians of Independence Square as a site of mourning and an appropriate location in which to appeal for constitutional rights, what "did not burn" on the grounds where the nascent nation's original compromises were made to justify the enslavement of black people was the literal and symbolic site of American origin. What did not burn was the mythical Hall, which had become "a shrine honored wherever the rights of men are honored" and "cherished wherever the principles of self-government on a federal scale are cherished" (National Park Service 2002, 1). What did not burn, among other priceless objects inside its rooms, was the renowned Liberty Bell, housed on resounding national grounds on which President Lincoln insisted, more than a hundred years before blacks gathered to mourn King and protest their continuing disenfranchisement, "that rather than preserve the Union by surrendering the principles of the Declaration, he would prefer to be assassinated on the spot" and that "to defend the legacy of Jefferson's Declaration . . . meant . . . that the city"—where, as both William Wells Brown and Frederick Douglass insisted, "prejudice against color is . . . rampant"—"must uphold the equality of all men in spite of itself" (Weigley, Wainwright, and Wolf 1982, 394, 386). The ideals animating Lincoln's statement—freedom, democracy, equality, the toll and toil of pursuing and preserving liberty, the glorious dream of a beloved community—resound in especially poignant ways in the presence of William Penn's welcoming shadow. Certainly, these black Philadelphians, assembling in early April 1968 on these grounds despite what may have been their ignorance of Lincoln's second inaugural address, were abundantly aware of the Hall's symbolic meaning and the Declaration's principles that had rarely been deemed by those with local, state, or national political power to apply to members of their race. These "thousands of blacks, angry and sullen," were engaged in as quintessentially American a ritual as Lincoln and the four million visitors who descended on the hallowed grounds annually during the 1960s and 1970s, their nonviolent protest honoring both King and the American experiment in ways that surpassed any gesture offered in the wake of his death of which I am aware.

Busy instituting a state of emergency and tired, perhaps, of wrangling with various members of the Philadelphia sports bureaucracy, with whom he had had to bicker over funding necessary repairs to the Spectrum, the 76ers' new arena whose roof had been blown off two months earlier by a "fierce gale" (W. Johnson 1968, 20–21), Mayor Tate was not involved in assessing whether the scheduled game between the 76ers and the Celtics should be played and the potential impact of such a decision on black residents. Boston's Mayor White, however, incorporated James Brown's concert into his multifaceted plan to limit rioting. Before the concert, he offered a statement that, if it did not rise to the eloquence of the remarks offered by presidential candidate Robert Kennedy when he announced to an Indiana crowd that King had been murdered the previous evening, similarly emphasized the importance of forging a lasting peace:

> Twenty-four hours ago . . . , Dr. King died for all of us, black and white, that we may live together in harmony. Now I'm here tonight to ask you to make Dr. King's dream a reality in Boston. This is our city and its future is in our hands. So all I ask you tonight is this: Let us look at each other, here in the Garden and back at home, and pledge that no matter what any community might do, we in Boston will honor Dr. King in peace. Thank you. (Whalen 2004, 7)

The renowned black music critic Nelson George has said of the entertainer whom Mayor White came to believe possessed both the showmanship and cultural capital to suppress riotous impulses in Beantown, "During the 1960s James Brown singlehandedly demonstrated the possibilities for artistic and economic freedom that black music could provide if one constantly struggled against its limitations" (1988, 98). Having made himself "a living symbol of black self-determination," Brown exhibited none of the self-doubt and fear of susceptibility to white manipulation that haunted Chet Walker. As a consequence, as the reports and grainy concert footage from that night attest, Brown produced a characteristically brilliant, quintessentially rousing performance.

Moreover, despite his emotional reactions to the death of the civil rights leader with whom he was acquainted, Brown remained sufficiently level-headed to (1) make live appeals for calm to listeners of his radio stations in Knoxville and Baltimore and tape other messages that could be played throughout the crisis, (2) renegotiate an appearance contract so that the concert could be broadcast without him subsequently getting into legal difficulties, (3) calculate the potentially calamitous financial implications for him of the announcement by city officials that the concert would be televised, and (4) most interestingly, discuss with one of Boston's black politicians the advantages and disadvantages of King's nonviolent philosophy. Brown and city officials were ultimately even more convinced than the basketball figures assembled in Philadelphia that performing would have a felicitous impact. After being "met at Logan Airport by Mayor Kevin White's limousine and a city councilman named Thomas Atkins," he was informed that "the National Guard was on alert and standing by" (Brown and Tucker 1986, 183–184) to stop rioting if it broke out in Boston on a large scale. Atkins informed Brown that

> city officials had spent the morning arguing about whether to let my concert go on. The mayor wanted to cancel it, but Atkins told him that would just make matters worse. If many people from Roxbury showed up downtown at the Garden and found a lock on the door, trouble would start. Atkins said he told the mayor he'd be lucky if his own office was left standing. Then somebody came up with the idea of televising the concert live. That way people could stay home and see the show, and the people who showed up wouldn't find a locked door. (184)

Fully aware that King's assassination would "bring a great deal of violence, burning, and death" nationally, Brown agreed to assist city officials who wanted to televise his show live to keep blacks indoors, sufficiently mesmerized by his performance that they would choose not to riot. And despite his chagrin that these officials had announced their plans to broadcast the show before consulting him, inspiring fans to travel to the Garden during the daylight hours of April 5 to return tickets to a concert they could now watch for free in the relative safety of their own homes, the singer chose to honor, and even to rework the terms of, his contract.

Brown, who perceived a direct relationship between his calls for restraint that were aired continuously on the Baltimore and Knoxville radio stations he owned and the fact that "those two cities had less trouble than most" (Brown and Tucker 1986, 183), insisted that his broadcasted concert helped Boston to get "through the weekend almost without any trouble at all" (187–188). The outsized sense of self-certainty that inspires these conclusions is also in evidence during his ride in the mayor's limousine from Logan Airport when he and Atkins discuss "how we felt about Dr. King."

I said, "I want to do a show tonight because I want to dedicate it to him. I didn't always agree with him, but he was a great man and he did a lot for all of us."

"He was remarkable."

"Yes he was," I said. If I was faced with some of the same situations he was—people beating me, throwing things at me, cursing me, spitting on me—I don't know if I could stay nonviolent, not as a matter of *philosophy*."

"I know what you mean," he said. "I once spent an entire night in Mississippi in 1964 arguing that point with him. I'm nonviolent if I have to be, but I don't want anybody to ever make the mistake of thinking they could hit me and get away with it."

"Brother, that's where I'm at," I said. "But I had the deepest respect and love for him." (185)

It is curious that, just hours after King's assassination, a black elected politician and Soul Brother Number One discussed the rationality of nonviolence. While it is certainly not their intention to blame King for his own demise, their exchange suggests that they did not consider the civil rights leader's guiding principle of nonviolence a viable way to address late-1960s struggles to assert black manhood, a quality that these men, dedicated to striking back at antagonists no matter what the cost, claim to have in spades. Though they profess to "respect and love" King, their conversation devolves into an endorsement of a rugged black masculinity that never lets "anybody"—any white male in particular—"make the mistake of thinking they could hit me and get away with it."

These men attest to admiring King because "he did a lot for us" at the same time that they deride him for having allowed white racists to curse at, spit on, throw things at, and ultimately murder him without exacting revenge or concerning himself with self-defense. The debate about how to react precisely to racial violence was, of course, the source of philosophical and, eventually, generational strife with which King dealt frequently. As he states in "The Power of Nonviolence," one of his many explanations of the principles that inform his notions of effective civil rights struggle,

There was always the problem of getting this method over because it didn't make sense to most of the people in the beginning. . . . We need to make it clear that nonviolent resistance is not a method of cowardice. It does resist. . . . The nonviolent resister is just as opposed to the evil that he is standing against as the violent resister but he resists without violence. This method is nonaggressive physically but strongly aggressive spiritually.

... Our aim is not to defeat [or] ... humiliate the white community, but to win the friendship of all of the persons who had perpetrated this system in the past. The ... aftermath of violence is bitterness. The aftermath of nonviolence is reconciliation and the creation of a beloved community. A boycott is never an end within itself. It is merely a means to awaken a sense of shame within the oppressor but the end is reconciliation, the end is redemption. (1986d, 12)

King's ultimate goal, the establishment of the United States as a beloved interracial community, could be accomplished only if whites looked critically at systemic racism, found it morally abhorrent, and disavowed it in favor of a version of *agape*, the Greek concept of "disinterested love ... in which the individual seeks not his own good, but the good of his neighbor," and which "springs from the need of the other person—his need for belonging to the best in the human family" (King 1986a, 19). Given the tenor of Brown and Atkins's conversation on the day after King's death, it is clear that, the civil rights leader's views of its courageous and "aggressive" dimensions notwithstanding, these men did not fully embrace a tactic that did not encourage a retributive response to racially motivated violence. Brown was far more accepting than the SCLC leadership of "the flash point of Negro rage" King identified as always "close at hand" (1986e, 65) in "Showdown for Nonviolence," a comparison of Black Power and nonviolent strategies for achieving black empowerment that appeared posthumously in *Look*.

While King remained "committed to nonviolence absolutely," having lived through three consecutive summers of intense rioting in American cities and the enthusiastic embrace of Black Power, he admitted "that if our nonviolent campaign doesn't generate some progress [particularly in the North], people are just going to engage in more violent activity, and the discussion of guerrilla warfare will be more extensive" (1986e, 69). In his view,

there is no longer a choice now between nonviolence and riots. It must be militant, massive nonviolence, or riots. The discontent is so deep, the anger so ingrained, the despair, the restlessness so wide, that something has to be brought into being to serve as a channel through which these deep emotional feelings, these deep angry feelings, can be funneled. There has to be an outlet ... , a way to transmute the inchoate rage of the ghetto into a constructive and creative channel. (69)

Rather than accept both nonviolence protests and riotous destruction as rational collective responses to racial injustice, King argues, Americans had to determine which expression of "inchoate rage" they would abide in a country whose white citizens "are [so] infected with racism" that, at least with regard to their examination of the lives of blacks, they often ignored the fact that they are "also infected with democratic ideals" (71). Recognizing both the volcanic black rage that he believed needed to be channeled through the orderly structures of nonviolent resistance and the necessity for politically and economically empowered whites to ameliorate the high levels of "unemployment and pitiful wages [that] are at the bottom of ghetto misery" and "undermine family life" (1986c, 191), King endorses a conservative notion of black gender relations. Echoing Daniel Patrick Moynihan's much-maligned report on black American families, King argues that

> the Negro male precedes his wife in unemployment. As a consequence, he lives in a matriarchal society within the larger culture, which is patriarchal. The cruelest blow to his integrity as a man are laws which deprive a family of Aid to Dependent Children support if a male resides in the home. He is then forced to abandon his family so that they may survive. He is coerced into irresponsibility by his responsible love for his family. (191)

Toward the end of his life, King spoke increasingly about male self-actualization. (This topic also comes to dominate the sonic landscape of R&B music, as I discuss in Chapter 2.) For example, he insists that "the Negro must rise up with an affirmation of his own Olympian manhood. . . . The Negro will only be free when he reaches down to the depths of his own being and signs with the pen and ink of assertive manhood his own emancipation proclamation" (1986f, 246). In this formulation, King offers points of entry to his philosophy of nonviolence more likely to resonate with the agitated masses concerned with restoring a putatively lost black masculinity than his earlier conciliatory emphases on reciprocal love, *agape*, *philia*, beloved communities, and mutually advantageous fellowship with whites. Despite King's emphasis on the courageousness of nonviolence, however, his philosophy came increasingly to be seen by many blacks as insufficiently masculine. In contrast to an emphatically retribution-minded Malcolm X, whom Ossie Davis famously dubbed "our manhood, our living, black manhood" (quoted in Haley 1965, 521), King, who insisted that he was seeking not "to humiliate or defeat the opponent, but to win his friendship and understanding" (1986d, 12, 13), appeared—at a time when the protection, articulation, and demonstrative exhibition of black manhood had become *the point*, for many activists, of sociopolitical agitation—to be what James Brown speaks of, in another context, as "girlish" (Brown and Eliot 2005, 71). Whatever else we might say about Brown's stated admiration of King, he was so opposed to the absolutist dimensions of the philosophy of nonviolence that he articulated his dissent as a prelude to planning a public commemoration of King and clearly doubted whether the martyred civil rights leader had provided a viable example of what one of his popular earlier releases terms "a man's man" whom "guys admire . . . [for his] strength and manliness[,] and look . . . [to] for direction" (71).

But having been compelled to perform at the scheduled Boston Garden concert, Brown confronted a dilemma not wholly different from Chet Walker's. Striving to honor King and to prevent rioting, he exposed himself to the sort of manipulation that regularly stymied the basketball star's nascent urgings toward resistance. In representing the messy fallout of the announcement, Brown connects his own anger with that of "the people who had tickets and the people who are excited about seeing it [his concert] at home"; thus, when he asserts that "instead of cooling things off, it's going to heat them up. The whole thing is a disaster. I want to stop riots, not start them" (Brown and Tucker 1986, 185–186), he, like Walker, recognizes that he was placed in a position in which refusing to participate in the "mess" created by others' responses to King's assassination means risking being held responsible for any resultant riotous behavior.

After Mayor White opens the concert by imploring blacks to "honor Dr. King in peace," Brown speaks directly to audience members watching in their homes, clearly ignoring the riotous potential of the roughly two thousand fans waiting to cheer, applaud, and generally have a funky good time with him in the Garden. He tells the television audience, "Let's not do anything to dishonor Dr. King. . . . Stay home. You kids, especially, I want you to think about what you're doing. Think about what Dr. King stood for. Don't just react in a way that's going to destroy your community" (Brown and Tucker 1986, 187). However pointedly Brown's message addressed the circumstances of viewers in the city's black neighborhoods, if the assembled fans gave in to destructive impulses once they left his presence, they would more likely have damaged the Garden, North Station, and Fanueil Hall, as well as historic national landmarks and a neighborhood populated primarily by affluent whites than their own, infinitely less well-maintained communities.

Brown concludes his autobiographical account of this concert by situating himself as mediator between members of the audience, whose emotions were driven to a state of frenzy by his performance, and the police force, whose tasks included protecting the singer and ensuring that a riot did not break out within or just outside the Garden. As I have suggested, caustic interactions between blacks engaged in seemingly transgressive behavior and aggressive, mistrustful white policemen precipitated riots in American cities during the summers from 1964 through 1967. Assembled in the Boston Garden, then, were the prime ingredients—excitable black citizens and suspicious white policemen—for an urban riot. In this case, however, the unsanctioned black behavior that law enforcement agents moved to police was essentially dramaturgical in nature, entailing the dissolution of an imaginary wall between audience and entertainer, between patron and wondrous display. This dissolution can be said to have been justified, perhaps even required, by long-established rules of black cultural performance that encourage a participatory relationship between leader and audience in forms of black expressivity, especially music and ministerial rhetoric, which rely on mutual inspiration, and in which, as I discuss elsewhere, "there is no sharp line between performers or communications and the audience, for virtually everyone is performing and everyone is listening" (Awkward 1989, 108).

From the vantage point of such participatory impulses, it is possible to argue that cultural differences led the white policemen to misconstrue the behavior of, and hence the potential threat posed by, the audience. Indeed, Brown's assumption of the role of expressive cultural leader and recognition that he is uniquely positioned to prevent a riotous maelstrom inform his reactions when audience members storm the stage:

> When we went into our finale, some of the fans at the Garden jumped up on their stage. They started dancing and shaking hands with me. That upset the police. They started to move in. I knew that all it would take to destroy everything I'd been trying to do all night was for there to be an incident with the police and have it televised. I stopped the music and asked the police to back off. "I'm all right," I said. "I'm all right. I want to shake their hands." . . . [W]e finished the show without any problem. (Brown and Tucker 1986, 187–188)

As William Van Deburg argues, the R&B singer of the 1960s and 1970s "evoked, embodied, and transmitted the warmth, pathos, and funkiness of group folk-life," presenting himself or herself as a "transparently extraordinary . . . member of the black extended family" who, because he or she is "capable of effecting spontaneous concert hall combustion within minutes," has been elevated "to the status of culture hero" (1997, 217–218). Certainly, no performer generated more combustion than Brown, whose propulsive grunts, gospel-influenced singing, polyrhythmic beats, and mesmerizing movements constitute archetypal examples of black American vocal and physical expressivity. Inspiring physical participation from his listeners is an essential point of Brown's music, as is generating sufficient levels of psychic release and emotional engagement to ensure that he, his musicians, and his listeners are all having—in the words of one of his hits—"a funky good time." If, as many observers have claimed, R&B helped to delegitimize the racial segregation of white and black youth in the South—for example, the Temptations' Otis Williams speaks of the removal of a rope separating blacks and whites at a South Carolina audience as "a step" toward racial "progress" (Williams and Romanowski 1989, 79)—the social function Brown performed included minimizing distinctions between hero and common folk. Indeed, he allowed audience members to be both engaged listeners and powerful participants, as its members' invasion of the stage demonstrated that he was a tangible, soulful presence, and underscored the differences between live and televised spectacle.

However else we might interpret them, Brown's actions "confirmed his power that the previous summer had led vice-president and presidential candidate Hubert Humphrey to give him an award for helping quell riots with public statements" (George 1988, 103). Given the interest of militants in retributive violence, Carmichael's concern about the singer's ability to get blacks to listen was obviously well founded. Hours after Carmichael extolled a crowd of angry, anguished blacks in D.C. to "go home and get you a gun and then come back because I got me a gun" for protection against "the white man . . . coming to kill you" (Brown and Tucker 1986, 145), and despite his own struggles with city officials who had helped create legal and logistical messes for him from which he had to extricate himself, Brown used the Boston Garden stage to urge his audiences to remain calm and nonviolent, and to pursue racial harmony.

Chet Walker sifted through the disparate rhetoric of black resistance articulated by leaders such as King, Malcolm X, and Carmichael in an effort to achieve a compatible mode of self-expression. Given his acknowledged familiarity with Malcolm X's dazzling verbal and political skills, it seems appropriate to return briefly at this point to Ossie Davis's eulogizing of Malcolm X as the quintessential black male leader:

[Malcolm] . . . knew that every Negro who did not challenge on the spot every instance of racism, overt or covert, committed against him or his people, who chose instead to swallow his spit and go on smiling, was an Uncle Tom and a traitor, without balls or guts, or any other commonly accepted aspect of manhood! (1965, 525)

According to these perspectives, Walker's decision to play reduced him to the status of a grinning, gutless race traitor, an emasculated Uncle Tom devoid of self-respect. Davis's characterization of Malcolm X resonates, in its opposition of righteous black manliness and treacherous (Uncle) tomfoolery, with Harry Edwards's explanation of why blacks would boycott the 1968 Olympics:

> I don't think any black athlete will go [to] the Olympics. If they do go, I don't think they'll come back. I am not threatening. I am not encouraging violence. I am assessing reality. I know the demeanor of the black people. They see a black man back from the Olympics, and they'll say, "Look at the devil, with his medal hanging around his neck." Some of them are going to have accidents. You can't live with the crackers and come back to Harlem. The athlete who goes will face ostracism and harassment. People are fed up with those shufflin' niggers. Them days are long gone. The black athlete who goes will be a traitor to his race, and will be treated as such. (Quoted in Bass 2002, 199)

From our current vantage point, it is impossible to imagine any black person living up to Davis's bombastic ideals. Certainly, Edwards's prophesy was called into question by a poll whose results appeared in the March 1968 edition of *Ebony*, in which "a massive 71 percent" of black athletes claimed to be "categorically against" an Olympic boycott, largely because they "don't like what they think is an infringement of their right to *individual* rather than *group* thinking" (Bass 2002, 202). Still, the inescapable implication of comments such as Davis's and Edwards's is that because Walker played in the game, he had engaged in an unmanly act of treason akin to the behaviors of "shufflin' niggers" and, hence, deserves to be ostracized. Walker's trauma, which he begins to resolve only when he can perceive of his end-of-career contract negotiations as structurally analogous to the treatment of his male ancestors as property, involves, among other things, his fear of being excluded from post–civil rights conceptions of black "Olympian manhood."

Discussions of King's assassination serve as tragic points of reference for autobiographical and historical accounts highlighting a growing pessimism about the possibilities of continued black social, political, and economic progress.[7] And like the sections of autobiographies by Chet Walker, James Brown, and Wilt Chamberlain that explore the implications of King's murder, Otis Williams's discussion of the "atmosphere of shock and disbelief" that "overwhelmed" the Temptations during the group's concert in Charleston, South Carolina on April 4, 1968 (Williams and Romanowski 1989, 130) hint at some of the myriad political and artistic implications of such performances. Unlike these other black cultural heroes, soul's most distinguished vocal group, whose music, beginning with "Cloud Nine," engaged political topics for the first time following King's murder, did not see its choice about whether to perform as having any potential impact on rioting either in their scheduled venue or nationally. Even though members of the group expressed "concern that King's assassination would spark racial violence," unlike the 76er-Celtic game, which was preceded by "a moment of silent prayer ... for Dr. King" that Walker viewed as a quintessential example of American sports' soulless "formalities" (Walker and Messenger 1995, 199), and Brown's concert, during which Boston's mayor and the Godfather of Soul urged blacks to honor King by resisting any riotous impulses they might be feeling, the Temptations "didn't even bother saying anything about King, because what was there to say" (Williams and Romanowski 1989, 130).

Chet Walker's passive response to the assassination constitutes a watershed episode for him, as his attendant psychological pressures led him to feel he had dishonored King's memory and the civil rights movement. It is positioned as the thematic center of his life story, the most resonant illustration of capitulatory tendencies that link him with earlier generations of black men who had been, or had been treated as, the property of powerful white Americans. And while a host of factors militated against his intervention—grief, confusion, disorganization, and the possibility of suspension, fines, and fan rioting—Walker's failure deeply affected him for the better part of three decades. Able neither to join other black Philadelphians in Independence Square to express dissatisfaction with a nation whose proclamation of "liberty ... unto all the inhabitants" continued to be little more than empty rhetoric on a cracked bell nor to provide an "outlet" for the "inchoate rage" surging through "the ghetto" that cried out for "a constructive and creative channel," Walker remained mired in a state of traumatic isolation and masculine failure. But if theorists of trauma are correct in their insistence that that state cannot be overcome until the survivor is able to communicate the details of his or her traumatic experience, Walker's memoir serves as an essential step in his quest for voice, historical continuity, and self-ownership. While James Brown insists that he was able to "pull . . . myself together" "when I was reminiscing about Martin . . . [and] I started to cry—just a few tears rolling out, you know, nothing anybody could really see" (Brown and Tucker 1986, 187)—and, hence, to manifest the psychic self-control required of a manly black cultural icon who could "stop riots" (186), Walker could not organize his thoughts sufficiently or "stop a basketball game." But if he was unable to lead members of his race who were "mourning and screaming in pain," telling his story appears to stem the flow of unrelenting pain caused by his failure and to push him toward the possibilities of his own racial healing.

2

Haunted Longings

*Nostalgic Black Musical Formulations of Masculinity
and the Patriarchal Family*

*Kenny Gamble (right) and Leon Huff, Philadelphia International Records visionaries
who produced pro-black family songs like "I'll Always Love My Mama" and "Family
Reunion." (Photo by BMI/Michael Ochs Archives/Getty Images.)*

*I*n September 1973, I began a three-year stint at Governor Dummer Academy (GDA), a northern Massachusetts institution that prides itself in being is the oldest boarding school in the United States. I had been deemed an acceptable risk by the school's administrators and by A Better Chance (ABC), a program that placed promising black and brown inner-city teenagers in excellent public and private high schools.¹ Having grown up in South Philly where, during the previous five years, I attended overcrowded, graffiti-, gang-, and apathy-infested schools, I spent my first months as a scholarship student acclimating myself to the lush, 450-acre grounds that I shared with more than 300 whites—including thirty knowledgeable and largely gifted educators—and about a dozen other nonwhites.

Because of my origins in a city renowned for its meticulous preservation of its hallowed history, its downtown stores brimming with plastic Liberty Bell replicas, its tourist centers offering daily performances of key- and kite-adorned Ben Franklins and sober, drably attired Quakers, I felt a sense of solace to be associated with an institution that also had a Colonial past. And like the brazen use of Philadelphia's sun-drenched yesterdays by my elementary and junior high teachers to school their young charges in the conventions of good American citizenship, GDA's history—which included a Massachusetts governor, Paul Revere, John Quincy Adams, and Booker T. Washington, Jr.— was invoked frequently by administrators and teachers to compel the illusion of full cooperation from its student body. Positioned literally and figuratively between two unquestionably superb prep schools, Exeter and Andover (the latter of which was founded by one of its own alumni), GDA's exploitation of its primacy reminded me of frustrated First City expressions of stark envy of a never-sleeping New York and a politically and legislatively incomparable D.C. Actually, being aware of its relatively modest place in the region's preppy hierarchy and mocking its name in a fashion that was also self-deprecating (which is a worse surname, I had asked, Awkward or Dummer?) helped me feel emboldened in my strange new world where, instead of being discombobulated by its workload, public bathrooms, and marshy owl-, skunk-, and snake-filled environs, I was overwhelmed by, and often felt diminished in the face of, the atmosphere's overwhelmingly cultural whiteness.

Indeed, pale skin, finger-combed and carefully brushed blond and chestnut brown hair, blue-veined behinds—it was, after all, the era of streaking—and New England-accented Standard English dexterity were less daunting to my narrow inner-city sensibilities than omnipresent Caucasian music. The offspring of doctors, businesspeople, lawyers, teachers, and one of the nation's most famous military generals, GDA's white students adorned their rooms with lacrosse and hockey sticks; tennis rackets; Humphrey Bogart, KISS, Marilyn

Monroe, James Dean, and Raquel Welch posters; and expensive stereo equipment on which they blasted pristinely maintained albums featuring screeching vocalists and electric-guitar-laden music whose assault on my unaccustomed eardrums was unremitting. Walking from my room to the bathroom, I traversed a hallway reverberating with the Moody Blues; Cream; the Who; Boston; Emerson, Lake, and Palmer; Jimi Hendrix; and, of course, the Rolling Stones. Eventually, when my hall mates and I grew familiar enough to inquire about one another's peculiarities—why I plaited my six-inch Afro every night, for example, and why my Alice Cooper–loving neighbor washed his hair only once a month—they lowered their systems' volume so that they could be heard extolling the virtues of Mick Jagger and Robert Plant. The voices of these singers, these rock aficionados explained, were steeped in the blues, as were the licks of Keith Richards and Jimmy Page, the guitarists accompanying them. Typically, I politely declined their requests that I acknowledge the excellence of music for which I had no appreciation, including—much to their consternation—the blues. In response, I asked why they settled for Mick's clipped, cloying vocals when truly great contemporary singers abounded, including Aretha Franklin, Stevie Wonder, Marvin Gaye, the Temptations, Donny Hathaway, and Harold Melvin and the Blue Notes, whose smooth vocal harmonies and deep-throated lead singer, Teddy Pendergrass, I admired partly because they hailed from my city and had come to represent the distant—and distinct—sounds of home for me.

I stood no chance of prevailing in debates over the respective quality of genres of racial music. Its musical and vocal excellence barely audible on my tinny Woolworth portable record player, Aretha's "Till You Come Back to Me" was drowned out by Led Zeppelin's incomprehensible "Stairway to Heaven." At a time when our English teachers were insisting that the enduring value of works from Romeo and Juliet *to* The Heart of Darkness *was the result of universal themes and highly metaphoric language, how could the literalness of Aretha's matter-of-fact, love-struck declarations compete with Led Zeppelin's booming assertions of the ambiguity of words? Even if Lady Soul explores the depths to which unrequited love can make us sink, Led Zeppelin's abstruse lyrics examine, my white peers told me, a far grander issue: the dissatisfied, erudite modern individual seeking to escape the superficial realm of base desire.*

Without an analytical leg to stand on, up against cultural forces that recognized imagistic and thematic ties between Shakespeare, Emily Brontë, William Golding, and Led Zeppelin that even the most divinely inspired R&B was not generally seen as possessing, I decided ultimately to stop advocating. Instead, at least until the O'Jays' 1975 release of the album Family Reunion, *one of whose songs bore the same title as Led Zeppelin's opus, I was content to listen behind* my tightly closed door—occasionally with other black students—to my short stack of soul records. Clearly referencing the rock anthem that begins with a materialistic woman hoping to buy her way into heaven, the persona of the O'Jays' song pursues a pirate's treasure, interested in neither multiple meanings nor elusive references but erotic pleasure and harmony exclusively. Isolated from the rest of the world by their passion, methodically unburdening themselves of the pressures of modern life as they approach ecstasy, the enthralled lovers confront nothing as confounding as—in the Zeppelin song—closed stores, the skeptical warbles of songbirds, a choice between equally attractive paths, or a lady bent on illuminating music's elusive power. Sensuous and emotional rather than ethereal and intellectual, the O'Jays' "Stairway to Heaven" emphasizes soul-exposing sexual arousal and release, especially in an extended, tour-de-force conclusion. Embodying R&B's capacity for earthly transcendence, its heaven seemed particularly inviting to a love-starved teenager. By contrast, Led Zeppelin's highbrow, assaultive song engaged a false paradise to which I was neither sonically nor emotionally attracted.

If I was frustrated that "Stairway to Heaven," the highlight of the 1975 O'Jays' Family Reunion, would never be appreciated by my white peers, I was also deeply ambivalent about the album's title track. While the song's sounds and pro-family sentiments were appealing—they made me miss my siblings, mom, aunts, and aspects of home immensely—its idealization of the nuclear family delegitimized my experiences and those of the majority of kids with whom I had grown up who were children of single mothers. A song that has become a quintessential Sound of Philadelphia and a staple at black family gatherings, including those facilitated by Temple University's Family Reunion Institute, though grounded sonically in a black American cultural particularity, stigmatized me and projected the realities not of inner-city black children but of my white schoolmates, as normal and highly preferable. Each mid-October, on Parents' Weekend, hordes of white adults crowded GDA's buildings, dormitories, and walkways, causing me to feel triply conspicuous: black, poor, and parentless. My mother remained safely in Philadelphia, away from the penetrating scrutiny of white parents whose curious glances I interpreted as pity and condemnation, even as they welcomed me to dine with their children who were also my friends. As I confronted early 1970s white upper-middle-class nuclear family intactness, the absence of my rolling-stone father, whom I did not know or care to know, caused me to feel deeply ashamed. These glimpses of abiding familial ties confirmed the O'Jays' notions not just of the necessity of heterosexual coupling but of the perversity—the brokenness—of households bereft of the guiding force of the benevolent father. Unable to see the poorly stitched rips in the fabrics of these and other seemingly ideal American *families, I wondered at times if, despite the opportunity for success that GDA and ABC provided me, my own fundamental abnormality—black fatherlessness—was an insurmountable obstacle.*

As I looked at white men who were dentists, doctors, lawyers, teachers, and psychiatrists, who drove nice cars and smiled brightly at their suddenly homesick children, the O'Jays' insistence that the father is the dominant family figure and source of guidance seemed like a taunt or a curse. At times, the song seemed like a harsh warning, sent from Philadelphia by people who seemed otherwise to understand my actual and imagined lives, that I was destined to fail because no matter how much I learned, my origins disqualified me from partaking of the good American life that was the destiny of classmates who had been correctly, paternally nurtured. At those moments, I felt doomed because of the absence of my deadbeat, good-for-nothing dad, even though he had not perfected a lucrative trade, won a court case, helped young kids learn algebraic equations, mastered the art of the business deal, or learned to win friends and influence people. To my knowledge, all he had achieved, besides fathering some children and leaving my mother with physical and psychological scars that never healed, was a determined departure just ahead of Philadelphia policemen and court employees, none of whom tried very hard to detain him or, after his escape, discover his whereabouts. Because of his absence and not what ought to have been disqualifying failings, when I was confronted with Parents' Weekend scenes and the sounds of "Family Reunion," I feared that I had already failed.

The Philadelphia International album that appeared in the middle of my GDA experiences, then, offered me cultural ammunition against pervasive whiteness and the climatic visions of romantic intimacy, as well as a portrait of the patriarchal family that marginalized me as dramatically as did exposure to the Rolling Stones' "Brown Sugar" and ruddy-cheeked adolescent jokesters who insisted that their fathers were paying for my scholarship. Looked at in the context of my peculiar struggles to comprehend the significance of race, culture, and upbringing, to reference the Led Zeppelin song that I learned not to despise, Family Reunion had at least two meanings, inspiring in me a state of upheaval that, ultimately, I found emotionally and intellectually invigorating.

Around the same time that I was struggling with this touchstone album and its implications, Elton John, the massively popular British singer influenced by Motown, Stax, and other forms of black and American music, released "Philadelphia Freedom." Dedicated to "BJK," the pioneering tennis star Billie Jean King, who defeated Bobby Riggs and captained Philly's World Team Tennis squad, and to "the Soulful Sounds of Philadelphia" produced by the Mighty Three—Thom Bell, Kenny Gamble, and Leon Huff—John's song also tapped into the bicentennial spirit that overtook the United States and was centered in large part on its First City. But as gratifying as it was for me to hear pop music's megastar extol my city's musical virtues and to imagine challenging white schoolmates to deny its contributions in the face of John's dedication, I was troubled by the fact that the song's meaning was as indecipherable to me as Led Zeppelin's "Stairway to Heaven." Why, I wondered, would a Brit claim to imbibe the revolutionary American spirit that, two hundred years earlier, soundly defeated and permanently weakened his own nation? What led him to leave home? Were the changes he referenced inaugurated by various civil rights groups that ultimately benefited the dedicatees of the song: black Americans who were largely responsible for the First City's place at the forefront of R&B, and homosexuals, an identity that King surreptitiously acknowledged as early as 1968 despite her marriage to Lawrence King and John himself later sought briefly to obfuscate by marrying Renate Blauel? What work is enabled by his silence? Why did he prefer not having family ties? How did this freedom imbue him with a sense of tranquillity never experienced by his own father?

What is clear, beyond its toe-tapping rhythms and seductive chorus and bass line, is that its disdain for or rejection of family places it thematically at odds with sentiments offered in lyrics and promotional materials connected to Philadelphia International. It is not coincidental that Philly Soul owes its orchestrated rhythms to a core group of stellar musicians who released albums under the name MFSB, an acronym for Mother Father Sister Brother. Unlike Motown's legendary Funk Brothers, the Philly label's house band was familiar to fans of R&B and pop, particularly after its "TSOP (The Sound of Philadelphia)" topped the pop charts in 1974, became the theme song of Don Cornelius's Soul Train, *and solidified the First City's place as the fulcrum of black popular musical production. Indeed, the label's primary ideological force and lyricist, coproducer and co-owner Kenny Gamble, insists in* Family Reunion's *liner notes that the "divided . . . family structure" has had disastrous consequences, halting "the flow of wisdom" from older to younger generations and "stifling the energy of the youth." Responding to Philadelphia's fraternal commitments with a more expansive notion of obligation, Gamble argues that "we must recapture the family structure—Mother, Father, Sister, and Brother"—and "put the 'unity' back into the family" if post–civil rights era children are to actualize their individual and collective potential.*

So while Elton John's "Philadelphia Freedom," released in February 1975 in part to honor the United States' two-hundred-year-old revolutionary spirit and encouragement of the pursuit of individual freedom, pays tribute sonically to Philly Soul, its representation of family as an obstacle to personal growth and self-fulfillment is fundamentally at odds with Philadelphia International's wistful familial yearnings. As gratifying as it was to know that my schoolmates had added a song honoring my city's music to their record collections, its anti-family individualism made placing it alongside Family Reunion, *for me, challenging and ultimately impossible. The pursuit of individual freedom, Gamble opines, has undermined the black American family, which in turn diminished the quality of its individual citizens' lives. According to this view, answers to life's important questions are discoverable not during solipsistic excursions in search of or governed by qualities John characterizes as "Philadelphia freedom" but in the institution of the black family, "recaptured" in all its patriarchal, pre–Great Society splendor, in which emotional support and the transference of wisdom are lovingly provided.*

Experiencing the song as falsely seductive, conveying nostalgic or utopian dreams of nuclear familial unity that could never come true for scores of black boys and girls in Philadelphia and throughout the nation, I began to take note of the increasing emphasis in R&B songs on the family unit generally and the role of fathers in particular. The commendable goals of integration notwithstanding, growing up in a neighborhood where paternal involvement was rare, I wondered what it meant for other fatherless black children to witness families that the O'Jays insisted looked, sounded, and were, indeed, normal in ways that ours could never be, no matter how much we learned, how hard we studied, and how diligently we strove to represent ourselves, our families, and our race in the best possible way.

The very questions we pose about the past are influenced by how we view the present. Which questions we choose to ask, as well as the answers we obtain, depends in considerable part on our approach to the politics of racism in the present.
—Robert Paynter, "Afro-Americans in the Massachusetts Historical Landscape"

In highly heterogeneous societies, meaning is more likely to result from a song's similarity to and difference from other songs within the total musical field, from the codes it activates and from the subject positions and competences it makes available to listeners that permit them to identify those codes. In this type of society, virtually anyone can be a "cultural insider" with respect to any type of music, although factors of class, ethnicity, and gender make some identifications more likely than others.
—David Brackett, *Interpreting Popular Music*

Authors . . . employ nostalgia and the tropes of home and home-
sickness to represent certain relationships between psychological
and cultural experience, including displacement and the poten-
tiality for imaginative repair. The idea of reparation presupposes
damage or injury. . . . [T]hat damage may be understood as emo-
tional/psychological—the narcissistic "injury" of separation that
inevitably occurs during infancy and childhood, and from which
most of us endeavor to recover.

—Roberta Rubenstein, *Home Matters*

D uring the first half of the 1970s, R&B continued its explorations of
social issues, a thematic swerve that, as we have seen, empowered
James Brown—whose music was less overtly focused on the machinations of romantic love than that of his contemporaries—to imagine a seamless
connection between funky grooves and sociopolitical progress. For example,
the considerations of R&B artists, songwriters, and producers were included
in the cacophony of responses to Daniel Patrick Moynihan's 1965 report on
the crumbling "Negro family in the urban ghettos" and its entrapment in a
"cycle of poverty and disadvantage" (i). On the surface, such songs—Brown's
own "Papa Don't Take No Mess," Gladys Knight and the Pips' "Daddy Could
Swear, I Declare," the Chi-Lites' "The Man My Daddy Was," and the Spinners'
"Sadie" among them—challenged Moynihan's notions of defective bonds
and limited opportunity, touting the long-standing health of components of
the black family by focusing on an individual parent's salutary impact on his
or her child. However, beneath the surface, these songs generally expressed
anxieties about the state of the institution and a palpable longing for its radical transformation, which would require, in Moynihan's words, "a unity of
purpose to the many activities of the Federal government . . . directed to a
new kind of national goal: the establishment of a stable Negro family structure" (1965, i). The black American family's stability, in other words, requires
recognition on the part of the government that that unit is "battered and ha-
rassed by discrimination, injustice, and uprooting" (4), as well as the altera-
tion of its "matriarchal structure which, because it is so out of line with the
rest of the American society, seriously retards the progress of the group as a
whole, and imposes a crushing burden on the Negro male" (29).

According to Moynihan, the black family's health necessitated the establishment of employment opportunities for fathers—emasculated because of their inability to be primary breadwinners in "a society in which
males are dominant in family relationships" (1965, 29)—that would, in turn,

inaugurate patriarchal order, altering the community's perverse gendered dynamics that reflect "American slavery['s] . . . lasting effects on individuals and their children" (15). Here, Moynihan echoes W.E.B. Du Bois's argument in *The Philadelphia Negro* and those of numerous other scholars that "slavery created laws and social norms that broke the bonds between fathers and children," producing a legacy of "family instability . . . [and] father absence in the African American families" because of "a caste-like status that isolates and carves for them a specialized and inferior niche within the social stratification system" (Lu et al. 2010, S2 50).

Despite or perhaps because of the successes of the civil rights movement, the institution of the black family has suffered tremendously since King's assassination according to almost every conceivable measure. Indeed, the 1970s witnessed the dramatic increases in out-of-wedlock black births in cities like Philadelphia, as well as in welfare dependency; paternal abandonment of financial, emotional, spiritual, and physical responsibilities; and losses of factory and other employment opportunities for relatively unskilled working-class and lower-middle-class black men. Because such developments led to the normalization of paternal absence and altered the social contours of black fatherhood radically, a number of songs emerging both from Philadelphia, the decade's preeminent producer of R&B, and elsewhere emphasized the longing of besieged sons for emotionally and financially supportive relationships with male progenitors. However, desires for paternal involvement and, hence, domestic wholeness often are expressed in such songs as nostalgia for the traditional patriarchal family, a structure whose foundations underwent energetic critique in the work of feminist intellectuals who deemed Moynihan's and other representations of the benefits of black patriarchal dominion highly objectionable.

In May 1973, the Intruders, a four-man R&B group whose members hailed from North Philadelphia, released *Save the Children*, whose title song shares a name and subject matter with the Marvin Gaye tune that Chet Walker mistakenly remembers hearing on the afternoon following King's assassination. Like these songs, the album's best-known track, "I'll Always Love My Mama," emphasizes the benefits of adult involvement in the lives of children. Featuring socially conscious lyrics and state-of-the-art sonic elements, this popular hit served as an early indication that the group's label, Philadelphia International Records (PIR), was on the verge of unseating Motown as the preeminent site of rhythm-and-blues invention.

Before *Save the Children*, the Intruders had been known primarily as an eclectic singles act that recorded both juvenilia like "Love Is Just Like a

Baseball Game" (1968) and "Me Tarzan, You Jane" (1969) and adult-oriented fare, lushly orchestrated tunes such as "Together" (1967) and the best-selling "Cowboys to Girls" (1968) that crossed over onto the top of the pop charts and served as sonic and lyrical templates for, and, indeed, the commercial foundation of, the Sound of Philadelphia. Like their predecessor, Berry Gordy, who during the preceding decade forged a symbolic association between his record company and Detroit's automobile industry, Kenneth Gamble and Leon Huff, PIR's co-owners and primary producers, connected the sounds and words emerging from Center City's Sigma Studios in the 1970s directly to a symbolically resonant American city. And what Philadelphia represented was not industry, as in the case of the Motor City, but *philia* (brotherly love) and the nation's founding—and, in the decade highlighted by the bicentennial, revived—commitment to liberty, freedom, and democracy. Those concerns were evident, for example, in the emphasis on social liberation that were discernible in the label's lyrics and its motto, "A Message in Our Music," as well as in its designation of its interracial studio group as MFSB (Mother Father Sister Brother) at a time of growing concern, particularly in black American communities, about the state of the fundamental social unit. The Philly Sound, in other words, embraced both family-centeredness—albeit, as we will see, often of a reactionary variety—and the city's legacy of inciting freedom.

Save the Children reflects many of PIR's persistent emphases. The album begins with covers of two songs focused on parents and their offspring: the title song, the work of the early 1970s' most consistently politically engaged black recording artist, Gil Scott-Heron, in which unspecified world problems threaten to hamper his offspring's pursuit of personal happiness and satisfying employment, and Paul Simon's "Mother and Child Reunion," in which a father reassures his anguished child that, despite his breakup with his former partner, the darling child will continue to have the benefit of his or her mother's loving presence. These angst-filled, family-centered covers set the stage for the album's signature tune, "I'll Always Love My Mama." This ode to maternal devotion in the face of obstacles such as abject poverty has achieved iconic status in black communities throughout the United States. Indeed, it is fair to say that the continuing popularity of this song serves as sonic confirmation of the overwhelming—and, according to the Moynihan Report, perverse—importance of mothers in black American families.

As I have suggested, the soul era abounds with songs that focus on the impact of parents on their offspring. Indeed, a sufficient number of father-centered songs emerged in the 1960s and 1970s to inspire historian Brian Ward to coin the phrase "father songs" (1998, 378). Their counterparts, mother songs, are a fascinating subgenre that includes Jerry Butler's "Only the Strong Survive" (1969), the Jackson 5's "I Found That Girl" (1970), and Cornelius Brothers and Sister Rose's "Too Late to Turn Back Now" (1972), all of which emphasize sage maternal advice offered to sons in matters of the heart. In such songs, mothers, well aware of the pleasures and pain of romantic love, share their hard-earned knowledge with starry-eyed or broken-hearted male offspring. In the case of the Jackson 5 song, a son informs his mother that in his relationship with his new love, he has experienced the overwhelmingly positive emotions she predicted he would feel when he had found a suitable mate, emotions that enabled him to comprehend—and come fully into—the exalted state of manhood. In contrast to the happy endings of which Motown's young family group sings, the two other songs I mentioned highlight heartbroken male recollection of maternal wisdom. "Too Late to Turn Back Now" focuses on a son, obsessed with a woman whose affection appears to be lukewarm at best, who recalls his mother warning him of the sense of vulnerability to which falling in love would subject him. Similarly, "Only the Strong Survive," a pre-PIR Gamble and Huff production, stresses a mother's efforts to implore her heartbroken son to persevere in the face of his desertion by his duplicitous former girlfriend, and to be prepared to meet some of the many well-intentioned girls who would appreciate his finer qualities. In these songs, in which mothers use the exigencies of heterosexual romance to instruct sons in the subtleties of masculine maturation, the role of fathers is peripheral. This absence may be said to reflect, among other things, a growing perception in the early 1970s that parental instruction—and parenting generally—had become, for the black audiences whose social realities these songs were attempting primarily to reflect, an almost exclusively maternal prerogative.

Like these mother songs, the version of "I'll Always Love My Mama" that was released as a single never directly engages the issue of fathers' absence. Instead, it concentrates on a son's praise of a self-sacrificing mother who works as a domestic to be able to purchase, among other items, new shoes for her son, and without whose patience and moral instruction he would have experienced permanent physical and psychological immersion in a gang-infested, hypermasculine urban culture. Beyond its discussion of the poverty that led the mother to perform arduous domestic labor, the single barely hints at the full scale of the problems faced by the son, which are detailed in the extended album track—problems that dedicated maternal attention is expressly intended to obviate. Indeed, it is not until after a lengthy instrumental break in the extended version of the song, in which Little Sonny, Big Sonny, Bird, and Phil discuss their hell-raising childhood activities, that listeners are offered a full rendering of the recuperative nature of the maternal love that is celebrated in its popular first half.

Edited out of the single version is the son's recollection that, in a North Philly environment marked by gang warring, cheap wine drinking, and acts of petty larceny, the mother's vigilance and insistence that her son "watch the things you doing out in that street" set him on the path to upstanding citizenship. Following this discussion of maternal attentiveness, one of his group mates, interested in learning of paternal contributions to his friend's social, cultural, and moral education, asks Little Sonny, "What about Pop?" While he initially challenges the appropriateness of addressing that particular issue during a celebration of maternal love—"we ain't talking about Pop"— ultimately Little Sonny begins a seemingly improvised conversation that yields a portrait of a black father in the throes of arrested development. Instead of offering an example of industriousness and self-sacrifice to supplement the mother's moral and practical instruction, Pop behaved like a carefree adolescent. Unlike the mother, whose travails outside the home are characterized by the now-mature son as exhausting, demeaning acts of domestic labor in the household of affluent—and, at this historical moment, undoubtedly white—employers, Pop would regularly "stay out all night, come home all wrinkled up, lint balls all over him," clearly engaging in precisely the types of irresponsible behavior in which the son had participated before his transformation. Recalling his own engagement in this sort of behavior compels Little Sonny to acknowledge that he had been the primary beneficiary of his mother's diminution. Instead of serving as a paragon of moral rectitude and industriousness, as the U.S. model of paternal uprightness that Moynihan suggests middle-class fathers generally appear to be, the song's father is a corrupt figure whose irresponsibility reflects and reinforces the surrounding urban culture's promotion of hedonistic and criminal male behavior. The "good old days" that the Intruders reference, then, have *nothing* to do with Pop. Instead, they are connected solely with Mama, who nurtures the son, enabling him to avoid following the father's antisocial lead. In the unedited version of the song, then, the benefits of maternal self-sacrifice endure, while the father's reckless boyishness, which the son diligently works to deny and repress, becomes, when his foibles are exposed (albeit accompanied by bemused, defensive laughter), stultifying flaws that maturing sons must to avoid repeating at all costs.

The extended version of "I'll Always Love My Mama" reveals paternal irresponsibility as an unacknowledged feature of mother songs, the flip side of black maternal love, if you will, and the subtext that makes devoted maternal instruction indispensable. Reading between the lines and listening beyond the break of these songs, then, focuses attention on the obstacles faced by impoverished black male urban youth seeking models of maturation: father lack, absence, and economic failure. These obstacles were the subject of or motivation for numerous songs, even when such songs attempted to avoid acknowledging black male shortcomings. Competing with images of confrontation-ready black masculinity, including the 1968 Olympic salute I discuss in Chapter 1 and rifle-toting Black Panther members, was the idea of a fundamentally flawed and bereft black male—many of whom are fathers—who needs to be redeemed, remade, or rearticulated if the race is to thrive. In R&B and other narrative forms, that rearticulation takes many guises, including men under the sway of nostalgic memory that encourages them to underplay or ignore altogether the harshness of pre–civil rights racial oppression.[2] In "I'll Always Love My Mama," that sentiment motivates Little Sonny's initial emphasis on intense mother love yet is not powerful enough to suppress the return of the repressed traumatic effects of paternal insufficiency.

As I show, these nostalgic songs are motivated by an impulse that feminist scholars have ascribed to conservative formulations of U.S. masculinity during the 1970s whose advocates believed that the dominant status of men had been compromised by the social, cultural, and economic advances women were making. As a consequence, such advocates sought to reinscribe a nuclear family ethos and traditional gender behaviors as the most natural and beneficial familial, communal, and social norms for a post-Vietnam, post-Watergate nation, its states wrestling, less than a decade following the implementation of Great Society initiatives, with court-mandated racial integration and gender equity. But, as is suggested particularly by R&B songs that address the politics of the family and of romance, conservative thinkers were forced to contend with an increasing mistrust of efforts to (re)establish black patriarchal authority through the promotion of a male-centered familial order, which, as is often the case in instances of ideology-compelled nostalgia, was never a firmly ensconced component of black American life in the first place.

According to recent scholarship on the subject, nostalgia is best understood as a self-protective response to, and resistance in the face of, radical social, political, and cultural change. Svetlana Boym, who speaks of nostalgia as "a longing for a home that no longer exists or has never existed . . . , a sentiment of loss and displacement, but . . . also a romance with one's own fantasy" (2001, xiii), suggests that such longing "inevitably reappears as a defense mechanism in a time of accelerated rhythms of life and historical upheavals" (xiv). Emphasizing its fundamentally defensive nature and its status as a longing for both a familiar place and "a different time—the time of our childhood, the slower rhythms of our dreams"—she insists that nostalgia is best understood as "rebellion against the modern idea of time, the time of history and progress." For Boym, nostalgia reflects a deep "desire . . . to obliterate history and turn it into private or collective mythology, to revisit time like space, refusing to surrender to the irreversibility of time that plagues the human condition" (xv).

Viewed in light of Boym's perspectives on the doomed efforts of nostalgia's adherents to counteract change and its cultural consequences, it is possible to consider the spoken dialogue that follows the lengthy instrumental break in "I'll Always Love My Mama" as inserting a marked rhetorical dissonance to highlight the protagonist's impulses "to revisit time like space." This musical narrative, in fact, is occasioned by an unabashedly nostalgic son's recollection of an earlier time when he was the focal point of exhaustive maternal attention.

And if, as Boym asserts, "the mourning of displacement and temporal irreversibility . . . is at the very core of the modern condition," if nostalgia constitutes "the promise to rebuild the ideal home that lies at the core of many powerful ideologies today, tempting us to relinquish critical thinking for emotional bonding" (2001, xvi), as feminist scholars such as Roberta Rubenstein suggest, the urge to inhabit a past time and a felicitous place is motivated by social, political, and cultural reformations that were instituted at the behest of an unwelcomed presence such as, for male-centered men, the modern feminist movement. Rubenstein notes that many women, compelled by pervasive feminist formulations "to regard home as a restrictive, confining space" and to resist "deeply-imbedded cultural scripts that defined women in terms of familial and domestic roles," came to "view . . . home not as a sanctuary but as a prison, a site from which escape was the essential prerequisite for self-discovery and independence" (2001, 2).[3] Further exploring women's notions of home, Rubenstein goes on to say that

> during the last third of the twentieth century and into the current century, women have felt the tension between private and public identities—between securing a professional life and honoring a private life that embraces elements of what is traditionally called "homemaking." Once domesticity became aligned with confinement and oppression, and once *home* became associated with a politically reactionary backlash against feminism, homesickness went underground, as it were. . . . Narratives that excavate and recover the positive meanings of home and nostalgia in effect represent "the return

of the repressed" in that they foreground, confront, and attempt to resolve that subversive longing. (3–4)

But if, for many women, nostalgia represents "yearning for recovery or return to the idea of a nurturing, unconditionally accepting place/space that has been repressed in contemporary feminism" (Rubenstein 2001, 4), for the sons in the aforementioned songs, it constitutes a longing to recover a domestic order whose focus was the physical and psychological needs and comforts of fathers and their male offspring, an order that is challenged by feminism's critique of traditional constructions of home. Of course, the domestic disrepair to which the extended version of the Intruders' song alludes appears to be tied to the urban dissolution that, by the end of the 1960s, had caused a radical increase in black American crime, poverty, and out-of-wedlock births and a retreat from ideologies of racial coalescence.

It is possible to argue that mother songs generally reflect what Rubenstein speaks of as

> a kind of haunted longing: figures of earlier relationships and places with which they are associated, both remembered and imagined, impinge on a person's emotional life, affecting her or his behavior toward current experiences and attachments. Implicit in the deeper register of nostalgia is the element of grief for something of profound value that seems irrevocably lost—even if it never actually existed, or *never could have existed*, in the form in which it is "remembered."
>
> The yearning of painful nostalgia is thus closely related to . . . mourning [and] other kinds of profound losses, including displacement from an emotionally vital domicile or cultural community. . . . I use the phrase cultural mourning to signify an individual's response to the loss of something with collective or communal associations: a way of life, a cultural homeland, a place or geographical location with significance for a larger cultural group, or the related history of an entire ethnic or cultural group from which she or he feels severed or exiled. (2001, 5)

If these songs can be said to communicate cultural mourning, that sentiment is most clearly discernible in their now-mature sons' grief over the perceived loss of masculine privilege, which motivates the songs' narratives and their accompanying dénouement. However else we may think of the 1970s, including its popular characterization as a decade of rampant narcissism, and because of or despite its association with black urban decline and disenchantment, it must also be understood as an era of black American historical self-inquiry that occasionally takes the form of nostalgia.[4]

According to Boym, "The study of nostalgia does not belong to any specific discipline: it frustrates psychologists, sociologists, literary theorists and philosophers . . . , tantaliz[ing] us with its fundamental ambivalence; it is about the repetition of the unrepeatable, materialization of the immaterial." She insists that "to unearth the fragments of nostalgia[,] one needs a dual archeology of memory and of place, and a dual history of illusions and of actual practices" (2001, xvi–xvii). We must be attentive, in response of efforts to reassemble the past via the modalities of memory, location, and ideological verity, to the dangers of nostalgic distortion. Pursuing such an idea vis-à-vis examples of R&B music that emerged from Philadelphia and elsewhere in the 1970s, I identify masculine yearning for an idealized black family as one possible cluster of fragments that can be productively pieced together to assess the Philly Sound and other representations of the meanings of blackness in the 1970s.

Exploring the concept of nostalgia within a national and gendered context, the feminist scholars Janice Doane and Devon Hodges argue that it "is a retreat to the past in the face of what a number of writers—most of them male—perceive to be the degeneracy of American culture brought about by the rise of feminist authority" (1987, xiii). Nostalgia, they insist, "permeates American politics and mass culture. While pulpits and podiums resound with the message that we need to restore American values and the American family, movies and television return us to the happy days of yore" (3). According to these scholars, such reactionary formulations are the work of "nostalgic writers [who] construct their visions of a golden past to authenticate women's traditional place and to challenge the outspoken feminist criticisms of it. . . . [T]hese writers [see themselves as] fight[ing] the false, seductive images of a decadent culture that they believe are promoted by feminist writing. The battleground is representation itself: feminism is envisioned as a source of degenerate writing that threatens male authority" (3). Doane and Hodges further insist that "each [masculinist] writer presents an indictment of contemporary culture that depends upon opposing the 'deteriorating' values of the present to the 'truer' values of the past, and each characterizes the 'liberated' woman as implicated in this movement toward degeneracy" (4). That degeneracy, caused by women's refusal to adhere to traditional gender norms, reflects the "tremendous desire" on the part of nostalgic male writers "for a 'natural' grounding principle, that is, a stable referent," that acts as an authentic origin or center from which to disparage the degenerate present and as the "truth" behind stereotypic sexual oppositions. It is always located in the past. . . .

Perhaps because of their doubts, nostalgic writers are defensively combative. They are fighting . . . to protect their turf: a language whose power resides in its claim to bring reality directly before the eyes of the reader. . . . The most important strategy employed by the writers we discuss is to maintain a system of oppositions that is at the same time a system of dominance and subordination. (8)

Further, Doane and Hodges seek to demonstrate that "nostalgic writers are entrapped by the illusion that their strategy of opposition creates: their mythic pasts become real" even when it is apparent that "they may be aware to some degree of the role representation plays in their stories of cultural decline" (9).

Later, I explore the O'Jays' "Family Reunion" as an act of "restorative nostalgia" that, Boym insists, "does not think of itself as nostalgia, but as truth and tradition." According to Boym, "restorative nostalgia . . . knows two main plots—the return to origins and the conspiracy—. . . [and] proposes to rebuild the lost home and patch up . . . memory gaps" (2001, xviii). Restorative nostalgic acts such as "Family Reunion" seek both to refurbish domiciles destroyed as a consequence of cruel time and cultural neglect and to spread the word that the refurbished place is again fit for habitation. Before I discuss this song's restorative intentions, however, I need to offer a context, gleaned from other artistic representations of black masculinity generally and black fatherhood in particular that were produced during the early 1970s, in terms of which the O'Jays' conspiratorial notions of familial dissolution and male-centered conception of gender's "absolute truth" can be measured. Those representations include black cultural nationalistic rhetoric, father songs, R&B ballads that center on male dissemblance, and a section of an influential novel that offers a race- and class-inflected rewriting of Freudian theories of male maturation as they relate to contentious father-son relations.

Echoing Doane and Hodges, Judith Kegan Gardiner, in her introduction to *Masculinity Studies and Feminist Theory*, argues that contemporary "masculinity is a nostalgic formation, always missing, lost, or about to be lost, its ideal form located in a past that advances with each generation in order to recede just beyond its grasp. Its myth is that effacing new forms can restore a natural, original male grounding" (2002, 11). But if there was never "a golden time of unproblematic, stable gender" (14), the period from the mid-1960s to the mid-1970s clearly represents a moment in which struggles for American racial equality were undertaken to restore black manhood to a position of uncompromised power. When, for example, Eldridge Cleaver insists in his controversial 1968 essay collection, *Soul on Ice*, "we shall have our manhood . . . or the earth will be leveled by our attempts to gain it" (1968, 63), he articulates the priorities of a range of cultural leaders who sought to reestablish black masculinity as the unchallenged center of black American life.

The era's theorists of an assertive black masculinity constructed it in opposition both to supporters of women's liberation and to black mothers who are said to have attempted "systematically to drive our manliness from our sons" by "securing the simple survival of their male children 'at the cost of their manhood'" (Ward 1998, 370). Black masculinity's emergence required the reconstitution of familial structures dominated by black women who were accused of being incapable of nurturing nascent signs of "virility, strength, and power" in their male offspring. Not surprisingly, at least if we take to heart Doane and Hodges's considerations of male indictments of the beginnings of U.S. gender equity, like King's efforts to render nonviolence masculine in the face of black American militants' embrace of a philosophy of redemptive violence, these formulations echo the Moynihan Report of 1965, which positions a heretofore repressed black patriarchy as essential to the economic and psychic health of struggling families. Moynihan argues that black prospects for significant socioeconomic advancement were compromised by the relative failures of black fathers and mothers to adopt traditional gender roles. While acknowledging racism's contributions to these problems, which include disproportionate numbers of unemployed or underemployed black males and, hence, heterosexual family units in which females were the sole or primary breadwinners, Moynihan insists that no significant black material progress will be achieved unless these aberrations are eliminated:

> At the center of the tangle of pathology [found in black American communities] is the weakness of the family structure. Once or twice removed, it will be found to be the principal source of most of the aberrant, inadequate, or antisocial behavior that did not establish, but now serves to perpetuate the cycle of poverty and deprivation. (1965, 30)

In response to Moynihan's notion of black manhood's "crushing burden" as a function of "the weakness of the family structure," we might suggest, along with Hortense Spillers, that such formulations imply that "the 'Negro

Family' has no Father to speak of—his Name, his Law, his Symbolic function mark the impressive missing agencies in the essential life of the black community" (2000, 58). Hence, concerns about black male identity formation reflect not merely anxieties about a castrating black female influence, but also socially marginalized, symbolically and literally absent, and legally nameless black males' frustrations about their putative inability to exert any significant influence whatsoever. Echoing, as does Spillers, Freudian notions of the centrality of the oedipal struggle to "the crucial issue of [male] identity," David Dudley, a scholar of black American male autobiography, speaks of the classical situation of "the male child who feels threatened by his father and who desires in some way to supplant his father" (1991, 2) as being inapplicable to the realities of an overwhelming number of black male sons and fathers. In such generational relationships, if Moynihan's and comparable notions can be believed, increasingly, the black father's shadow is faint, if it is at all visible, and the sense of threat he represents for his heir is less a function of the older male's accomplishments than of his failure to provide a sufficiently impressive presence against which the son must struggle to achieve a self-determined male identity. In other words, the disruption of traditional Western notions of masculine succession appears to be a haunting *precondition* within black families rather than the goal of intergenerational male conflict. Hence, the maturation of the impoverished black male is marked by a fear not of being erased by the father's overwhelming presence but of being doomed to repeat his literal and/or symbolic social, economic, and domestic absence.

Later, I explore some of the challenges that impoverished black male performances of patriarchy present for sons in father songs. Keeping in mind Moynihan's aforementioned 1965 government-sponsored report on the detrimental impact for the family of black males' limited power, I look at two songs, Clarence Carter's "Patches" and the Temptations' "Papa Was a Rolling Stone," that challenge the notion set forth in the O'Jays' "Family Reunion" that the male-dominated family "is the solution to the world's problems today." Offering a nostalgic vision of wise governing fathers, mothers focused exclusively on domestic chores, and compliant children fated to replicate in their own heterosexual families their parents' traditional performances of gender roles, the O'Jays' song stands with the works of Robert Bly, John Irving, and other nostalgic male writers of the 1970s that present the instability of gender identity as injurious to the society as a whole. Like such writers who imagine "mythic pasts" in their work that "become real," they seek to replace the gray, degenerate present with golden memories of a phallocentric social logic that served the needs of all of its members. In the case of "Family Reunion," however, as we will see, the longing for the return of the nuclear family is directly at odds with the era's emphatic representations of whites' historic denial to black men of sufficient power to form the sorts of patriarchal clans that "Family Reunion" fondly recalls. To examine the nostalgic elements of the O'Jays' song most effectively, we must consider it alongside concomitant examinations of how the legacy and perseverance of racism affect black males' performances as men generally and as fathers in particular. In the world of R&B, two father songs in particular, Clarence Carter's "Patches" and the Temptations' "Papa Was a Rolling Stone," help set the tone for the 1970s as it relates to representations of black male vulnerabilities and their impact on sons struggling to construct gender identities in the face of their progenitors' troubling—and troubled—masculinity. In addition, I explore these songs alongside an amazingly insightful literary examination of these issues, Toni Morrison's *The Bluest Eye*, which depicts black American paternal vulnerability in a manner that sheds further light on the psychic costs—for black fathers and their families—of failing to recognize the consequences of striving for an always unreachable patriarchal normality.

The engagement of social themes in R&B songs during the 1960s and 1970s was influenced by the politicizing of black American cultural production. Much of R&B, a heretofore romance-obsessed genre, reflected—and reflected on—black social, economic, and political conditions, manifesting the widespread impact of formulations of cultural nationalists such as Ron Karenga, who insisted that "all art must reflect the Black Revolution, and any art that does not discuss and contribute to the revolution is invalid" (quoted in Werner 1999, 120). To respond effectively to songs that emphasize paternal lack, we must consider them both as sociopolitical interventions and in terms of their contributions to an artistic form, one of whose major features is its male contributors' resolute display of emotions. Given the commitment to expressing uncontrollable male pain in R&B songs such as Little Anthony and the Imperials' "Tears on My Pillow," Otis Redding's "These Arms of Mine," Solomon Burke's "Just Out of Reach," Donny Hathaway's "Giving Up," Jimmy Ruffin's "What Becomes of the Brokenhearted," and Al Green's "How Can You Mend a Broken Heart," it is interesting that an era that gave rise to father songs examining phallic weakness also featured a subgenre of male romantic tunes that emphasizes elaborate acts of male dissemblance whose goal is to hide or disguise male vulnerability. The songs that are concerned with both fatherhood and heartbroken male dissemblance, I believe, are influenced by sociopolitical efforts to restore black male power, reflecting anxieties that characterize this and other periods about the appropriate social and aesthetic performance of an always-deferred black patriarchy.

"Patches" and "Papa Was a Rolling Stone" were released within a three-month period in 1970 by Atlantic and Motown Records, respectively, two of the era's reigning sites of black popular music production. Music critic Dave Marsh, who considers "Patches" one of the best singles in rock-and-roll history, speaks of Carter's song as "the ultimate soul opera" (1989, 564), while Bill Dahl, a contributor to the *Blackwell Guide to Soul Recordings*, views it as a "maudlin narrative of death, destruction, and redemption" (Dahl 1993, 245). Exploring the struggles of an eldest son to live in accordance with the notions of appropriate masculine behavior he learns from his father, "Patches" is one of a group of soul songs that "depicted dutiful fathers who took care of their families as best they could" (Ward 1998, 378). Brian Ward juxtaposes songs such as "Patches," which resist the hypermasculine, man-and-a-half posturing that characterized much post–civil rights discourse, with the Temptations classic that "revealed the ravages wrought upon the black community by the interplay of racism, poverty, and macho irresponsibility" (378). In Carter's song, a poor sharecropper passes down to his son his sense of the virtues of hard work, self-denial, prideful endurance in the face of backbreaking obstacles, and a highly developed sense of familial responsibility. Set in the backwoods of Alabama and featuring sparse instrumentation and the black preacherly cadences and blues inflections of Carter's speaking and singing voices, respectively, "Patches" marks itself as an explicitly rural Southern narrative whose guiding force holds that self-denial and paternal responsibility will be rewarded by God or are, at the very least, their own reward. By contrast, "Rolling Stone" explores an urban father disinterested in fruitless or purely symbolic black paternal self-sacrifice who is instead partial to hedonistic pursuits of self-fulfillment.

"Patches" offers a stark depiction of the tragic possibilities of black masculinity, particularly when its adherents measure themselves against what Antony Easthope calls "the masculine myth." In *What a Man's Gotta Do*, an engaging study of male representations in Western popular culture, Easthope argues that "men are invited to recognize themselves in the masculine myth . . . [which] posits masculinity as natural, normal and universal" when, in fact, "it embodies a particular definition of masculinity with its own particular structure" (1990, 166). "Patches" and "Rolling Stone" provide seemingly conflicting responses to the recognition that the narrow formulations of black American manhood prevent men from partaking wholly of or seeing themselves as embodying the full promise of the myth of masculinity. If patriarchy is a "social organization marked by the supremacy of the father in the clan or family, the legal dependence of wives and children, and the reckoning of descent and inheritance in the male line" (116), black American masculinity, as it is portrayed in these songs and in the Moynihan Report to which these songs and numerous black American fictive and investigative narratives of the period respond, is bereft of determinative social and, hence, familial, power.

According to the psychoanalytical paradigm on which Easthope relies, male maturation depends on the ability of the son "to separate the real father from the symbolic role he only imperfectly performs." He insists that that separation occurs when the son "discovers that the father is not a real presence but a name. . . . Castration, lack, the recognition that . . . paternity [is] only a name, all these work together to encourage him to take up his own place in the system as father and possessor of the symbolic phallus" (1990, 120). Historically, representatives of white American male hegemony have operated as if they are in possession of "the symbol of male power, the phallus" (121), and seek to deny even the illusion of its power to black men, whose most salient quality is not self-generative possibility, but phallic lack. What place, then, can black sons such as Patches assume if the black father has neither a name that can be passed on to subsequent generations nor a presence that can help shape the values, perspectives, and fortunes of the family generally and of the male line in particular?

Before I explore in detail how this issue is represented in these father songs, I turn briefly to a novel that appeared in the same year as "Patches" and "Rolling Stone," Toni Morrison's *The Bluest Eye*, because of its astute exploration of how impoverished forms of black masculinity deviate from the psychoanalytical script. A fourteen-year-old Cholly's initial encounter with white Southern masculinity's apparent omnipotence and its insistence on burdening black males with castration complexes ironically occurs during his sexual initiation. Following the funeral of his aunt, Cholly pursues pleasure in the woods with a female peer, but just as he feels a sexual "explosion threaten, Darlene froze and cried out. He thought he had hurt her, but when he looked at her face, she was staring wildly at something over his shoulder. He jerked around" ([1970] 1994, 115).

White male power—symbolized by two white hunters who appear, from Darlene's perspective, over Cholly's shoulder—deflate him with the threat of castration. The giggling, titillated white hunters order Cholly to "get on wid it, nigger," transforming his initiatory sexual activity into a perverse scene of triangulated desire in which, in response to what amounts to dictatorial stage directions, he "begins to simulate what had gone on before" because "he could do no more than make-believe" (Morrison [1970] 1994, 118). The black (hetero)sexual act is transformed by the presence of well-armed white masculinity into a perverse interracial performance in which black female subjectivity goes largely unnoticed.[5]

Reduced by his powerlessness to an essentially feckless enactment of potentially procreative sexual intercourse, Cholly's fear and sense of humiliation create a "vacancy in his head" (Morrison [1970] 1994, 118). Experiencing black masculinity, then, as a bloodless identity devoid of self-determination, the demoralized teenager "cultivated his hatred of Darlene. Never did he once consider directing his hatred toward the hunters. Such an emotion would have destroyed him. They were big, white, armed men. He was small, black, helpless" (118). Consumed by his powerlessness to control either his sexuality or his body's natural functions, he transfers his self-hatred and disdain for the sadistic white hunters onto Darlene, whom he fears he may have impregnated during his simulations of intercourse. Bent on escaping parental responsibility, Cholly follows in his father's footsteps, a father whom he sets out subsequently to find.

> Cholly knew it was wrong to run out on a pregnant girl, and recalled, with sympathy, that his father had done just that. Now he understood. He knew then what he must do—find his father. His father would understand. Aunt Jimmy said he had gone to Macon.
>
> With no more thought than a chick leaving its shell, he stepped off the porch. (119)

But instead of finding a father that he had long imagined, a "larger version of himself" who would sympathize with his youthful quest for generational connection, he encounters, "at the far end of the group" of men "gathered . . . for and about dice and money" (121), a short, "pitiable," balding man with "a hard, belligerent face" who fails to recognize their biological connection despite the fact that the abandoned son has "his eyes, his mouth, his whole head" (122). Mistaking him for "Melba's boy" coming to collect a debt, "he stood up and in a vexed and whiny voice shouted at Cholly, 'Tell that bitch she get her money. Now, get the fuck outta my face!'" (122, 123). Samson Fuller's completely compromised masculinity, manifested in his total irresponsibility, childish voice, and reliance on games of chance instead of hard work, stands as a chilling example of the power of American racism to obliterate any illusion that black masculinity partakes of transcendent masculine power.

If, as Easthope contends, "the masculinity myth keeps coming back to the idea that the father is absolutely *all there*, that sons are perfect copies of him, that they are masculine all the way through," if, according to this myth, "men are masculine and only masculine because they possess the symbol of male power, the phallus" (1990, 121), black masculinity constructed under the threat of white erasure can present itself as being in full or partial possession of the name or law of the Father only by submitting mainstream society's script of appropriately manly behavior to strategic misreading and/or revision. If black men under such conditions stand up to white male threat, if they seek to enact traditional heterosexual familial narratives despite a denial to them of even the illusion of real social or symbolic phallic power, then they appear doomed to exaggerate or overvalue those features of masculinity to which they have access because they do not threaten white male power. If, on the other hand, such men seek to escape dictatorial white male control, they may, like Cholly, be limited to pursuing antisocial and antifamilial freedom. Ultimately, Cholly—"abandoned in a junk heap by his mother, rejected for a crap game by his father," a male whose sexual initiation teaches him of the omnipotence of white masculinity—comes to recognize that "he was alone with his own perceptions and appetites, and they alone interested him" (126). Consequently, he is

> free. Dangerously free. Free to feel whatever he felt—fear, guilt, shame, love, pity. Free to be tender or violent, to whistle or weep. Free to sleep in doorways or between the white sheets of a singing woman. Free to take a job, free to leave it. (125)

That perverse freedom, linked to other myths of masculinity that hold that adventure, mobility, and spontaneity are prized attributes, involves the compulsion which playwright August Wilson identifies in *Fences* as "them walking blues." These "blues" take the form of "a fellow moving around from place to place . . . , woman to woman . . . , searching out the New Land" (A. Wilson 1986, 51, 50).[6]

Looked at in light of these literary formulations, "Patches" appears to be a representation of black masculinity whose distinguishing feature is not dangerous freedom but, rather, the overwhelming burden of familial responsibility. The song begins with Carter's establishing the narrative's geographic and socioeconomic circumstances, focusing, in a spoken introduction, on the ragged clothes his character was forced to wear as a child and his father's responses to and pained participation in his son's mocking derision.

> *I was born and raised down in Alabama on a farm way back up in the woods*
> *I was so ragged the kids would call me "Patches"*
> *Papa used to kid me about it*
> *Of course deep down inside he was thinkin' he had done all he could do*

Carter's persona manifests an acute sensitivity to his father's pain that appears to compel him to ignore his own. Patches's clothing, his paternal inheritance, symbolizes both the father's laborious efforts to achieve a modicum of financial success and the purely functional nature of his attempts to disguise the gaps or rips in the myth of masculine power. In the father's performance and attitudes, then, black masculinity, marked by inescapable economic failure rather than the illusion of omnipotence, is characterized by dissemblance (patches that both cover and call attention to the rips in the fabric of masculinity), persistence in the face of repeated failure, a self-deprecating sense of resignation, a privileging of efforts over results, and, as we see later, bequeathing to the son the belief that, taken together, these behaviors constitute a coherent cultural practice.

Because the song uses tattered garb to point out masculinity's constructed nature, it is helpful to consider "Patches" in terms of Marjorie Garber's provocative formulations of our "vested interests" in using clothing both to mark and, in moments of transgression, to unsettle the categorical meanings of race, gender, and class in the West. According to Garber, figures like the transvestite help produce significant cultural anxiety through the use of clothing, serving to "disrupt, expose, and challenge, putting into question the very notion of the 'original' and of stable identity," and allowing us to recognize "'category crisis' . . . not as the exception but rather the ground of culture itself" (1992, 16). By "category crisis," Garber means "a failure of definitional distinction, a borderline that becomes permeable, that permits border crossings from one (apparently distinct) category to another: black/white, Jew/Christian, noble/bourgeois, master/servant, master/slave" (16). But while Garber includes class as a borderline whose permeability clothing can expose, in the case of Carter's song, the tattered garb can be said to symbolize the intractability of problems confronting the impoverished black family. In such cases, what is passed to the next generation is not category crisis but, in fact, a racially inflected *economic* crisis that persists despite the relative success of civil rights struggles to increase the velocity of black American class crossing.

In its exploration of efforts to cover inconsistencies in black male performances of masculinity, "Patches" uses the rhetorical devices and strategies of dissemblance that appear in numerous R&B love songs focused on the subject of romantic failure. Patches's father responds to the mocking assemblage of his masculine lack by joking with his son about his appearance, hoping to disguise his own sense of shame and to teach him to approach the blues conditions of his life with a sense of humor. The father, then, contributes to his son's harassment rather than choosing to become himself a "victim of the joke,"[7] employing self-protective humor reminiscent of the efforts of soul men to mask tearful signs of the emotional vulnerability that enables and/or accompanies romantic heartbreak. Smokey Robinson and the Miracles' "The Tears of a Clown," a hit three months after "Patches," is the paradigmatic articulation of this persistent male desire to disguise vulnerability.[8] Its bouncy, danceable rhythms are sonic approximations of attempts by the song's persona to disguise heartache behind a mask of carefree frivolity. Greater than the persona's pain is his need "to camouflage my sadness," to wear the mask of masculine invulnerability even if he looks and feels foolish doing so.

Again and again, R&B songs of this period equate masculinity with dissemblance, with performances that cover over emotional accessibility. And even if, as the Miracles' thematically similar "Tracks of My Tears" suggests, the vulnerable man desperately hopes that the departed lover will return to him precisely because she is able to discern his agony, the ability to assume a masculine pose publicly—which, according to Warren Farrell, entails refusing to show emotion, "vulnerability, empathy, or doubt," along with having "an answer to all problems at all times," and resisting any and all "forms of introspection" (1979, 32)—is ultimately more critical to his sense of well-being. If Easthope is correct that, for the man bearing the "burden of having to be one sex all the way through," the "struggle to be masculine is the struggle to cope with his own femininity" (1990, 6), and if, as Bruce Schulman asserts, for American men during the 1970s, "more than anything else manliness meant not to be womanly" (2002, 179), the staged responses of these heartbroken male personae demonstrate that masculinity is largely a charade, the result of decisions not to perform the U.S. culture's notion of femininity (weakness, emotionality, and vulnerability). In these songs, the phrase "emotional crisis" aptly describes the permeability of the border between masculinity and femininity for the suffering male. To hide his awareness that gender is a façade and his fear that he is not a man "all the way through," the heartbroken male will go to any length: become "the life of the party" despite his overwhelming anguish; pretend to have fun with another girl despite his conviction that his former lover is "the permanent one"; even, in the case of the Temptations' "I Wish It Would Rain," entrap himself within a space—the home—overwhelmingly figured in the R&B songs of the period as female, waiting for bad weather.

These songs of male heartbreak help illuminate the gendered charade in "Patches," where masculinity's desires to "control what threatens it both from within and without" (Easthope 1990, 166) are no match for economic circumstances that force generations of black males to wear their lack literally on the sleeves and the knees of their tattered garb. In the son's eyes, the father is heroic, a great man, not because of widely recognized accomplishments—he is uneducated, barely able to pay their bills, and psychically deflated by life—but because of his skillful public dissemblance, his capacity to disguise his sense that, according to American capitalist standards he certainly does not reject, he is an abject failure. Unable to partake of the masculine myth's full range of empowering possibilities, he clings to invulnerability, passing on his patched text of masculine performance to his overburdened son whom he imagines being able, like the lovers in ballads of romantic woe, to see beyond the dissemblance.

The father's death shifts the burden of impoverished masculinity to his eldest son on his deathbed, bequeathing the role of familial caretaker to his pubescent son, whom he warns, "It's all left up to you." Unlike Cholly in *The Bluest Eye*, who retraces the path of the father who deserted him in favor of "dangerous freedom," Patches assumes a daunting responsibility that he sets out to meet on his own, armed only with a patched masculinity and seven or eight years of a backwoods formal education. However, failure marks his initial efforts to be the man of the house as thoroughly as it does those of his father. Unable to devote himself full time to his farm duties—his father insisted that he not interrupt his education—he assumes both his father's burdens and his own, the combination of which is so overwhelming that he considers abandoning his family and his inherited duty: "So every morning 'fore I went to school / I fed the chickens and I chopped wood too / Sometimes I felt that I couldn't go on / I wanted to leave, just run away from home."

Patches rejects the "walkin' blues," but instead of redemption, he finds evidence that impoverished black male struggles to attain masculinity's symbolic and material plentitude are essentially fruitless. Motivated by his father's dying decree, the dutiful son, having endured the departure of his siblings and the death of his mother, experiences his cursed fate as a destiny he pursues for its own sake rather than to support anyone else economically.[9] And while he insists that he is spurred on by memories of his father's example and instructions, rather than enable his maturation or class mobility, his ethos of black male invulnerability entraps him thoroughly. So when Patches acknowledges that his difficulties have reduced him to tears, when he throws off the mask of black male dissemblance, his admission appears to be a sign that the solitary figure is preparing to join his dead father, if not literally, then symbolically. Because he offers no indication that he has broadened his sense of the options available to him as a gendered performer beyond his father's tragic example, public vulnerability for Patches apparently is possible—as was the case for his progenitor—only if death is imminent. Indeed, only death would free him from the scrutiny and pejorative judgment of a community whose members would condemn him, as they did when he was a child, for wearing his vulnerability on his sleeve.

Like "Patches," the Temptations' "Papa Was a Rolling Stone" is an R&B song in which a son measures the meanings and possibilities of his own life against those he discerns in the stories passed along to him about a deceased father. To invoke modes of black masculinity introduced earlier, "Papa Was a Rolling Stone" describes the contours of a man's life lived fully under the sway of the "walkin' blues" and the impact of his "dangerous freedom"—his Rinehartesque ability to reinvent himself perpetually—on his son. Hearing of the demise of his mysterious father, this son questions his mother about the veracity of the "bad talk goin' around town" about a man he has never met. Neighborhood reports about his father's activities differ radically from the honorific commemorations circulating throughout a backwoods community about Patches's ineffectual but persistent father. Neither bogged down by a philosophy of masculine self-sacrifice nor tied to a single impoverished domestic space, the father in "Rolling Stone" manifests a level of flexibility that allows him to feel, literally and symbolically, that "wherever he laid his hat was his home."

If the father's practice of black masculinity is marked by a self-defeating rigidity in Carter's song, the "Rolling Stone" progenitor can be said to thrive because, lacking a single defining role or core identity, he possesses a great deal more social flexibility. By turns a storefront preacher "stealing in the name of the Lord," an adulterer with "three outside children," and an alcoholic, he is a veritable jack of all trades and master, apparently, of none, except avoiding ontological entrapment. Unlike the Sisyphean patriarch of "Patches," who is tied to a life of backbreaking, and ultimately fruitless, labor, this "rolling stone" is, like Cholly, "free to feel whatever he felt."

Clearly, these songs depict divergent modes of male social performance: a dogged, family-centered, utterly self-consistent form of masculine responsibility, which is, at most, its own reward in "Patches" and polymorphic flexibility and changeability emerging paradoxically, in "Rolling Stone," from a selfish practice of selflessness. And while the sons adopt conventional views of their fathers—Patches expects us to share his admiration of his dad, while the son in "Rolling Stone" chastises his father for his irresponsibility and his trickster behavior—our assessments may be more complicated than they anticipate. Ultimately, we might view Patches as cursed rather than ennobled by his paternal legacy. And even if, like Carter's protagonist, the son in "Rolling Stone" wonders whether his father is driven to "an early grave" by his irresponsible performance of masculinity and his failure to be "the same thing all the way through," we also might recognize him as wholly ill-equipped to shoulder the awesome burden of unrewarding black American masculine consistency.

"Patches" and "Rolling Stone" are both concerned about the dilemmas endemic to impoverished black masculinity. Interrogating the songs in such terms proves difficult, however, because they lack both a coherent expression of black social consciousness and a sufficiently pointed critique of the inequities of American capitalism that might justify such a reading. Carter's song fails to explain precisely why the efforts of the father go unrewarded, and the Temptations song, which assumes the perspective of the ignorant son, cannot examine why the absent, rolling-stone patriarch acted in such an irresponsible manner. Such a context is available if we consult historical analyses and literary texts of the period, whose discussions of white patriarchy's determination of the limits of black masculinity at crucial points of male psychosexual and socioeconomic self-definition suggest the deforming implications of American racial oppression. Equally illuminating, for my purposes here, are other R&B songs that discuss black fathers, deal with black male vulnerability, and describe black social reality in ways that are informed by Black Power imperatives.

Like "Patches" and "Rolling Stone," numerous R&B songs from this period explore fatherhood, but these songs generally do not speak insightfully about the social obstacles these men seek to overcome. I want, therefore, to reference the examination of such matters contained in another Temptations hit, "Masterpiece," which offers a chilling vision of social conditions faced by members of the urban underclass such as the dramatically irresponsible father in its currently more cherished predecessor. Dominated more by producer Norman Whitfield's extended psychedelic soul orchestration than by the voices of the quintet, which had by this point lost three-fifths of its classic original lineup, this song speaks of the inner city as a place devoid of legitimate means of achieving social mobility ("getting ahead was strictly a no-no / 'Cause nobody cares what happens to folks who live in the ghetto"). A Darwinian nightmare landscape where "only the strong survive," where mere sustenance is often unavailable, and infestations of crime, rats, and roaches raise the stress levels of its inhabitants, "Masterpiece" portrays an inner city on which civil rights protests and Great Society programs have had frighteningly little impact. In these environs, whose homes are in catastrophic physical and institutional disrepair, not even the most committed patriarchs can protect "strung-out kids" or material possessions, as such violations are seen as "an everyday thing in the ghetto."[10]

In the urban American jungles the song envisions, masculinity is asserted most powerfully through forms of antisocial behavior generally and criminality in particular. If the rural Southern setting of "Patches" limits our sense of its engagement with post–civil rights social chaos, "Masterpiece"— and, by inference, "Rolling Stone"—equates modernity and urbanity with forms of disorder that render traditional modes of gendered behavior utterly inappropriate. Nothing—and, indeed, no one—can cover over or patch sufficiently the human devastation imagined in this song and by the architects of the United States' Great Society programs, which strove to create possibilities for black males to be men in traditional, patriarchal ways. The Temptations songs, viewed in tandem, reflect the logic for impoverished black males of refusing to embrace traditional formulations of masculinity and fatherhood. And while they offer no plausible solutions, no instructions for abandoned sons desperate to comprehend and practice personally and socially beneficial forms of black masculinity, they acknowledge the perils and virtual impossibility for black lower-class males of trying to be "the same thing all the way through." As products of or participants in poor urban families, such males appear fated either to experience the curse of impoverished (Southern) black masculinity or to harm others because of the seductiveness of "dangerous freedom."

In assessing the nostalgic themes of the O'Jays' "Family Reunion," it is useful to keep in mind the skepticism animating in the aforementioned songs, which are concerned with projecting a consistently manly or a fully liberated black male presence. The liner notes of the 1975 album for which it serves as the title song—an album that also includes "Unity," which urges divided and conquered people to speak in a single voice against the forces of oppression; the popular hit "I Love Music"; and the Quiet Storm classic "Stairway to Heaven"—examine the post-1960s American family. Penned by Kenny Gamble, who composed most of the socially conscious lyrics that dominated the trio's corpus during the 1970s, the notes evince what Svetlana Boym terms nostalgia's "two main narrative plots—the restoration of origins and the conspiracy theory, characteristic of the most extreme cases of contemporary nationalism fed on right-wing popular culture" (2001, 43). The notes read:

> The generation gap is another evil plan. The result of which divided the family structure, therefore creating a halt to the flow of wisdom from the wise to the young, and stifling the energy of the youth which is the equalizer to wisdom and age. . . . Being of truth and understanding in all things, we must recapture the family structure— Mother, Father, Sister and Brother—and give respect to everyone.
>
> Remember the family that prays together stays together. Put the "Unity" back into the family.

Articulating Gamble's solution to the problem of the generational divide, a widely debated phenomenon because of the notorious rebellious nature of 1960s U.S. youth culture, this statement distinguishes "they"—those who plotted, and profit from, the people's disenfranchisement—from the "we" whose understanding of this master plan will enable us to unite the divided factions within the nonruling classes. After defeating the forces that launched this "evil plan," the heretofore divided family will restore the generational "flow of wisdom" from adults to children.

Typically, responses to PIR's conservative, sometimes even reactionary, concerns focus exclusively on praising Gamble and Huff for their willingness to take on important cultural issues. Indeed, even when it recognizes troubling aspects of the lyrics and other facets of this company's remarkably successful musical output, analysis of its often complex and contradictory ideological interventions fails to submit PIR's general promotion of conservative gender politics to serious scrutiny. For example, in *The Death of Rhythm and Blues*, Nelson George notes that "Gamble developed a tough, male-dominated, anti-materialist perspective" (1988, 145) but refuses to test this perspective—and, moreover, his view that the company offered a salutary vision of (comm)unity—against the book's intriguing thesis that an obsession with crossover success during the 1980s precipitated the demise both of a psychically nurturing black popular music and of a unified black America. From a feminist perspective, how ideal was male domination to begin with, even when it was delivered in melodic, sonically appealing bursts of toe-tapping, soul-powered beautiful music?

Craig Werner's insightful *A Change Is Gonna Come* also briefly notes Gamble's "commitment to a morally upright, patriarchal community" and a "potentially explosive tension, nearly a contradiction" in the celebrated "message in our [PIR's] music" (1999, 200). But despite Werner's recognition of the implications of "patriarchal community," the tension that concerns him is not connected to its naturalization of women's subordination. Instead, he emphasizes the contradictions between PIR's promotion of a potentially unified, informed, multiracial community, on the one hand, and on the other, more pessimistic, Afrocentric songs like "Ship Ahoy," a haunting "recount[ing of] the brutal experiences of the Middle Passage" (202).

Of course, rather than being thrown analytically by PIR's signaling of both transracial and black nationalist concerns, we might recognize possible distinctions between local and national (and, for that matter, global) cultural registers in order to account for such tensions. If, as Andy Bennett suggests in *Popular Music and Youth Culture*, popular black styles signify, for blacks, local and/or global dimensions of racial distinctiveness and, for whites, "a symbol of community into which local white youth are included" (2000, 30), then we can see instances of black cultural style such as the self-consciously mass-marketed music of PIR as fulfilling a similarly "dual function." But the studies that I reference are concerned with PIR's status as *black Americanist* discourse. Hence, in interpreting its sociopolitical musical message, they seek to acknowledge both its "inclusive vision of human unity" and its awareness that "the society around them seemed on the verge of resegregation. . . . [Consequently] it became harder and harder to believe that the legacy of slavery could be consigned to the past" (Werner 1999, 201–202). What is also not consigned to the past, however, and what PIR seeks to promote, is a sonically appealing vision—and, indeed, the naturalization—of male domination during an era whose preeminent struggle was over the rights of women.

Because of my concern in this study with culture's continuing local meanings despite—or even because of—its participation in national and global markets, Werner's attention to black artists' efforts to work both identifiably racial and potentially transracial registers proves particularly suggestive. Still, I want to consider some of the problems that the achievement of Gamble's dream of patriarchy's reassertion might pose. Despite the admiration I share with George and Werner of aspects of Philadelphia International's significant cultural work, it is not possible for me to ignore the often retrograde nature of its message concerning gender roles. I do not want, in other words, merely to praise PIR's contributions to black political discourse while failing to deal with what these R&B analysts doubtlessly recognize are the limitations of Afrocentric patriarchy, as much as I have myself witnessed the benefits of Gamble's commitment to the "healing powers of music" (Jackson 2004, 200).

In the histories of soul and R&B, PIR operates generally as evidence of the plausibility of a series of narratives about the meanings and sonic circulation of post–civil rights blackness, one of whose features is resistance to dehumanizing and deracinating white oppression. Because Philadelphia International recordings examine racial oppression energetically, when analysts concerned about the problems of patriarchy take note of Gamble's strivings for a patriarchal community, they do not always feel compelled to engage that nostalgic urging as a significant subject. The refusal of critics seeking to determine or confirm PIR's historical meaning and message to critique its gendered conservatism energetically can be attributed, I think, to their investment in *monumentality*. This concept is influenced by Boym's notion of constructing what she calls an "intentional monument." As Boym persuasively argues:

> What is involved in the restoration of an "intentional monument" is
> a recuperation of a single moment in history, made exemplary for the
> purpose of the present. Restoration of intentional monuments makes
> a claim to immortality and eternal youth, not to the past; intentional
> commemoration is about victory over time itself. . . . Revelation of
> mortality is of no use for group identity. (2001, 78–79)

If the point of highlighting black social, political, and aesthetic achievements
is, in part, to identify and legitimize their status and potential meaning-
fulness as racial discourse, the unwillingness of commentators to critique
PIR is understandable. Despite the contemporary music that continues to
be released under its name, like its predecessors Stax and Motown, whose
abandoned physical spaces now serve as tourist attractions for the cities of
Memphis and Detroit, respectively, PIR has become a veritable mausoleum
housing ghostly echoes of its formerly dominant, still-resonant sounds. Indeed, these places have become what Boym terms "modern ruins," which
"point . . . at [the] coexistence of different dimensions and historical times in
the city" (79). I am interested less in aiding in the preservation of products of
Philadelphia than in examining them for residue of disputes over the meanings of black American racial identity that emerged specifically in the wake
of Martin Luther King's assassination. Hence, I am compelled to engage PIR's
aurally seductive patriarchal family-centered music and mission statement in
a critical manner, recognizing them as what Boym calls "memorial places in
the city [that] have to be seen in the process of continuous transformation"
(79). If, "in stable countries [such as the United States that are] forgetful of the
past, monuments become invisible" (79), we must be willing to destabilize
PIR's meanings if it is to remain culturally evocative. And like all memories
with which we are actually engaged, its dreams of black patriarchal supremacy must be recognized as continually "moving, traversing, cutting through
place, taking detours" (80).

Doing so enables me to resist the impulse metaphorically or literally to
carve PIR's cultural meanings in stone via a process I call *black discursive
monumentality*. I use the phrase to describe a tendency among commentators aware of mainstream U.S. society's general historical refusal to recognize
black American contributions to praise rather than interrogate individuals
and institutions whose efforts have not yet been widely or sufficiently acknowledged. In each of its manifestations, *black discursive monumentality*
constitutes a mode of recognition with beneficial symbolic potential and
can be an intellectually nuanced activity. Perhaps the best available example of its virtues is the creation of a genre of novelists that Ashraf Rushdy

(1999) terms "neo-slave narratives" including *Beloved, Dessa Rose, Oxherding Tale, Kindred, Middle Passage, The Price of a Child,* and *The Known World,* to name some of this subgenre's most highly lauded and well-known titles. In a symbol-drenched United States where powerful forces have sought to wish away or otherwise ignore slavery's incommensurability with American ideals, where presidents and members of Congress viewed apologizing for slavery as unseemly or as tantamount to political suicide until 2009,[11] where no national monument recognizes its countless victims, such novels confirm and remember the facticity of systemic black American degradation. In other words, especially in the absence of official recognition, neo-slave narratives describe—and inscribe—the stain this peculiar institution left on America's soul, its impact on blacks' continuing skeptical participation in the myths of America, and its broad cultural significance.

At its worst, however, black discursive monumentality operates as a mode of uncritical racial nostalgia. Discussions of PIR have typically reflected this latter tendency. One such example appears in *Just My Soul Responding*, in which Brian Ward insists that

> male Rhythm and Blues from the late 1960s to the mid 1970s [saw] . . . a marked revival of the sexism and sexual hostilities which had been so much a part of r&b before the birth of the modern civil rights movement. . . . [A]s a progressive movement fuelled by radical equalitarian ideals splintered, a form of retrogressive entrenchment took place. Frustrated, angry and increasingly desperate and alien-ated, black men, particularly the masses who failed to escape into the black middle class, where they could practice a different, more main-stream, form of patriarchy and sexism, sometimes took refuge in a peculiarly intense form of racial and sexual chauvinism. The revival of black macho and the myth of matriarchy in soul were cultural manifestations of that phenomenon. (1998, 380)

Citing the work of James Brown and Wilson Pickett as evidence, Ward de-scribes black patriarchal retrenchment as a significant feature of R&B during the period in which PIR achieved its greatest popularity. Still, while agree-ing with George's reading of Gamble's perspective as "male-dominated," his discussion of PIR rushes to explore subjects other than the implications of masculine biases: the label's status as "the second biggest black-owned corpo-ration in the country" (1998, 418); its deep implication "in the steady corpo-ratization of black—and white—popular music during the period" (419); the 1971 Harvard University Graduate School of Business report on the music business that led CBS Records to strike a distribution deal with Gamble and Huff; and the report's recommendation "that CBS should make a concerted effort to develop its meager black music catalogue" and suggestion that "with the right sort of crossover material and access to black radio and the black retail market, Rhythm and Blues could provide CBS with a springboard to the much greater riches of the mainstream market" (419). Exempting PIR from the gender analysis that infuses his study, Ward speaks of it solely as an exemplary enterprise whose success at integrating the music business takes precedence over its reactionary gender norms. Certainly, we can remember the glorious heyday of Philadelphia International Records, note its stunning accomplishments, and still interrogate—even energetically critique—its representations of gender.

The notion of *restorative nostalgia* helps us understand the otherwise myopic "conception of good and evil" animating "Family Reunion." The song can be said to reflect what I identified earlier as the phenomenon's "two main narrative plots—the restoration of origins and the conspiracy theory." Boym says about the latter:

> The conspiratorial worldview is based on a single transhistorical plot, a Manichaean battle of good and evil and the inevitable scapegoating of the mythical enemy. Ambivalence, the complexity of history and the specificity of modern circumstances[,] is thus erased, and modern history is seen as a fulfillment of ancient prophecy. "Home," imagine extremist conspiracy theory adherents, is forever under siege, requiring defense against the plotting enemy. (2001, 43)

Looked at from such a vantage point, Gamble's formulation of ideal familial roles cannot be seen as anything other than a reflection of male nostalgia for, in the words of Mieke Bal, "an idyllic past that never was," but which nonetheless can "be empowering and productive if critically tempered and historically informed" (1999, xi). Calling attention to both the mythic and conservative aspects of Gamble's formulation need not be seen as tantamount to offering a blanket dismissal of his or PIR's tremendous contributions. Particularly when we consider instances of nostalgia whose purpose is to counteract the historical effects of systemic oppression, we can recognize that, like sentimentality and other modes of cultural memory, nostalgia can best be seen as what Bal describes as "a structure of relation to the past, not false or inauthentic in essence" (xi).

In an essay that interrogates his Jewish family's pre-Holocaust photographs, Leo Spitzer insists that nostalgia signifies

"loss" in a more generalized and abstract way, including the yearning for a "lost childhood," for "irretrievable youth," for a "world of yesterday" from whose ideals and values one had become distanced and detached. In this usage, nostalgia became an incurable state of mind—a signifier of "absence" and "loss" that could in effect never be made "presence" and "gain" except through memory and the creativity of reconstruction. (1999, 90)

Liberating nostalgia from the "sharp reproach" of detractors who deem it "'reactionary,' 'escapist,' 'inauthentic,' 'unreflective,' and as a 'simplification' if not 'falsification of the past'" (91), Spitzer argues that the creative reconfiguration of "nostalgic memory . . . serves as one source through which" oppressed people can build "a new communal culture and construct . . . a new collective identity to serve their changed needs" (92). Such aims are best served when nostalgic memory—"the selective emphasis on the positive from the past"—is accompanied by its "complicating 'other side,' critical memory," which incorporates "the negative and the bitter" (96). However temporarily empowering nostalgic memory is because it serves "as a potential anchor for personal and group stability and identity," if oppressed groups are to arrive at a nuanced comprehension of their historical place, ultimately they must incorporate "a more complete memory of a past in which both its negative and its positive aspects would be acknowledged and employed" (101).

In my view, the assassination of Martin Luther King, Jr. caused the traumatizing rupture and absence that has destroyed any real chance that the dream of a post–civil rights black American collective identity and community could be achieved. Responding to the death of the possibility of racial wholeness—a death often attributed to black women's economically essential workforce participation, which was seen as undermining masculine authority and, hence, deforming black American families—"Family Reunion" traffics in nostalgic memory of patriarchal dominion that ignores "the negative and the bitter" fact of racism's historic repression of black male labor and proffers it as "a new communal culture and construct . . . to serve their changed needs." At the same time, the song condemns critiques of gender norms that position the father as (according to the spoken-word second half of the O'Jays track) "the head, the leader, the director," suggesting that such critiques, rather than the deforming phenomenon of U.S. racism, are the family's most daunting obstacle.

If PIR's nationalist inclinations place black and white men at odds concerning the overall message in the music, members of these groups were certainly able to agree on the sociocultural damage caused by feminists who view "rhetoric about separate male and female natures, traits or abilities as parts of the 'tool-kit of oppression' practiced by the patriarchy" (Schulman 2002, 164). Following a conventional first section in which the O'Jays' Eddie Levert—father of the late R&B crooner Gerald Levert—expresses regrets about the infrequency of familial gatherings and longing for deceased grandparents, "Family Reunion" devolves into a didactic track that, like the second part of the Intruders' "I'll Always Love My Mama," is spoken rather than sung and illuminates the song's beginnings. While gender is masked as a major concern in the first part of the song except, perhaps, in the distinction the lyrics make between the deceased grandparents—the nurturing grandmother noted for "her warm and tender embrace" and the proud grandfather-progenitor whose loins produced the reuniting clan—it is the overwhelming subject of its second part. The members of the family, an institution of healing and "solution to the world's problems today," adopt conventional gender roles: the father as leader, the wife as empathetic helpmate, and male and female offspring imitating the gender practices of their parents. And unlike humanity's obsession with superficial differences ("color, race, creed"), the gender differences whose acceptance constitutes the family as a healing structure are ordained by a god whose sacred words enable inhabitants of a conflict-filled, war-torn world to recognize themselves as members of a "universal family" united by "one divine purpose and one divine Father."

Certainly, we would be hard pressed to suggest that King's death *caused* the post–civil rights era black family's demise. Still, the primary manifestation of that demise—the normalization of paternal absence—indicates black Americans' rejection of the civil rights leader's preeminent goal, integration, since, as Moynihan argues, matriarchal structures that "evolved within the isolated world of the Negro folk" (1965, 18) cannot propel men, women, and children toward mainstream success. "Family Reunion" posits an incompatibility between black social progress and mainstream feminist notions: in the song, race and religion are deemed inessential markers of difference, whereas gender represents the sole unassailable, divinely ordained mark of differentiation. Hence, the patriarchal reunion, a coalescence of dispersed people tied together by blood, ultimately offers a tradition-bound vision of black American collective identity and imagined community whose members embrace their roles within God's male-centered plan.

Speaking of "Family Reunion" in terms of its racial resonances, then, we can say that instead of seeing black strivings for equality as of a piece with other liberationist efforts of the 1960s, Gamble isolates black collectivity from feminist, gay, and other quintessentially progressive formulations. In fact, according to his patriarchal, heterosexist vision, it is precisely such formulations, and not the conservative forces against which 1960s youth culture struggled, that threaten black familial unity. If, at the end of his life, King's antiwar activism and redistributive economic plans demonstrated that he had moved beyond a regional racial politics and had embraced some of the most radical perspectives of the 1960s, Gamble's mid-1970s response looks back nostalgically to pre-1960s, pre-integration formulations of black family that U.S. racism never allowed to become a general norm, while at the same time taking advantage of cultural transformations that allowed him to figure the patriarchal family as a "universal" solution.

Given their similarly conservative takes on the sources of American familial dissolution, it is not difficult to recognize points of connection between Gamble's notion of family and James Dobson's rhetorical justification of his conservative group, Focus on the Family. Like Gamble, Dobson built a family-centered institution in response to developments during the 1960s—the sexual revolution, in Dobson's case—that littered the United States with children whose lives had been torn apart by "divorce, abuse, and other forms of familial strife. . . . I became convinced that the only hope for these broken and disillusioned kids—as well as for future generations of kids—lay in the strengthening of the family unit and returning to the Judeo-Christian concepts of morality and fidelity" (quoted in Gilgoff 2007, 21–22). Ann Burlein describes Dobson's perspectives in the following way:

> The Right has launched its bid for hegemony, not by stubbornly insisting on speaking only its own language, but by reworking and appropriating precisely those cultural memories, discourses, and images that the Left thinks of as its property: memories of protest and popular resistance associated with the 1960s. (1999, 217)

Dobson challenges the left by preserving "memory of our Christian heritage even though every effort has been made to extinguish it" (220). Through his nostalgic act, Dobson wages war against

> "the humanist value system" that emerged out of 1960s popular youth culture with its fascination for Black Power, feminism, gay rights, and Eastern spiritualities. As Dobson tells it, in just a few short years the "humanistic system of values" popularized by these

movements "outstripped Judeo-Christian precepts" to capture "most of the power centers of society," moving from 1960s counterculture to 1990s mainstream. (Burlein 1999, 210)

While insisting that the 1960s revolutions were the result of a "'well-thought out and coordinated' secular humanist conspiracy to exterminate all memory of the nation's Christian heritage" (Burlein 1999, 211), including the patriarchal family, Dobson does not demand a rejection of youth cultural concerns. Indeed, he recognizes "the truth of certain feminist criticisms regarding masculinity and the cultural devaluation of women" but promotes a return to the ideals of the traditional family, in which women's honest communication of their feelings, coupled with men's willingness to "get in touch with their feelings and involved with their families" (211), can heal the ruptures that that decade's rhetoric overemphasized and exploited. As Burlein puts it, "By remembering the 1960s in ways that pit social movements against the family, . . . Dobson deploys a rhetoric of remembrance to create social and symbolic spaces from which people can discipline, evade, and silence difference in the name of connection and compassion" (213). One of the differences Dobson evades is race or, more specifically, the persistence of racism and its impact on the constitution of the black family, and on blackness as a mode of opposition. Fully cognizant of the attractiveness of King's dream both to blacks and to others in the United States frustrated by the intractability of the problems associated with black urban poverty, Focus on the Family, in Burlein's words, "professes the ability of the family to conjure African-Americans out of poverty and into the middle class" (215).

In Gamble's nostalgic rhetoric, the post–civil rights family, like Dobson's organization, is capable of mighty things if and only if it reconstitutes itself by rejecting a disempowering 1960s humanism. For Gamble, the recuperated family offers "the solution to the world's problems today." In its seductive expression of affection and longing, the sung first portion of "Family Reunion" only hints at the conservative patriarchal reformation contained in the spoken words that conclude the song. Accompanied by pleasant instrumentation that assumes a soothing, largely nonintrusive, mid-tempo beat, Levert declares, "It's so nice to see all the folks you love together," an increasingly rare event presumably because family members have left their neighborhoods and hometowns in pursuit of educational and employment opportunities. Despite the pleasures of reunion, however, the persona quickly recognizes that essential family members are absent, including his grandparents. In the song's last formal verse, he expresses his longing for the presence of both his grandmother, whose identification as an unmodified face and a soothing embrace compels the listener to regard her as an irreplaceable source of nurturance, and his grandfather, whom he imagines would see the gathering as evidence of his impressive generative power.

However, the spoken-word conclusion lays bare Gamble's recuperative intentions, associating personal and human salvation with family members' assumption of traditional roles and notions of gender—and generational—identity. While, like the male in Dobson's family, Gamble's father is described as "not domineering," he is indisputably in charge. Certainly, there are a variety of ways to interpret the sincere expression of a desire for "all the fathers in the world to stand up and be fathers," including one that focuses on the potential benefits that accrue in intact families when adult males embrace traditional masculine leadership roles. But given the song's coding as "black music" (in Levert's church-trained voice and PIR's status as a 1970s, post-Motown hit factory), it is difficult not to see these suggestions as addressed primarily to poor black American men who, as Moynihan predicted would be the consequences of continuing black male socioeconomic and domestic marginalization, were abandoning their families in increasing numbers and thereby causing their offspring and former mates significant emotional and economic hardship.

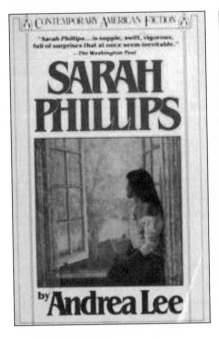

3

A "Genuinely Afro-American Narrative"

Sarah Phillips *and the Politics*
of Black Textual Authenticity

Contrasting visions of race and freedom: the covers of Andrea Lee's Sarah Phillips, *which is set in suburban Philadelphia and was published first by Random House (1984; left) and, following its commercial failure, as part of Northeastern University Press's Library of Black Literature series (1993; right).* (Photo by LaSonia Forte.)

*T*he May 13, 1985, bombing of the steel-fortified, heavily armed head-
quarters of the antiestablishment Philadelphia group MOVE, which
was at war both with city officials and with modernity, exposed radically divergent notions of black American identity in the post–civil rights era.
The group's abhorrence of what it deemed the physically, psychologically, and
spiritually toxic nature of postindustrial U.S. life created unclean, pest-ridden
living conditions for its neighbors. In addition, the group's amplified proselytiz-
ing, complaints about the local and national legal systems, and acts of physical
intimidation turned initially sympathetic residents of two middle-class communities vehemently against it, leading these residents to plead repeatedly with
city officials for assistance that, on two occasions, devolved into lethal police
intervention.

On August 8, 1978, in the racially integrated neighborhood of Powelton
Village that abuts two universities, a lengthy standoff and exchange of gunfire
culminated in the apparent friendly-fire death of a police officer; the severe
beating of a surrendering member of MOVE for which the policemen who were
involved were never punished despite taped evidence of their transgressions;
the arrests of nine members of the group, who were sentenced to lengthy jail
terms for the officer's murder; and the bulldozing of the home from which the
city had been attempting to evict the MOVE tenants. The aforementioned 1985
incident, which took place on the 6200 block of Osage Avenue, involved the
use of military-grade explosives to dislodge a protective bunker on the roof of
the MOVE residence, which ignited a can of gasoline. Faced with an increasingly dangerous situation, city officials present at the scene and reporting to the
city's first black mayor, W. Wilson Goode, ordered firefighters not to extinguish
the resulting blaze, which ultimately destroyed an entire city block in a thriv-
ing black neighborhood. This decision led to the immolation-related deaths of
eleven members of MOVE, who remained in the burning house rather than
face the bullets of policemen who opened fire on them as they attempted to exit.

These events have been explored in numerous articles and books about the
hostilities between MOVE and the City of Philadelphia, including a commis-
sioned report that, while highly critical of Goode and the fire and police department commissioners, among others, concluded that none of these city officials
should be held criminally responsible for the group members' deaths, the destruction of sixty-one homes that displaced 250 city residents, and the traumatization of many of the city's inhabitants.[1] One such publication, MOVE: Sites
of Trauma, speaks of the bombing as "one of the most tragic events" (Dickson 2002, 12) in the city's long history and as affecting "everyone who lived in
Philadelphia at the time." According to its author, Johanna Dickson, both the
bombing itself and the city's efforts "to bury the event and its physical remains"

have made psychic recovery virtually impossible both for individuals who were directly involved and for Philadelphia as a whole. Describing the city as a "post-traumatic environment," Dickson insists that its recovery is contingent on the "communalization of the trauma—being able safely to tell the story to someone who is listening and who can be trusted to retell it truthfully to others in the community." Such dialogue, according to the researcher Dickson cites, Jonathan Shay, is necessary because "unhealed trauma . . . destroys the unnoticed substructure of democracy, the cognitive and social capabilities that enable a group of people to freely construct a narrative of their own future" (12).

As remarks occasioned by the twenty-fifth anniversary article in the Philadelphia Inquirer *about the aftermath of the bombing indicate, one of the traumatized survivors struggling to construct such a narrative is former Mayor Goode, who earlier characterized the massive governmental miscalculations as having "killed two birds with one stone—MOVE and me" (Rosenberg 2010). A fundamentally decent man hopelessly at odds with himself about the tragedy's psychic impact on the city, the nation, and himself, Goode insists that others recognize that the bombing holds an "aberrant" place in his otherwise exemplary American life, despite his at least tacit endorsement of the decision to release a lethal explosive that caused generations of black and nonblack Philadelphians to experience "the darkest day in the [post–civil rights era] history of the city." Throughout a lengthy public life, he distinguished himself as a man of gritty determination: as the consumer-oriented leader of the Pennsylvania Utilities Commission; the hardworking, supremely competent city manager under Mayor Bill Green; the two-term mayor from whom, even after MOVE, much good was expected by residents from across multiple racial divides; and, currently, executive director of a well-regarded national program that provides mentors for children of incarcerated parents. Still, even if it is the case that, as Goode asserts, during his travels throughout the United States, at no point has "the issue of MOVE . . . been raised with me," no Philadelphian who watched the surreal images of the siege—the piercing volleys of water projected at the MOVE home, the massive police presence, the burning bunker and the slowly spreading flames engulfing adjacent houses—will forget the day that the birthplace of American liberty earned the moniker "The City That Bombed Itself" (Rosenberg 2010).*

Goode's twenty-fifth-anniversary descriptions of his reactions to the catastrophe suggest that he remains traumatized to such an extent that he cannot construct a coherent narrative about events that altered his life permanently. Insisting in his conversation with the Philadelphia Inquirer's *Amy Rosenberg that he has "no explanation as to why it happened or how it happened" and that "it is something that should never have happened," Goode expresses ambivalence about the current state of the psychic, moral, and spiritual wounds—his own and those of others—resulting from this tragedy. Indeed, he insists at one point in the interview that this mid-1980s event was "just one day in the life," "an aberration" that was not "part of a continuum in my life" (Rosenberg 2010). Chafing at the notion that he is defined as a human being and a public servant in part by this administrative debacle and expressing doubt that "people think about it any more," he nevertheless acknowledges that he drives "daily . . . by the block where it occurred," that "every week, I talk with people who live there who were hurt by what happened," and that he feels compelled "to make up for it every day." So impactful is this day of destruction that, because of the failures of his own and subsequent administrators to rebuild the 6200 block of Osage Avenue (the incredibly shoddy work of builders contracted to replace the homes has rendered many of them unlivable), Goode, like visitors to the ruins of Ground Zero a decade after 9/11, considers the gaping wound left in the city's landscape an utterly fitting "monument to what happened" (Rosenberg 2010).*

For the former mayor, identifying precisely what the Osage Avenue wreckage symbolizes appears to be impossible, because what it can be said to monumentalize changes frequently. Does it reflect, for Goode and for others, MOVE's virulent disdain for modernity, its thoroughly fed-up black middle-class neighbors' fractured pride and conflicted sense of racial loyalty, the anger of policemen who remembered that one of their brothers-in-arms was killed less than a decade earlier during a similar altercation with this dreadlocked group, or the anguish of firefighters ordered to wait out distrustful occupants who chose immolation instead of surrender to executioners of unjust laws who were bent on exterminating them? Does it reflect the death of the possibility of interracial brotherly and sisterly love, of dreams of black social progress, of truly transformative black leadership of major cities? Does it represent Goode's internal struggle to maintain faith in his own fundamental decency, the soundness of his judgment, or the possibilities of justice for all? Can it be said also to signify the anguish he feels, given what he knows has been the traumatic nature of his people's experiences in the United States generally, to be partially responsible for one of the most horrific losses of black American life in the city's history?

The bombing of MOVE remains sufficiently unassimilated by Goode that he can hardly speak of "it" publicly and can admit that he "has never discussed MOVE with his wife, Velma, or his three children" (Rosenberg 2010), two of whom I knew when they were undergraduates at the University of Pennsylvania. His angst seems also to be deeply familial, a sense of trauma resulting from a husband's and father's role in an event that has stained the heretofore well-respected Goode name in so significant a manner that the resulting pain and sense of shame cannot be spoken of even in the privacy of their home. Nor can they be addressed publicly even by the son who has followed nominally and professionally in the former mayor's shoes, Philadelphia councilman W. Wilson Goode, Jr., whom I remember as a diffident student in one of the first classes I ever taught and whose service to the city has been by all accounts admirable, even exemplary. According to Rosenberg, Goode, Jr. "refused to discuss even the idea that the family did not talk about the subject" (Rosenberg 2010).

Quite honestly, I share the Goode family's reticence about discussing the city's gaping, unhealed wound. Hoping to formulate an answer to pointed questions for more than a decade about why I did not want to include MOVE in this study, I have read thousands of pages about the group, watched footage and numerous analytical accounts, and certainly thought about this tragedy as extensively as I have about the subject I have chosen to represent black Philadelphia during the 1980s, Sarah Phillips *by Andrea Lee, a fictive examination of a Main Line suburban black girl's upbringing in and around the First City during the civil rights movement. I believe that the concerns addressed in this chapter—the deindustrialization of the inner city, the racial responsibility of the black middle class, the burdens of racial history, and the urge to codify the meanings of black authenticity—constitute important issues with which black Americans were grappling during this decade. The chapter on Lee's novel is the one I drafted first, soon after I returned to Philadelphia to teach at Penn following a decade in Ann Arbor, and is a chapter whose interdisciplinary emphases and concern with trauma and intraracial difference set the terms for the rest of the book. Also,* Sarah Phillips *allows me to interrogate issues with which I feel comfortable, emotionally engaged, and, frankly, at ease.*

I have long felt unsettled by the MOVE saga and by MOVE. I remember this group as a noxious presence in downtown Philly when I was a teenager. Invariably during my window-shopping trips to Center City as a teenager, I had to walk past assemblages of protesting MOVE members, blocking my way, seeking to recruit people in front of or behind me to their ill-defined cause, disturbing my shopping pleasures with condemnations of the hopelessly fallen modern world. Holding my breath as I passed them, I imagined foul odors emanating from their raggedy clothes and dusty dreadlocks, and I saw them as a sign of urban decay, which, I subsequently learned, was precisely how they viewed me and virtually everyone else they encountered. I saw them as a crazy cult whose hatred for the city and its representatives was, however understandable—fully aware of Frank Rizzo's decades-long crusade against young black males, I recognized how such disdain could come to seem justifiable—ultimately self-defeating.

Then the MOVE tragedy on Osage Avenue happened, which I watched all day, in a state of shock. I saw the hoses aimed at the house, its piercing water reminding me of scenes of soaked black Southern protesters who had assembled to demand the privileges of U.S. citizenship that documents composed in Philadelphia insisted were their birthright. I saw thousands of policemen gathered in front of this drenched structure, awaiting orders about how to remove a longtime irritant because of which a policeman had died less than a decade earlier. And I waited for Mayor Goode—the patient, empathetic man who had roamed Philly's streets confidently as its city manager and shattered its political glass ceiling by making his resolutely unflashy, meat-and-potatoes, just-up-from-Dixie blackness an asset to his pursuit of political power—to show up. In his autobiography, In Goode Faith, he later insisted that he had watched the events of the day unfold on television because "three people who had always provided me with reliable information . . . had obtained information alleging that if I went to the MOVE scene, I would 'catch a bullet with my name on it!' It would be made to look like an accident, but they told me unknown members of my own police force had targeted me for death if I came near Sixty-second Street and Osage Avenue" (Goode and Stevens 1992, 217–218). And then I watched the bomb drop, the bunker burn, and the fire workers fail to respond. I watched the raging fire spread to adjacent homes. The mayor stayed away, and I wondered about the responses of his children. Were they watching "it," too?

After hearing about the deaths, the charred bodies and the irreparable damage done to the houses, and the devastated psyche of the street's inhabitants, I told myself I had to see "it" for myself. "It" was less than three miles from where I was living, on the way to my Aunt Peggy's house, but in the subsequent days, months, and years, I could not bring myself to go to see this street in either its charred or its hastily rebuilt state. Even when I resolved to include MOVE in some way in this book, even when I returned from Ann Arbor during research trips to Philly to see the Constitution Center and its hallowed historic sites, I did not venture to Osage Avenue. I could not, and still cannot, bring myself to walk on a site I think of as a graveyard. I am afraid of the dreadlocked ghosts, young and middle-aged, who may continue to roam this street, full of a rage I cannot fully understand. I am afraid of the pain of their neighbors— those who returned and those who fled—all of them seeking in vain an end to "it." And I am afraid of encountering an aged former mayor, a goateed ancient mariner tirelessly traversing Osage Avenue, asking its last stubborn residents how he can help. I am sure, too, that he hopes these displaced former neighbors of MOVE are concerned about how they might help the man who shows up almost as regularly as the dreadlocked ghosts whose faces are familiar to them

and whose pain—like that of the First City's first black mayor—they recognize
as intricately tied to their own, endless anguish.

———————

[T]ruths compete with each other for power within a social
system.
　　　　　—John Fiske, *Reading the Popular*

The politics of identity is always questionable, and . . . can readily
lead to ethical and social disaster.
　　. . . [D]rawn to bind myself to the shared values of other
people . . . , I become what . . . I can sincerely profess. . . . There is
an element of hope or prediction involved; I should be able in fact
to steady my beliefs in this way and live under the social requirements of this shared identity. What I have to ask myself . . . is
precisely whether I can live without fantasy while accepting these
understandings.
　　　　　—Bernard Williams, "The Politics of Trust"

Entire groups of people keep bumping into "something" as they
walk down a particular road or pass by a particular house. This
"something" is a living nexus of material forces, occasionally
abstract, sometimes personified but always real, a "ghost" ready
to grab hold of anyone passing by. This rememory [is] . . . always
haunted by the power relations and violence that have accompanied the formation of blackness itself.
　　　　　—Hershini Bhana Young, *Haunting Capital*

———————

In *Behind the Mule*, a compelling examination of black political attitudes
in the United States, Michael Dawson argues that black Americans possess a sense of "linked fate," having "adopted the worldview that individual freedom can be realized only within the context of collective freedom,
that individual salvation can occur only within the framework of collective
salvation" (1994, 99–100). Connecting politics and religion through such
concepts as "collective salvation," he draws his epigraphs almost exclusively
from Martin Luther King, Jr.'s writings, highlighting the civil rights leader's
views of the importance for blacks to "work passionately for group identity . . . in order to participate more meaningfully at all levels of the life of

the nation" (69). Following King's assassination, this vision of an intensely political group identity is best understood as what Dawson calls "the black utility heuristic," a strategic calculation on the part of black Americans that, notwithstanding the insistence of pluralists that "individuals may indeed have multiple social and political identities . . . , not all of those identities are equally salient" (46). In determining black political behavior, Dawson argues, the most salient feature of identity is not class, religion, or region, but, rather, race: "The relationship between a black person's sense of his or her own interests and the same person's sense of the interests of the racial group is the key to the apparent political homogeneity of African Americans. It is also key to understanding how perceptions of racial group interests shape black public opinion and political behavior" (45–46).

Dawson insists that this sense of racial solidarity is threatened both by the emergence of "a growing, if vulnerable, black middle class" whose size doubled between 1960 and 1991, and by the employment woes of unskilled black Americans at the other end of the economic spectrum who, over the same period, became "three times more likely to live below the poverty line than whites" (1994, 9). As he further asserts:

> This heuristic suggests that as long as race remains dominant in determining the lives of individual blacks, it is "rational" for African Americans to follow group cues in interpreting and acting in the political world. This tendency of African Americans to follow racial cues has been reinforced historically by institutions developed during the forced separation of blacks from whites during the post-Reconstruction period. These institutions, particularly the black church, tended to transmit the lessons of how to respond to the shifts in race relations, economic climate, and political environment across generations. (58)

This information appears to support a conclusion that widespread faith in the rationality of this heuristic requires that the black middle and lower classes remain in general geographical, political, and philosophical proximity to one another. But as Dawson, William Julius Wilson, and other social scientists have helped us recognize, the suburbanization of the former and the criminalization of the latter have begun to break down, if not totally obliterate, the links that heretofore bound black Americans under the constitutive cloak of (cultural) blackness. If the late 1970s inaugurated a period marked by what Wilson terms a "declining significance of race" (1978), incontrovertible signs of that transformation during this period include myriad intraracial class struggles to determine the meanings of blackness itself.

Indeed, at the end of the 1970s, as more affluent blacks experienced greater access to elite institutions of higher education and, subsequently, to corporate and public sector employment, poor blacks saw their social mobility hindered by "higher unemployment rates, lower labor-force participation rates, higher welfare rates, and, more recently, a slower movement out of poverty" (W. Wilson 1978, 134). These changes led Wilson to conclude that "there is a deepening economic schism in the black community" and that there are "clear indications that the economic gap between the black underclass (close to a third of the black population) and the higher-income blacks will very likely widen and solidify" (134). This schism, Wilson recognizes, has less to do with a "collapse of traditional discriminatory patterns in the labor market" than with shifts in the dominant forms and sites of production:

> as a result of the decentralization of American businesses, the movement from goods-producing to service-producing industries, and the clear manifestation of these changes in the expansion of the corporate sector and the government sector, a segmented labor market has developed resulting in vastly different mobility opportunities for different groups in the black population. (120–121)

Along with market requirements that prospective employees be significantly better educated and/or trained than their counterparts just a decade earlier to meet the demands of an increasingly technology-oriented marketplace, these changes led to skyrocketing black unemployment after World War II. As Wilson asserts, "in the nation's twelve largest metropolitan areas, the central city's proportion of all manufacturing employment dropped from 66.1 percent in 1947 to less than 40 percent in 1970" (93). Because of such trends in manufacturing and other industries, which decimated Philadelphia's heretofore remarkable industrial base, radically transforming an economic system that had accommodated black unskilled workers during the period between two world wars who flocked to the First City and others in search of livable wages and less racial antagonism, the United States experienced a middle-class exodus to outlying suburbs that devastated cities' economies. If the patriarchal black American family was imperiled by limited employment opportunities for black men in the 1970s, as Chapter 2 insists, these trends rendered it statistically anomalous by the middle of the 1980s. According to the authors of *Philadelphia: Neighborhoods, Division, and Conflict in a Postindustrial City*, "By 1960 the suburbs had gained more than half of the region's residents; by 1980 the suburban share had grown to almost two-thirds of the total population. Employment followed people to the suburbs" (Adams et al. 1991, 16). This exodus—spearheaded by more than 30 percent of Philadelphia's whites between 1955 and 1980, who joined the vast majority of "white migrants into the region" (96)—included a contingent of well-educated, upwardly mobile blacks, many of whom, like their white counterparts, wanted both the convenience of residing in close proximity to their suburban places of employment and distance from an increasingly unlawful black working class.

If transformations in the American economy improved the prospects of a college-educated black middle class and decreased the likelihood of upward mobility for the black poor in cities like Philadelphia, their vastly different fates have both a class dimension and significant spatial implications. As the city's center and its traditional—often ethnically and/or racially diverse—surrounding communities were perceived as disadvantageous places to reside, they became, for all intents and purposes, increasingly marginal to U.S. technological maintenance and expansion. Investigations of the consequences of divergent black American residential patterns and economic opportunities necessarily locate us in the realm of symbolic space, which we might consider in terms of such formulations as the politics of place or, perhaps better for our purposes here, the geography of identity. According to such theorizing, space is distinguished from place by its "extrinsically storied or narrated" quality, acquiring interpretive significance as a consequence of the fact that its meanings are shaped by human hands and minds. The terrain in relationship to which people locate themselves is transformed by human contact into what Patricia Yaeger calls "themed space."

> As space that is precolonized and prefabricated around an idea or point of view, a themed land suggests a subject of representation that is blatant, repetitious, and blandly revelatory. . . . Clever theming guarantees coherence and readability and . . . has the capacity to be embodied or expanded. . . .
>
> Themed space is not only coherent and analyzable: it tries to be convincing. . . . Theming . . . gratifies much more than a whimsical desire for homogenized, coherent space; it suggests a longing for incorporation, a longing to inhabit credible space. (1996, 18)

Until the transformations that Wilson argues created discernible class differences within the race, "credible space," for blacks in Philadelphia and elsewhere, reflected much greater cultural coherence than it did a uniformity of economic circumstances. But if Wilson's interpretations and Dawson's predictions concerning the black utility heuristic are persuasive, even that undoubtedly contested coherence was threatened during the period in which, as a consequence of the desegregation of American society, the black poor and middle class generally became separated geographically, if not politically. That separation is perhaps most provocatively manifested in the class dimensions of debates to determine the "credible space" of blackness. However contested its precise meanings were when blacks occupied the same communal space, the schism precipitated new types of struggles to *place* black American authenticity—that is, to determine whether well-maintained middle-class urban and suburban lanes or increasingly grimy city streets best manifested the race's constitutive features.

Before this residential divide, black themed space was widely believed to be defined in accord with heartfelt desires to see the nation's ideals of freedom, liberty, and equal opportunity actualized for its residents. But as race declined in significance as a socioeconomic indicator, blacks' embrace both of constitutive features of U.S. ideology and of less easily idealized avenues to material advancement became progressively more economically determined. During the post–civil rights era, the increasing significance of class divided large numbers of blacks into differentiated, though psychically contiguous, even intersecting, themed spaces. The lower classes embraced their marginality, refining narratives that cast themselves in roles as alternately romantic, victimized, and outlaw subjects. Conversely, upwardly mobile black Americans more and more viewed blackness as a site of resilience and of resistance, as both impermeable protection from the dehumanizing excesses of American racism and an obstacle to their full embrace as important contributors to and participants in the comforting ideology and burgeoning opportunities that the United States offers its fully assimilated citizens.[2]

For black Americans in the post–civil rights era, complex patterns of interactions, movement, and change resulted in an escalation of class-based attitudes. While we might, along with journalist Ellis Cose, view the reactions of an emerging black "privileged class" (1993)—to glass ceilings, real and imagined slights, racist law enforcement practices, and so forth—as constituting rage, clearly, some of that rage has been directed at inner-city blacks whose disproportionately antisocial behavior helps to perpetuate, or at the very least to reinforce, racist white views of black criminality and inferiority. Attentive to these realities, we must devise theories of blackness that move convincingly beyond the wearying mindset that luxuriates in calling into question the racial commitments of those who embrace middle-class perspectives and mainstream norms of behavior.

By the 1980s, the 1960s vision of a Great Society was neither energetically pursued nor even, for that matter, fondly remembered, as the woes of the poor became an impolitic topic of political conversation. And the separation of blacks into separate class spheres affected inner-city youth, who were unable to witness the negotiation of the postindustrial American economy by the parents of their middle-class peers, which was fueled in large part by their higher educational attainment. Hence, to validate their isolated culture and their meager economic prospects, the black lower class increasingly saw the pursuit of formal education as deracinating and, in the words of anthropologist John Ogbu, "detrimental to their collective racial identity and solidarity" (2008, 91). Certainly, the categorization of behavior as racial did not begin in the post–civil rights period, but the devaluation of formal education signals a significant swerve away from a view, previously widespread among blacks, that its energetic pursuit was crucial for individual and group advancement. While the sources of such contemporary attitudes are obviously complex, their prevalence diminishes the already infinitesimal possibility that inner-city blacks will become valuable assets in an increasingly suburbanized and service-oriented job market.

If, as Kai Erikson argues, collective trauma can result from "a continuing pattern of abuse" of members of a group, "the tissues of community" heretofore linking black Americans have been significantly—and, perhaps after King's assassination, irreparably—harmed. The education-related class tensions between black Americans may constitute one manifestation of that harm if collective trauma is "a blow to the basic tissues of social life that damages the bonds attaching people together and impairs the prevailing sense of community" (Erikson 1994, 232–233). Before the deindustrialization of cities such as Philadelphia and the class-determined geographical separation of black Americans, black community, which had heretofore provided "a cushion for pain . . . , a context for intimacy . . . , the repository for binding traditions" (234), ceased to link black Americans regardless of their varying class positions. Instead, the notion of black community became a source of conflict and a sign of disharmony between urban and suburban black Americans, as members of these increasingly isolated groups were compelled to deal, in increasingly disparate ways, with the implications of their racial heritage.

Michael Dawson argues that the black utility heuristic—resulting from and in the group-centeredness of a politically unified black American "local life"—develops "in opposition to the American liberal tradition" (1994, 100) whose "metaphysical and ontological core," according to Anthony

Arblaster, "is individualism" (1984, 8). Arblaster asserts that liberal individualism "involves seeing the individual as primary, as more 'real' or fundamental than human society and its institutions and structures. It also involves
attaching a higher moral value to the individual than to any society or to any
collective group. In this way of thinking the individual comes before society
in every sense" (1984, 15). For Dawson, immersion in black communities,
institutions, and social networks "serve[s] to limit the reduction of black political homogeneity. . . . As ties with the black community and community institutions became progressively weaker, one would expect to see a decline in
group consciousness in this stratum" (1994, 58). Without the mediating presence and pressure of "familial and other ties between the new elite and the
less affluent African Americans" (59), heterogeneity—including the privileging of an "individual calculus" by members of the black middle class—can be
expected inevitably to emerge.

Thus, it should not be surprising that the expanded geography of blackness significantly affected the constitution and contestation of the contours
of black identity. As Bernard Williams insists in "The Politics of Trust," "An
identity is something that each of us individually has, but it is also something
that is essentially shared: it is a group identity, such as an ethnic, religious, or
(in certain cultural surroundings) sexual identity" (1996, 379). But, Williams
further argues,

> an identity cannot be simply a matter of decision. . . . I might find out
> as a matter of fact that I do belong to an ethnic group but be quite
> indifferent to the idea that it contributes to my identity, and if in good
> faith and without evasion I can live with that idea, then this is in-
> deed not my identity. The relevant notion here is acknowledgment.
> Someone may come to acknowledge a certain affiliation as an iden-
> tity, this being neither a mere discovery nor a mere decision. It is as
> though the identification were forced upon the person in a way that
> recognizes its authority to structure and focus that person's life and
> outlook. (379–380)

Inherited ties to people who were traumatized during slavery and Jim Crow
need not be seen as shaping someone's identity if that person does not acknowledge, and therefore attempt to alter his or her behavior in accord with,
socially constructed notions of group membership for which these terroriz-
ing epochs are particularly momentous. But if someone deems links to these
slavery and Jim Crow to be constitutive, that person must generally adhere to

at least aspects of the social constructions of black American identity that are informed by extant analyses of the meanings of these horrible epochs.

While acknowledgment does help determine behavior, this formulation does not sufficiently recognize the fact that geographies of ethnic, racial, and gendered identities are themselves contested terrains where readings of identity, of sameness and difference, constantly compete with one another for determinative power. Identity is enacted in themed space, but we do not necessarily stand powerless to resist any particular attempt to define our own and others' constitutive features. The eponymous protagonist of *Sarah Phillips*, for example, is free to resist embracing whole-cloth, as it were, notions of black American identity that are dominated by historical trauma and a concomitant sense of group shame.[3]

If blackness can be said to occupy a largely class-bound social space, its expansion "toward infinity," as Yaeger puts it (1996, 25), and the seeming persuasiveness of aspects of its categorizations are influenced by our proximity to other, equally highly contested, geographies of identity. Dawson's reading of the costs and consequences of economic dispersion encourages us to supplement our geographical discourse with one possessing quantitative resonance:

> Affluent African Americans with weak ties to the black community are likely to have biased calculations in favor of the individual calculus. . . . The information obtained by these African Americans would be drawn largely from their white colleagues. While such information might include mixed signals about their own worth and achievements, it would also convey the individualistic norms and values prominent among white citizens. . . . These norms would tend to bias the African American's calculations toward the individual calculus. (1994, 67)

Affluence and its pursuit increase the likelihood that blacks will embrace American ideologies of rugged self-determination. The constant engagement of mainstream values, along with the decreased influence of geographically dispersed institutions such as the church and the family, severely weakens the impact of the black utility heuristic on the black middle class. The individual calculus that causes blacks to reject community in favor of self-determination is a reflection of the outcome of one in an endless number of individual battles between competing formulations of racial identity.

In the pages that follow, I use the foregoing formulations of identity, positionality, and racial identification to explore Andrea Lee's 1984 novel,

Sarah Phillips. Lee's text, set largely in suburban Philadelphia during the social, political, and cultural turmoil of the civil rights movement, examines its protagonist's sense of the incommensurability of black identity and upper-middle-class status. For Sarah, none of the long-standing markers of authentic blackness—including Southern identity, inner-city residency, poverty, radical marginality, psychically debilitating oppression, and cultural difference—informs her social identity. In each of the chapters of the novel, Sarah is forced to confront formulations of traumatized black subjectivity that generally exclude her as a result of her suburban upbringing and relative indifference to racial history. In Lee's examination, the city of national self-making reflects the socioeconomic and political trends of which Dawson and Wilson speak, on the one hand, and, on the other, the themed nature of place that Yaeger highlights.

Sarah Phillips is notable in part because of its initial *unpopularity* within black American intellectual circles, some of whose contributors saw it as a racially treacherous narrative. After being serialized in the *New Yorker, Sarah Phillips* was published first in book form in an attractive hardback edition published by Random House in 1984 and, a year later, in Penguin's prestigious Contemporary American Fiction series. Despite its appearance at the height of the black American women's literary renaissance,[4] the novel went out of print relatively quickly, having made hardly a dent in the collective consciousness of academicians and general readers despite its enviable beginnings. It remained unavailable until 1993, when it was saved from the dustbins of American literary history by Northeastern University Press, which republished it, along with an introduction written by black feminist literary critic Valerie Smith, in the press's Library of Black Literature series, edited by Smith's former UCLA colleague, Richard Yarborough.

In her contribution to *Changing Our Own Words*, a collection of black feminist literary criticism and theory that appeared four years before *Sarah Phillips*'s rebirth, Smith points out that in reviews of the novel, two prominent figures in black American women's letters, critic Mary Helen Washington and poet and novelist Sherley Anne Williams,

> suggest a point of contrast between Lee . . . and other contemporary black women writers who construct fictional communities of privilege. . . . But as Susan Willis has written, [in Toni] Morrison's novels, black middle-class life is generally characterized by a measure of alienation from the cultural heritage of the black rural South. Her characters are saved from "the upper reaches of bourgeois

reification" by "eruptions of 'funk'"—characters or experiences that invoke the characters' cultural past and repressed emotional lives. (1989, 51–52)

Smith is primarily concerned with probing the dialectic between self and other, cultural insider and outsider. In her estimation, this dialectic structures most of the novel's sections, evincing, in its equations of "that 'other' with the historical or the material," the sort of hierarchical relationship between "theory" and "practical criticism" that obtains both in the academy and elsewhere (52).

More important for my purposes, however, is Smith's referencing of Susan Willis's (1989) investigations of the alienation of black middle-class characters from their Southern, folk cultural heritage in Morrison's work. As Smith implies, unlike Morrison's bourgeois characters, Sarah is at least two generations removed from that heritage and, hence, from ties to funk that Rickey Vincent, in a study of the phenomenon's musical manifestations, describes as "an aesthetic of deliberate confusion, of uninhibited, soulful behavior that remains viable because of a faith in instinct, a joy of self, and a joy of life, particularly unassimilated black American life" (1996, 4). In other words, funk is unassimilated black cultural difference undetermined by qualities that are deemed constitutive of the white middle-class mainstream. A rejection of puritanical worldviews and Nordic aesthetics, funk constitutes an oppositional stance vis-à-vis a variety of emotionally repressive U.S. social norms under whose regime blacks have both historically suffered and often felt compelled into envious emulation. In *The Bluest Eye*, which I discuss in Chapter 2, Morrison speaks of the costs for blacks whose attempt to obliterate what musical icon George Clinton refers to as the "uncut funk" of blackness evinces a measure of racial self-hatred:

They learn . . . , in short, how to get rid of the funkiness. The dreadful funkiness of passion, the funkiness of nature, the funkiness of a wide range of human emotion.

Wherever it erupts, this funk, they wipe it away; where it crests, they dissolve it, wherever it drips, flowers or clings, they find it and fight it until it dies. They fight this battle all the way to the grave. The laugh that is a little too loud; the enunciation a little too round; the gesture a little too generous. They hold their behind in for fear of a sway too free; when they wear lipstick, they never cover the entire mouth for fear of lips too thick, and they worry, worry, worry about the edges of their hair. ([1970] 1994, 68)

As Lee's novel makes clear, Sarah's light complexion, Nordic features, and Main Line Philadelphia upbringing limit her access to the pleasures and burdens of funk's physiological and cultural difference. During her formative years, she witnesses no celebratory immersion in funk, no unambiguous or tangible familial relationship to modes of marginalized cultural being that offer a means of resisting "bourgeois reification" or from whose vantage point she can see the soul-killing errors of her racially unconscious ways. Unlike canonical constructions of black fictional characters such as Morrison's, for whom black difference is a not-too-distant personal memory that they have sought to reject as a significant element of their bourgeois existence, "dreadful funkiness" is, for Sarah, confined to an unremembered racial past which she views as archaic.

Despite the existence of "other contemporary black women writers who construct fictional communities of privilege," one reviewer of Lee's novel insists that

> the time has come for the black novel to move beyond the recall of poverty and prejudice that has given it distinction up to now, and deal with the challenges in an era of integration. Although Lee takes a transitional step in this direction, she is somewhat awkwardly preoccupied with the posture her heroine ought to assume in any given circumstance. (Kapp 1984, 6)

If Lee is a "somewhat awkward" transitional figure in what the reviewer, Isa Kapp, sees as the necessary movement by contemporary black American writers toward the subject of integration, her novel, according to Patricia Vigderman, "does not fit easily into the Afro-American tradition, and may even meet with some disapproval" (1985, 23). In her estimation, such disapproval will result from the fact that unlike Zora Neale Hurston, who "spoke for a distinctly black cultural identity and ridiculed the black intellectuals of her own day who seemed to be imitating white culture," Lee creates, in the character of Sarah, a black bourgeois figure who "is not imitating anything. She is as firmly in possession of the culture we share as (white and middle class) I am" (23).

The aforementioned women of letters also assess *Sarah Phillips*'s relationship to formulations of a black literary tradition. Specifically, Sherley Anne Williams asserts that as opposed to Harlem Renaissance figures such as Hurston, Sterling Brown, and Langston Hughes, who "celebrate the rich verbal and musical culture of the black masses—music and lore that the black middle class deplored as examples of the backwardness of the lower classes and as reminders of the slave past[—] . . . what Lee's first novel holds up to mockery is not the pretensions of her upper middle-class heroine, but the 'outworn rituals' of black community" (1985, 71). Rather than being in step with a tradition that "treated the black bourgeoisie as the object of scorn, deriding them for intellectual superficiality and conspicuous consumption, as well as for their shame of the slave past," *Sarah Phillips*, in Williams's estimation,

> resembles . . . Richard Wright's autobiographical *Black Boy*, one of the most searing accounts of a deprived boyhood in the literature. In *Black Boy*, Wright literally and figuratively renounces oral culture and black traditions for personal autonomy. Andrea Lee seems bent on something of the same sort in *Sarah Phillips*. (71)

In her review, Mary Helen Washington bemoans the fact that Lee's novel, whose first chapters "seemed to represent a strikingly new consciousness in Afro-American literature"—one controlled by "the kind of perceptive narrator who understands that her 'peculiar' freedom is a form of estrangement, separating her from her culture and her people"—devolved into an unfortunate representation in which "the privileged kid had become the privileged narrator, no longer willing to struggle over issues of race and class, unable to bear the 'alarming knowledge' that these issues must reveal" (1985, 3). While Williams believes that *Sarah Phillips* fails to critique black bourgeois false consciousness that forms at times to repress the trauma of blackness, Washington sees it as enabling "instructive comparisons" with James Weldon Johnson's *Autobiography of an Ex–Colored Man* (1912) and Nella Larsen's *Quicksand* (1928): "Sarah Phillips is struggling with [the questions] . . . : how does the privileged black narrator consciously explore the subterfuge in being considered an exception? What masks does the elite black wear in the white world? . . . Sarah threatens to investigate these masks, but she never does" (72). We might ask some additional questions: Must the consciousness of members of the black American middle class always be derided? How, precisely, do the children of this class develop a sense that their fates are linked to those of the less fortunate members of the race? What difference, indeed, does class make?

In Washington's view, Sarah's perception of herself as a rebellious spirit is "undercut by the narrator's passivity" (1985, 4). To support her contention, Washington cites the fact that "when she poses nude for photographer-friend Curry, it is his photography, not her poetry that is the focus of the chapter" (3).[5] Instead of exploring the doubtlessly important issue of Sarah's alternately rebellious and passive behavior, I want to consider another facet of the apparent irony to which Washington points in this particular example and the distance between protagonist and narrator that she references. As I show, these textual features can be connected in illuminating ways to the novel's general patterns of intertextual activity—specifically, the narrative gap between the rendered and the repressed, the unspoken and/or underutilized, the shown and the told.

Throughout *Sarah Phillips*, there are notable disparities between the narrator-protagonist's myopic observations about race and Lee's informed allusions to black-authored texts. While Sarah engages works with European or Euro-American origins, the author slyly invokes crucial images, tropes, and scenes from the black American literary tradition. Sarah goes to great lengths to demonstrate that hers is not a traumatized black subjectivity informed by the "dreaded funkiness" of black folk cultural behavior, leaving many reviewers and scholars concerned about the novel's thematic challenges to long-standing and emerging doctrines of black identity and textuality unable to attend to Lee's interrogations of black American sociopolitical and authorial responsibilities. In other words, while Sarah self-consciously rejects expressive cultural texts and racial contexts that might help her position herself in terms of social constructions of blackness, Lee intentionally references tropes and crucial scenes from works that, during the early 1980s, were beginning to be widely regarded as powerful artistic representations of the traumatic consequences of racial, gendered, and class oppression.

In one form or another, scholarly notions of the constitutive features of texts deemed appropriate for entry into the black American literary tradition during the 1980s emphasized their cultural specificity, the formal and thematic interrogations of funk or, in Henry Louis Gates, Jr.'s resonant phrase, the particulars of a "signifying black difference" (1988, xxii).[6] This tradition's contours were determined by Mary Helen Washington, among others, whose anthologies helped significantly to shape our sense of which black female–authored texts were both aesthetically and ideologically worthy of serious consideration. In addition, strategies for investigating its contours were offered in three suggestive explorations of black American literary tradition that were published in the ten-year period that bracketed the appearance of *Sarah Phillips*: Robert Stepto's *From Behind the Veil* (1979), which investigates revision within a male lineage of slave and fictive narratives in terms of characters' quest for literacy and freedom, and their immersion in and ascent from black cultural spaces; Houston Baker's *Blues, Ideology, and Afro-American Literature* (1984), whose deconstruction of received archaeologies of American literary knowledge helps specify the contours of what he terms the "genuine black literary text"; and Henry Louis Gates, Jr.'s *The Signifying*

Monkey (1988), which links textual revision to forms of black vernacular jousting.

Much of the intellectual and institutional power of these studies derives from their efforts to use mainstream critical theories within black American literary-cultural contexts. Those gestures include testing the appropriateness for black American literary study of the emerging theoretical consensus—in deconstruction, in feminist criticism, in postcolonial studies, and elsewhere—insisting that categories such as race, gender, culture, class, and more esoteric concerns such as literary inheritance had historically been constructed to serve and to justify white male power dynamics. Indeed, like these studies, and the academic trends to which they contributed, *Sarah Phillips* can be read as an assault on notions of black racial essence.

The covers of both the Random House and Penguin editions of *Sarah Phillips* feature a painting by Namiko Shefcik. In it, a young, fair-skinned, casually dressed woman sits staring out of a sumptuously paned, expensively curtained double window, her clasped hands resting on her right thigh as the oversized neckline of her shirt exposes her thin left shoulder. The woman gazes inquisitively or appreciatively at the world outside, and the painting's airiness, light, and soft tones—its diaphanous beige curtains spotted with white flowers, its bright white windowpanes and the protagonist's white blouse, the pallid tint of the scene on which she stares—could be said to project any number of moods, including calm, serenity, longing, depression, guilt, grief, and despair. Whatever mood the painting evokes in its spectators, we are nonetheless always aware of its indecipherability. Because of the artist's decision to obscure crucial features of the scene, including the race and facial expression of the subject, as well as precisely what she sees, observers are forced to attend to other visual cues to read the painting; the indecipherable vistas that lie before her, however, offer no definitive interpretive assistance whatsoever. If the painting is meant to signify aspects of the novel, what precisely is the viewer to make of it beyond its resistance to full comprehension? One might see what, from the spectators' vantage point, is the indecipherability of the space before her as representing for the painting's—and the novel's—subject the opportunity to determine its precise meanings. The open window could be said to signify literal or imaginative freedom or entrapment, the potential to determine the contours of what lies ahead by dint of one's cognitive effort or the inability to read its necessarily ambiguous natural objects that have nonetheless been shaped to serve human agendas. Absent the text of the novel, this figure is someone whose race and other circumstances, including class, observers must determine, if they are so inclined.

By contrast, the Northeastern edition categorically places Lee's novel visually and discursively within a black social and literary context. The name of the series—the Library of Black Literature—is boldly inscribed on the novel's cover, serving to point out the racial concerns of a novel whose protagonist insists on the book's first page that her greatest wish is to avoid the consequences of racial classification. The marketing of the salvaged *Sarah Phillips*, then, establishes it as a black American text via the prominent display of the series title, the renowned black feminist critic Smith's prefatory remarks, and the edition's cover art, a purple and white, quasi-realistic woodcut of a middle-aged black woman seated in a church pew, staring straight ahead of her, enraptured by the word of God made flesh in the mouth of the preacher who performs just outside our visual range. Her hands are clasped tightly together, and she holds, or perhaps better, *restrains* a seemingly restless, pigtailed young girl too large to fit comfortably on her lap. Unlike her adult guardian, the girl stares not at the pulpit but away from it and in the direction of stained-glass windows.

As a pictorial representation of a resonant image in and theme of the novel—competing notions of spiritual and racial community—its cover art situates *Sarah Phillips* in terms of the modern dialectic between spiritual faith and existential despair whose intellectual formulations, beginning with slave narratives that ponder the ironies of white oppressors' use of Christian doctrines to rationalize slavery, are numerous enough to constitute a unifying trope of black self-investigation at least as provocative as the notion of literacy that dominated scholarship on the black American tradition at the time Lee's novel was published. And as in the Random House/Penguin art, the head of the Northeastern edition's younger, even prepubescent, cover girl is turned toward a window, toward what is, in the earlier representation, a site of vast interpretive possibilities. On the cover of the reissue, Sarah's motive for window gazing is much less ambiguous; encircled—trapped, if you will—in the woman's grasp, she contemplates escape. The closed stained-glass windows, however, permit no access to scenes energized by the possibility of either spectator (re)making or sublime interpretability. Instead, the restrained child, inattentive to the exhortations of the preacher and to the nearby Bible, turns dramatically away from both of these crucial elements of institutional indoctrination.

This Bible is adorned with a cross, indisputably the central symbol of Christianity. Noticeably enlarged, the crucifix—and the Northeastern cover generally—compels us to consider the protagonist's religious experiences as a thematic center of *Sarah Phillips* or, at the very least, as a key to comprehending other challenging images and situations in the novel. The cross, then, not only stands in symbolic relationship to the sprawling, multivoiced narrative text whose crucial moments include Christ's torturous assumption of the burden of humanity's sins and articulation of fears of paternal abandonment. (Reading this as an image unifying readers and protagonist, we must also note here the crosses we have to bear in the face of centuries of debates over whether the Bible's meanings are most clearly illuminated by pursuing literal or figurative readings.) In addition, the cross speaks figuratively to the religious, cultural, and social conditions to which Lee's protagonist is trying to accommodate herself.

It would be useful here to explore in detail some of the symbolic resonances on which the Northeastern artwork draws to demonstrate the plausibility of my reading of its intertextual density. An important factor in Sarah's decision to return to the United States after an "aimless and sometimes bizarre" stay in Europe following the death of her minister-father and her graduation from Harvard is her "horrid dream in which I was conducting a monotonous struggle with an old woman . . . [who] smelled like one of the old Philadelphia churchwomen who used to babysit for me" (Lee [1984] 1993, 14). While her decision to repatriate has several motivations, she describes her nocturnal adversary not merely as a former babysitter but as a member of her father's church, a characterization that suffuses her self-described "complicated return" with explicitly religious overtones. After her period of "experimental naughtiness" (15), she plans to explore the implications of her familial, racial, and national "ties," seeking to fulfill her "nameless," ill-defined social responsibility.

Sarah's insistence on the inescapability of her (racial) fate connects her, as I discuss in some detail shortly, to canonical black American protagonists like Helga Crane, Janie Crawford, Milkman Dead, and Avey Johnson. But it also connects her to Christ, whose burdens, like Sarah's, are symbolized on the cover of the books under artistic scrutiny in the Northeastern artwork. As the Bible narrates vividly, Christ is nailed to and dies on the cross, whose symbolic placement at the center of Christian religions, all of which claim to be the institutional site where his teachings are most effectively actualized, is fraught with compelling irony. The Christian church's dominant image is offered as a resonant example of what we have seen Michael Dawson, in another context, describe as "linked fate," where Christ's willingness to submit to corrupt social authority and, hence, to a prophesized death enables human souls to achieve everlasting life. The religion's most profound model of sacrifice is Christ's choice to die in order to save souls from eternal damnation. Through that sacrifice, which creates the possibility of salvation closed off by Adam and Eve's inability to resist satanic temptation, Christ absorbs and dissolves humanity's sins, presenting himself as a supreme metonymic figure whose suffering is a precondition for God's embrace and forgiveness. The cross speaks, then, to the coexistence of death and life, of life-in-death. Even if Sarah has chosen not to join her father's church, and her relationship to dominant notions of blackness remains at best problematic, her decision to return to the United States forces her to confront the sometimes burdensome consequences of an always politicized black American identity or "linked fate." At least in terms of Sarah's sense of blackness as conferring on her inescapable, preordained responsibilities, her return is tied visually and thematically to Christ's sacrifice.

Her inability to "cut off ties with the griefs, embarrassments, and constraints" of black American identity (Lee [1984] 1993, 15)—to abandon, in other words, what others have forced her to consider her racial destiny—is signaled by the aforementioned dream, which she has on the heels of her return to the United States. Clearly, the dream has its genesis in a childhood episode in which a frenzied churchwoman, a former babysitter to whom she and her brother, Matthew, refer as Aunt Bessie, tries to pull Sarah to the edge of the baptismal pool, where she can signal her preparedness for ritualistic immersion. On the Northeastern cover, the girl is depicted as confronting not only her guardian's tightly clasped hands and encircling arms but also the stern warnings directed at the entire congregation by an unseen father-preacher ordained to interpret the Bible's persistent emphasis on both sin's inevitability and the necessity of working to avoid sinful transgression if one is to escape permanent banishment from heaven. And while we cannot see the specific object of her gaze, her head and eyes are turned toward the right edge of the frame, a space occupied by a stained-glass window.

The novel's second chapter, "New African," makes at least two references to the church's stained-glass windows. In the first, Sarah unflatteringly compares the church, which she frequents out of a sense of duty, to the suburban quiet of her tree house:

> There was shade and wind and a feeling of high adventure up in the treetop, where the air seemed to vibrate with the dry rhythms of the cicadas; it was as different as possible from church, where the packed congregation sat in a near-visible miasma of emotion and cologne, and trolleys passing in the city street outside set the stained-glass windows rattling. (Lee [1984] 1993, 17)

Sarah greatly prizes the "high adventure" of her lookout over the noxious atmosphere of New African Church, whose windows rattle from the movement of modern mass transportation and fail to admit light or air to an enclo-sure. Instead, Sarah suggests, these windows are vehicles of white ideologi-cal transmission, adorned with images of "a hollow-eyed blond Christ . . . who stood among apostles on the stained-glass windows of the church" (17). Rather than serving as a permeable boundary between inside and outside and, hence, a locus of liberating interpretation, like the window on the Ran-dom House/Penguin cover, the closed windows of New African are stained with images white hegemony's institutional control.

In the discourse of symbolic geography, the room of worship in which the girl is trapped is literally a closed themed space, which Yaeger speaks of as "precolonized and prefabricated around an idea or point of view" (1996, 18). As is the case in all such spaces, its ideology—religious and racial in emphasis—survives in part because its rules permit only limited interroga-tion of the veracity of its visions of the world. Indeed, Christianity's reliance on faith, belief in the absence of ocular proof, challenges the post-Edenic will to knowledge, particularly in the postindustrial age wherein hereto-fore myth-inspiring events—hurricanes, solar eclipses, tornadoes, and the "rattling" of earthquakes, of which the trolley's passing is reminiscent—can be explained, or even anticipated, by means of advanced technological divination.[7]

However, that tension—between, among other things, science and myth, legibility and indecipherability—is played out in the differences between the Northeastern art, whose theme is trapped racial being, and the Random House/Penguin painting, which obscures the object of the spectator's gaze, thereby heightening the interpretive possibilities signified by the artwork's interrogation of racially ambiguous embodiment. While both covers can be read as conveying deep-felt longing, the Northeastern artwork suggests the restrictions—and restricted nature—of themed space, while the image af-fixed to the major publishing house versions of Lee's text appears to cede determinative power to its female subject and to the book's readers.

In "New African," Sarah insists that access to her minister-father's prepa-ration of sermons and symbolic accouterments of church services allows her to make "a game of dispelling the mysteries of worship with a gleeful secular eye" (Lee [1984] 1993, 19). Because Sarah and her brother, Matthew, "knew how the bread and wine were prepared, and where Daddy bought his robes (Ekhardt Brothers, in North Philadelphia, makers also of robes for choirs, academicians, and judges)" (19), they can reduce religious "mysteries" to the status of ritual. In this posture, even events like baptism, whose "unassail-able magic" she recognizes, are considered merely theatrical performance. As Sarah puts it,

> I felt toward it the slightly exasperated awe a stagehand might feel on realizing that although he can identify with professional exactitude the minutest components of a show, there is still something indefinable in the power that makes it a cohesive whole. Though I could not have put it into words, I believed that the decision to make a frightening and embarrassing backward plunge into a pool of sanctified water meant one had received a summons to Christianity as unmistakable as the blare of an automobile horn. (19–20)

Later in the chapter, Sarah speaks of black folkways as backward, "archaic," and "already passing into history and parody" (24–25). In her description of baptism as "a frightening and embarrassing backward plunge," she equates the mumbo-jumbo of black folkways with Christianity's "embarrassing" reliance on myth and ritual, ways of systemizing world order that she deems inappropriate in a technocultural age. They are especially inappropriate at a time when symbolic behavior such as her father's sanctification of tap water required a suspension of scientific disbelief. Figuring godly summoning in terms of one of the twentieth century's greatest inventions, the automobile, Sarah demands from her father's God a call to religious faith she can experience as a form of sensory stimuli and that, consequently, is interpretively "unmistakable." Like all such institutional realms governed by discourses we use to determine and stabilize meanings, New African Church is a themed space whose status as "a cohesive whole" relies on the capacity of its members to respect its descriptive—and proscriptive—power over them and their ways of constructing their relationships to the world. In part, that power derives from the church's capacity as a rule-governed institution to repress or accommodate seemingly competing perspectives on, points of view about, and interpretations of relatively minor features or large aspects of that institution.

If New African Church is, indeed, cohesive, it is certainly not without competing perspectives or discourses. Such competition is manifested in the remark of "Mrs. Gordon, a stout, feeble old woman who always complained of dizziness , . . . that at the rate the air-conditioning fund was growing, it might as well be for the next century" (Lee [1984] 1993, 16); the fans used by Sarah's mother and her aunts, supplied by "the Byron J. Wiggins Funeral Parlor," which "bore a depiction of the Good Shepherd: a hollow-eyed blond Christ holding three fat pink-cheeked children" and which "resembled the Christ who stood among apostles on the stained-glass windows of the Church"; Deacon Wiggins's "thoughtful" counternarrative, "a few dozen fans bearing the picture of a black child praying" that were "rarely . . . in use" (17); the distracting presence of white college students who admired Reverend

Phillips's sense of social responsibility and who, amid the angry whispering of church members about their informal dress, insisted after church that they had never heard "a more beautiful civil right sermon" (21); Reverend Phillips's "two very different ways" of preaching—"the delicate, sonorous idiom of formal oratory" and the "hectoring, insinuating, incantatory tone, full of the rhythms of the South he had never lived in, linking him to generations of thunderous Baptist preachers" (22); the "staid congregation's" relatively limited participation because most of its congregation thought of New African as "not the kind of Baptist church where shouting was a normal part of the service," and Miss Middleton's disruptive "fits of rapturous shrieks," which Sarah's mother and aunts viewed as "incomprehensibly barbarous behavior" (23); and "the running dispute between the choirmaster and the choir" over whether to perform music that reflected Jordan Grimes's attraction to Handel or the choir's to "artistic spirituals performed in the lush, heroic style of Paul Robeson" (23).

While these discourses may have other functions in the narrative, they are manifestations of competing versions of black performance, and the cohesiveness of the church as themed space depends not on their obvious repression, which doubtlessly would create animosity, but on their continued peaceful coexistence. Jordan Grimes and Miss Middleton can be accommodated, as can Mrs. Phillips's whispered injunction to Sarah to "run up to the side of the pool" to join other unbaptized children who watched the ceremony of religious immersion from the front of the church. Less easy to accommodate, however, are unexpected breaks in protocol, such as Bessie's maniacal reaction to Sarah's refusal to heed whispered entreaties to submit to the backward plunge of Christian faith.

In addition to babysitting the Phillips children, occasions during which she revealed that she had "strict ideas on child-rearing [that] had evolved over decades of domestic service to a rich white family in Delaware" (Lee [1984] 1993, 24), Bessie was also "a fanatically devout Christian." In characterizing the "link between us" in language that is profoundly suggestive, Sarah speaks of Bessie's

> worshipful respect for my father . . . , [which] was exceeded only by her pride—the malice-tinged pride of an omniscient family servant—in her "white children," to whom she often unflatteringly compared Matthew and me. It was easy to see why my mother and her circle of fashionable matrons described Bessie Gray as "archaic"—one had only to look at her black straw hat attached with three enormous old-fashioned pins to her knot of frizzy white hair. . . . She talked in ways

that were already passing into history and parody, and she wore a thick orange face powder that smelled like dead leaves. (24–25)

This passage works by establishing stark polarities: between acceptable and unacceptable behavior, "white children" and "Matthew and me," "fashionable matrons" and a "family servant," modish contemporaneousness and "archaic" belatedness. If Sarah and Bessie are linked, theirs is a pairing like fire and water, or traditional formulations of blackness and whiteness as categories of identity, with the capacity both to help define and to destroy each other.

But if Sarah is oppositionally connected to her antagonist, her words link her delineations of self and other to black female protagonists in such twentieth-century novels as Nella Larsen's *Quicksand* ([1928] 1986), Zora Neale Hurston's *Their Eyes Were Watching God* ([1937] 1998), and Toni Morrison's *The Bluest Eye* ([1970] 1994). A servant of a rich white family like the self-loathing Polly Breedlove in Morrison's novel, for example, Bessie, like Polly, negatively compares black children to her white charges. And like Janie's grandmother in Hurston's novel, who "slapped the girl's face violently, and forced her head back so that their eyes met in struggle" ([1937] 1998, 13) in order to compel her granddaughter to act in accord with the former slave's vision of severely limited black female possibility, Aunt Bessie resorts to physical force to get Sarah to accept her ideological perspectives.

In fact, the attitudes attributed to Bessie, on whom the Phillips family bestows a familial appellation in compliance with black folk notions of extended kinship, are described by Sarah, her mother, and her aunts as "already passing into history and parody." Fittingly, given Sarah's privileging of vibrant natural scenes over the emotional and olfactory "miasma" she experiences at church, she insists that Bessie "smelled like dead leaves." Here, *Sarah Phillips* uses imagery from Hurston's novel, wherein the older woman's attitudes, which fail to register the incremental social progress blacks have made since the bygone era during which those attitudes were formed, are figured through a discourse of death. As Nanny approaches her granddaughter, whose appreciation of a "blossoming pear tree" occasions some of the most beautiful writing in twentieth-century American literature, Hurston describes the former slave as someone whose

head and face looked like the standing roots of some old tree that had been torn away by storm. Foundations of ancient power that no longer mattered. The cooling palma christi leaves that Janie had bound

about her grandma's head with a white rag had wilted down and become part and parcel of the woman. (Hurston [1937] 1998, 12)

The connections between Hurston's and Lee's representations of these
women are indisputable. In and of itself, however, recognition of what Pierre
Macherey calls "the allusive presence of those other books against which it [a
text] is elaborated" (quoted in Collins 1989, 44) is virtually meaningless if the
critic is unable to assign an interpretively compelling outcome to the use of a
prior text that helps him or her explore vital aspects of both texts. That outcome must reflect, in part, writerly interrogation of the implications of succession, an issue with which many canonical artists struggle to some degree
or another. In that regard, Julia Kristeva's insistence "that every text is from
the outset under the jurisdiction of other discourses which impose a universe
on it" (quoted in Collins 1989, 44) is particularly persuasive. Seeing discursive revision as a necessary outcome of the effort to exercise textual power
helps explain the *hyperintertextuality* of these descriptions of old women's
dictatorial treatment of their blood or nominal relatives.

Hurston's passage most clearly references biblical scenes and images—for
example, Nanny's "christi leave[d]" crown recalls Christ's crown of thorns,
whose coterminous invocation of life and death occupies the same symbolic
family as the cross—while Lee's description of Sarah's struggles with Aunt
Bessie draws self-consciously on a range of black women's texts, including
Their Eyes Were Watching God. I have already alluded to Bessie's occupa-
tional and attitudinal affiliations with Polly in *The Bluest Eye*. Other intertextual references in the chapter titled "New African" are largely nominal.
They include Lee naming the choirmaster Jordan Grimes, inviting the reader
to recall John Grimes, the protagonist of *Go Tell It on the Mountain*, James
Baldwin's depiction of intergenerational strife as it is played out in sacred and
domestic themed spaces, and Aunt Bessie Gray, who shares a surname with
Quicksand's Ann Grey, whose ambivalence about notions of racial value is
metaphorized in her name.

Perhaps as important, Lee's novel reflects a telling self-referentiality in
that "New African" echoes the first chapter's climatic invocation of Sarah's
dream, which prompts—or at least confirms the wisdom of—her decision
to return to the United States. As she tells us in sometimes painful detail—
a pain resulting from the historically conditioned nature of the inescapably
racial behavior in which she participates—Sarah journeys to Europe in the
hope of achieving a state of personal and cultural "amnesia" by "discard[ing]
Philadelphia [and] . . . everything that made up my past" and "cut[ting] off

communication" (Lee [1984] 1993, 5, 4). But after suffering the sting of racial insults from her French lover, Henri, who jokes that she is "a savage from the shores of the Mississippi" and is the product of the rape of an Irishwoman by "a jazz musician as big and black as King Kong, with sexual equipment to match," Sarah comes to recognize with "blinding clarity the hopeless presumption of trying to discard my portion of America" (11, 12). After accepting, with a troubling sense of resignation, the "weird accuracy" of Henri's "absurd political joke," Sarah acknowledges that she "felt furious and betrayed by the intensity of nameless emotion it had called forth in me" (12).

Even before this moment in the novel, the parallels between the European exoduses of Sarah and *Quicksand*'s Helga Crane are startling. For example, Helga accedes to her Danish aunt's and uncle's suggestions that she wear "bright things to set off the color of your lovely brown skin. Striking things, exotic things" befitting her status as "young . . . , a foreigner, and different," making her feel "like a veritable savage" (Larsen [1928] 1986, 68, 69). Sarah is similarly objectified during her European visit, both in Henri's aforementioned racial insults and during her participation in "a game called Galatea, in which I stood naked on a wooden box and turned slowly to have my body appraised and criticized" (Lee [1984] 1993, 6–7), evoking not just Pygmalion's beloved milky white statue[8] but also slave auction block appraisals of black bodies. Because their reactions to their sexual objectification reflect the strikingly different mores of the historical times in which the novels are set, the characters' reactions are quite dissimilar. Thus, Larsen references prominent early twentieth-century notions of black female sexuality: the black middle-class view that racial uplift required a debunking of myths of black female hypersexuality and the belief that blacks possessed a superior psychic and sexual health because they were unable to partake fully of the bitter fruits of modernity and industrialization. As David Levering Lewis explains in *When Harlem Was in Vogue*:

> There existed a common conviction that Western civilization had been badly maimed by an omnivorous industrialism. . . . From such convictions the rediscovery of the Afro-American followed logically and psychologically, for if the factory was dehumanizing, the campus and the office stultifying, and the great corporations predaceous, the Afro-American—excluded from factory, campus, office, and corporation—was the perfect symbol of cultural innocence and regeneration. "One heard it said," Malcolm Cowley remembered, that the Negroes had retained a direct virility that the whites had lost through being overeducated. (1981, 91)

Such attitudes are reflected in the perspectives of Helga's bohemian artist-suitor, Axel Olsen, who, after he proposes marriage, insists that she has "the warm impulsive nature of the women of Africa, but . . . , I fear, the soul of a prostitute" (Larsen [1928] 1986, 87). Olsen's sense of Helga as a soulful harlot is reflected in the portrait he paints of her, which, though unanimously praised by local "collectors, artists, and critics," was not, "she contended, herself at all, but some disgusting sensual creature with her features" (89). Moreover, in a passage that can be positioned as a direct intertext of Sarah's injunction that she "felt furious and betrayed by the intensity of nameless emotion" as a result of her own inability to react to Henri's racism with the sort of emotional cool she prizes, Larsen writes of another of Helga's suitors' "cold asceticism":

> Robert Anderson's inexorable conscience . . . had been the chief factor in bringing about her second marriage—his ascetic protest against the sensuous, the physical. Anne had perceived that the decorous surface of her new husband's mind regarded Helga Crane with that intellectual and aesthetic appreciation which attractive and intelligent women would always draw from him, but that underneath that well-managed section, in a more lawless place where she herself never hoped or desired to enter, was another, a vagrant primitive groping toward something shocking and frightening to the cold asceticism of his reason. Anne knew also that though she herself was lovely—more beautiful than Helga—and interesting, with her he had not to struggle against that *nameless and to him shameful impulse*, that sheer delight, which ran through his nerves at the mere proximity to Helga. (94–95; emphasis added)

Exploring intertextual relationships between these novels helps us comprehend Sarah's passivity, among other aspects of *Sarah Phillips*. While the European adventurers Sarah and Helga share a desire to reconcile themselves to their racial responsibilities, their efforts are limited by their own and others' notions of the meanings of blackness. For Sarah, responsible return is precipitated by a dream of generational battle: "I awoke with a start from a horrid dream in which I was conducting a monotonous struggle with an old woman with a dreadful spidery strength in her arms; her skin was dark and leathery, and she smelled like one of the old Philadelphia churchwomen who used to babysit with me" (Lee [1984] 1993, 14). This dream, inspired by and coupled with Henri's formulation of American race relations, reinforces Sarah's burgeoning awareness of the socially prescribed limits to individual black American self-determination:

Before that afternoon, how wonderfully simple it had seemed to be ruthless, to cut off ties with the griefs, embarrassments, and constraints of a country, a family; what an awful joke it was to find, as I had found, that nothing could be dissolved or thrown away. . . . It was clear, much as I did not want to know it, that my days in France had a number, that for me the bright, frank, endlessly beckoning horizon of the runaway had been, at some point, transformed into a complicated return. (14–15)

Sarah resolves here to embrace a still-unsettled notion of blackness, to engage the implications of ancestral connection and responsibility when, like Helga, she recognizes the transnational fact of racial stereotyping. Helga's journey back includes a nascent comprehension of her black father's choices: his "facile surrender to the irresistible ties of race" that caused him to abandon his white mate and mulatto child, ties to "the inexhaustible humor and the incessant hope of his own kind, his need for those things, not material, indigenous to all Negro environments" (Larsen [1928] 1986, 92). Conversely, Sarah, who never seems to understand her own father, fails to manifest an abiding connection to any notion of cultural blackness and its discursive manifestations, such as the funky "wailing undertones of 'Swing Low, Sweet Chariot'" (92), in which Larsen's protagonist recognizes aspects of herself.

Unlike Helga and, for that matter, Avey Johnson, the protagonist of Paule Marshall's *Praisesong for the Widow* (1983), Sarah has never experienced a period of cultural immersion. The musical sounds of black culture "struck into [Helga's] longing heart and cut away her weakening defenses," forcing her to recognize her own "incompleteness" (Larsen [1928] 1986, 92). Similarly, Avey, who, before succumbing to the glitter of bourgeois materialism, had sustained herself psychically with examples of black American culture—music like "Flying Home," "Take the A-Train," and "Stompin' at the Savoy," the "black voices" of "The Southerneers, The Fisk Jubilee Choir, Wings over Jordan (which was her favorite of the groups), The Five Blind Boys of Atlanta, Georgia," the poetry of Langston Hughes, and the perspectives that she shared with her husband, Jay, who, during their lovemaking, felt himself "surrounded by a pantheon of the most ancient deities who had made their temple the tunneled darkness of his wife's flesh" (Paule Marshall 1983, 127). Additionally, through her Great Aunt Cuney, Avey had developed an transformative connection to Ibo Landing during her childhood visits; her great aunt taught her the familial narrative of Ibos gifted with "second sight" who, just after their arrival on slave ships, "left the white folks standin' back here [on Ibo Landing] with they mouth hung open and they taken off down the river on foot." This narrative ended with Aunt Cuney's recitation of her own grandmother's (and Avey's namesake's) Du Boisian formulation of the bifurcated black American condition: "Her body she always usta say might be in Tatem but her mind, her mind was long gone with the Ibos" (39).

I have spoken about Marshall's novel at some length because its exploration of the particulars of Avey's journey back are at once so similar to and, precisely because of the protagonists' vastly different cultural upbringings, so distinct from those of Lee's protagonist. Like Sarah, Avey dreams of physical contestation with an older woman who seeks to deliver the younger woman from her cultural amnesia. In Avey's dream, "she found herself being dragged forward in the direction of the Landing" by her forebear, who divests her now-matronly great-niece of her trappings of material comfort—her mink stole, "the spring suit, the silk blouse, the gloves" (Paule Marshall 1983, 44–45)—whose pursuit robbed Avey of the pride in black heritage and cultural values that her aunt had helped instill in her. Aunt Cuney's exhortation, "Come / O will you come," prompts the dreamer to compare her forebear to "a preacher in a Holiness church imploring the sinners and backsliders to come forward to the mercy seat" (42), and to resist. Their confrontation devolves into a "tug-of-war [that] was suddenly a bruising fist fight," with Avey and her great-aunt, whose flesh she had, as a child, considered "too awesome for her to even touch" (44), battling to determine the younger woman's psychic, spiritual, and cultural direction.

Because of the loving relationship she had enjoyed with Aunt Cuney, Avey possesses a solid—albeit, for much of her adult life, buried—foundation that provides her with the cultural grounding to recognize, ultimately, the psychic dangers of mindless capitalist consumption. As a consequence of otherworldly haunting or a "subliminal flash" of racial sensibility (Paule Marshall 1983, 59) during her cruise on the *Bianca Pride*, Avey is able ultimately to recognize the pleasure ship as a free-floating signifier of white hegemony's enduring legacy. She has, in other words, a funky narrative of prideful blackness—"back home after only her first summer in Tatem she had recounted the whole thing [the story of Ibo Landing] almost word for word to her three brothers, complete with the old woman's inflections and gestures" (38)—in terms of which she can place and recollect herself.

By contrast, Sarah's relationship to blackness is at best ambivalent, if not, as in the case of her responses to Aunt Bessie and proffered narratives of slavery, hostile. In a scene teeming with echoes of, among other moments, Avey's aforementioned dreams, Sarah finds herself in heated battle with Bessie, who seeks to force the minister's daughter to take a literal step toward the baptism

pool and toward the symbolic place in the front of the church of both her
minister-father and to God:

> Aunt Bessie *seemed to lose her head*. She stood up abruptly, pulling
> me with her, and, while I was still *frozen in a dreadful paralysis, tried
> to drag me* down the aisle toward my father. The two of us began
> a brief struggle that could not have lasted for more than a few sec-
> onds but that seemed an *endless mortal conflict*—my slippery patent-
> leather shoes braced against the floor, my straw hat sliding cockeyed
> and lodging against one ear, my right arm twisting and twisting in
> the *iron circle* of the old woman's grip, my nostrils full of the *dead-
> leaf smell* of her powder and black skirts. (Lee [1984] 1993, 27–28; em-
> phasis added)

Again, we are confronted with *Sarah Phillips*'s hyperintertextuality: echoed
here are Frederick Douglass's battle with the slave breaker Covey; Richard's
and his mother's paralysis in *Black Boy*; Nanny's "dead-leaf" worldview; and
Marshall's use of images of slavery to describe Avey's dream of a "tug-of-war"
with her great-aunt, Cuney, with her "hand with the feel of a manacle . . .
around her wrist" (43).

But as I have suggested, this scene's references extend as well to the novel's first chapter. Like the rest of the novel, "In France," which mentions *Jules
and Jim*; spaghetti westerns; the painter Poussin's *Paradis Terrestre*; *Gone
with the Wind*; the cartoon canary, Tweety, whose French name is "TiTi";
Jane Birkin; "the spirit of Bruderschaft"; "Dixie"; "Home on the Range"; John
Denver's "Country Roads"; Edward Hopper's paintings; and the film *Il Etait
une Fois Dans l'Ouest*, evinces Sarah's willed indifference to or practiced silence about black American texts and connections. At the height of the Black
Power movement, prevailing notions of slavery's total institutional effects on
the culture of black people were being radically revised, and Afros, dashikis,
and the phrase *Black Is Beautiful* were ubiquitous. Also, black students were
discovering *Native Son*, *Cane*, and the Harlem Renaissance and, as I discuss
in the Introduction, successfully lobbying college administrators for black
studies programs in the wake of King's assassination. And as Lee's protagonist informs us, at this time, Frantz Fanon was a popular enough figure in
the United States to have had a reading group named for him at Harvard. At
a time when so much attention was being paid to the recovery and creation
of powerful representations of blackness, it is noteworthy that Sarah chooses
"The Literature of Adventure in Nineteenth-Century America" as the subject

of her senior thesis. Having acknowledged early in her life that she feels no connection to slaves, she chooses to write not about Douglass's or Harriet Jacobs's harrowing narratives, whose struggles with white hegemony might have provided her insight into her own challenges, but about picaresque white adventures. Such an emphasis undoubtedly bracketed, if not utterly ignored, the racial dramas surrounding slavery: the abolitionist movement, slave escapes and revolts, the passage of the Fugitive Slave Law, the near-rupturing of the New World adventure of democracy that culminated in the Civil War, and a Reconstruction that ultimately left the great majority of freed slaves and their descendants bereft of the capacity to pursue the political and socioeconomic bounty constitutive U.S. citizenship.

The novelist's sly echoes of, among other black-authored works, *Their Eyes Were Watching God* and Douglass's *Narrative*, coupled with Sarah's emphatic refusal or inability to see her life circumstances as connected with such representations or to the black masses, provide the heretical text with a telling, and bitter, irony. While the author constructs Sarah's dilemmas out of black American cultural tropes and fragments of its canonical texts, attesting to her understanding of a racially "linked fate," her protagonist's individualism dooms her to repeat the mistakes of her unacknowledged precursors, as she is unable or unwilling to avail herself of a compensatory wisdom or sense of cultural situatedness that blacks who recognize their historically marginalized cultural place are able to access. Like Avey, she feels the pull of racial trauma, which Marshall figures as the restricting manacles of slavery. Unlike Marshall's character, however, Sarah has never viewed slavery as a governing condition or as possessing any significance in her life. So while Avey's journey back is enabled by her recognition of the inextricable connections between personal and racial history, between the *Bianca Pride* and her ancestors' traumatic experiences during the Middle Passage, even Sarah's gestures toward community at the end of "In France" are in conflict with her acceptance of the "weird accuracy" of Henri's nigger joke in which an "embarrassingly primitive" black man rapes a "part redskin," "part Jew" "Irlandaise" (Lee [1984] 1993, 13, 112). Sarah is sent scurrying back to the United States by her lover's strategic repression of white male responsibility for the sexual violation of black women, which is, of course, the most historically plausible explanation of "why," in Henri's words, "our beautiful Sarah is such a mixture of races, why she has pale skin but hair that's as kinky as that of a Haitian" (11). And like white men throughout U.S. history who have used violence and its threat to compel black Americans' nominal embrace of such self-serving readings, Henri seeks to force Sarah to accede to his narrative offense:

He reached over and pinched my chin. "It's a true story, isn't it, Sarah?" He pinched harder. "Isn't it?"

"Let me alone!" I said, pulling my head away. . . .

There was a short silence, in which Henri's eyes were fixed cheerfully and expectantly on mine, as if he were waiting for a reward. (11)

Unlike her protagonist, then, for whom black oppression and self-affirming responses thereto hold no significance, and whose evasion of the racial themes with which her life resonates is suggested by her decision to leave America "to study French literature in Lausanne, intending never to come back" (4), Lee manifests an authorial awareness of central black American cultural tropes and literary texts and of historical and experiential continuities whose recognition Sarah studiously avoids.

In his study *Blues, Ideology, and Afro-American Literature*, published in the same year in which Lee's novel appeared, Houston Baker deconstructs the assumptions of the governing American metanarrative of democratic destiny by means of which founding fathers and their white descendants evaded or rationalized their constitutive failures vis-à-vis dark-skinned peoples. In place of nationalist formulations that historically have failed to contend adequately with the challenges of racial difference, Baker posits an "ideological analysis of discursive structure" that

discovers the social grounding—the basic subtext, as it were—that necessarily informs any *genuinely Afro-American narrative text*. What I want explicitly to claim here is that all Afro-American creativity is conditioned by (and constitutes a component of) a historical discourse which privileges certain economic terms. The creative individual (the black subject) must, therefore, whether he self-consciously wills it or not, come to terms with "commercial deportation" and the "economics of slavery." The subject's very inclusion in an Afro-American traditional discourse is, in fact, contingent on an encounter with such privileged economic signs of Afro-American discourse. The "already-said," so to speak, contains unavoidable preconditions for the practice of Afro-American narrative. (1984, 38–39; emphasis added)

If American slavery, writ large, represents the "preconditions," the traumatic "already-said" of subsequent formal and thematic articulations, *Sarah Phillips*, whose eponymous character does not perceive that her fate is linked to those of "ancestral" figures who suffered under slavery and Jim Crow, appears to resist what, following Baker, we might refer to as "genuine" black

American narrative thematic compulsions. However, Lee's situation of Sarah's experiences in terms of canonical scenes and tropes of black American narrative confirms the author's recognition of, if not wholehearted embrace of, the constellation of views out of which Baker's formulations emerge. Like Bessie's and Sarah's struggles within the highly suggestive symbolic realms of generation, region, and class, the author's and subject's less easily detectable struggles for—and against—intraracial placement animate, if not the dreams, certainly the textual experiences, of *Sarah Phillips* for "practice[d]" readers.

In addition to the moments I have already mentioned, we might note, for example, *Sarah Phillips's* apparent reference to key scenes in Toni Morrison's first two novels. In considering her chilly reception at Prescott, the prestigious, heretofore all-white suburban Philadelphia private school that she is the first black to attend, Sarah highlights the radical differences between her generally innocuous experiences and one of the most compelling representations of the violent struggle for school integration in the South.

> Classes were easy for me, but friends were hard. A few years earlier I'd seen a picture of a southern black girl making her way into a school through a jeering crowd of white students, a policeman at her side. Prescott didn't jeer at me—it had, after all, invited me—but it shut me off socially with a set of almost imperceptible closures and polite rejections. (Lee [1984] 1993, 54)

In response to her marginalization both from the whites and from images of Southern black schoolgirl courage, Sarah mimicked the Marxist rhetoric of her outcast friend, Gretchen, while longing for inclusion. She notes this suppressed longing in terms that echo Pecola's nightly prayer for blue eyes in Morrison's first novel:

> I wanted to fit in, really fit in, and if Lissa Randolph or Kemp Massie, rulers of the Olympian band of suntanned, gold-bangled popular girls, shimmering in their Fair Isle sweaters, had so much as crooked a finger at me, I would have left Gretchen and followed the way the apostles followed Christ. No one knew my secret—not my parents, who bragged with relief about my levelheaded *adjustment*; not my brother, Matthew, who might have understood. At night I gloated over a vision of myself transformed by some magical agency into a Shetland-clad blonde with a cute blip of a nickname. (56; emphasis added)

Lee references the language and deconstructive impulses animating *The Bluest Eye*, even repeating the key term "adjustment," borrowed by Morrison from James Baldwin's famous critique of Richard Wright's *Native Son* to describe Claudia's suppression of her impulse to dismember "blue-eyed, yellow-haired, pink-skinned doll[s]," "which all the world had agreed . . . [were] what every girl child treasured" (Morrison [1970] 1994, 20). In her description of Sarah's desire for acceptance and aesthetic superiority, Lee conflates Claudia's "adjustment" and Pecola's prayer for a religious and alchemical "miracle" that would allow her to be graced with Nordic features. Positioning Sarah's desires for mainstream acceptance self-consciously in terms of *The Bluest Eye* allows Lee to demonstrate that if her character has ignored such interrogations of the negative consequences of the repression of funk, "the creative individual" examining such impulses clearly has not.

While not all of her intertextual references are as thematically resonant—for example, although, like the protagonist of *Sula*, Sarah's childhood acquaintance and Harvard friend, Curry, has a facial birthmark, that "long tear"–like mark lacks the symbolic richness of Sula's, which resembles, among other things, "a stemmed rose" (Lee [1984] 1993, 45) and a tadpole (134)—even such moments challenge the notion that Lee seemed bent on renouncing black traditions. Recognizing the tensions between Sarah's renunciation and Lee's referencing of "genuine" black American narratives and themes, in fact, allows us to see *Sarah Phillips* as a much more sophisticated novel than either its condemning reviewers or its confounded defenders have demonstrated. Its sophistication results, in part, from its capacity to disguise Lee's sly critique of Sarah and/or the patterns of black bourgeois self-segregation that, whatever their positive features, tend to produce children for whom traditional formulations of blackness are deemed "archaic" and inessential to their self-perceptions.

No moment more effectively suggests the origins and consequences of Sarah's alienation than her mother's refusal to permit her to accompany her parents to the 1963 March on Washington where King delivered his eloquent "I Have a Dream" speech. As Sarah tells us, she is forced to remain at home because of her mother's fear of "exposure":

> In August my brother and I watched the Washington march on television. . . . As I had known, there had been no question of my going along with my parents: my mother, ever practical, had immediately squelched the idea for fear of stampedes and what she called "exposure"—by which she meant not sun and wind but germs from possibly unwashed strangers. (Lee [1984] 1993, 51)

While Sarah fails to specify precisely what sort of "unwashed strangers" her mother seeks to protect her from, the novel's general concern with intraracial class differences suggests that her mother's intent is to limit her daughter's contact with the funkiness of black difference. Her parents, whose commitments to black equality are beyond dispute, participated in the middle-class exodus from the inner city to integrated suburbs during the 1950s. In fact, though Sarah believes she is escaping "the cautious pomp" of "the hermetic world of the old-fashioned black bourgeoisie," her inability to recognize constitutive features of the racial past and present—including the traumas of slavery, the psychic costs of poverty, and unending white domination—as linked to her own marginalized suburban condition is a direct result of a childhood where figures with whom she shares a white aesthetic like Bessie are deemed archaic and her own experiences are measured, in large part, by her capacity to distinguish and protect herself from members of her race who manifest a traumatic black subjectivity. Instead of constituting a unifying and transcendent occasion, King's energizing speech, and the March on Washington more generally, underscores, for the Phillips clan, the intractable challenges of class—and, hence, experiential—differences.

Growing up in a household that, unlike Avey's and Jay's Halsey Street dwelling in *Praisesong for the Widow*, is largely devoid of serious consideration of black cultural difference and the traumas of black American being, Sarah perceives funk as a contagion from which she needs to be protected, just as the interior of New African and its suburban congregation are protected from "bottles and papers and loungers" (Lee [1984] 1993, 18) by the urban church's closed, stained-glass windows, onto which the church's founders affixed pictorial representations of white hegemony. Sarah cannot establish a sense of racial and cultural (comm)unity because blackness, as a sign of ontological presence, is devalued both outside and within the themed spaces she occupies. It is devalued: just outside the church, whose undoubtedly black "loungers" are equated with the debris they carelessly strew onto heretofore middle-class streets; in her Main Line neighborhood, where interloping gypsy furniture makers insist that "it's a crime for colored to live like this" (43); within the "embarrassingly primitive" church; and in her own suburban household, where her father's playful signifying on and serious critique of black people ("there's nobody like us for spoiling a community" [43]) are incomprehensible to a daughter who is neither acculturated enough to recognize in-group verbal jousting nor interested enough in her father's activities to want to emulate them or to understand such racial behavior.

In fact, unlike her father, who is able to speak both the standardized dialect of mainstream institutions and the idioms of the black South and urban poor, Sarah is, discursively and otherwise, a black cultural outsider. Indeed, what distinguishes her suburban town, Franklin Place, is the fact that it is a place where Sarah feels "snug and protected" (Lee [1984] 1993, 42), especially from the funky eruptions of black (vernacular) difference. In fact, *Sarah Phillips* highlights the family's insistence on containment of "the intensity of nameless emotion" that Henri's racism precipitates, making her feel "furious and betrayed" (12); of the "something frightening and wild about" the gypsy woman whose "long breasts . . . swayed back and forth in a way in which our mothers' well-contained bosoms never did" (43); and of the hurt inspired by the romanticizing of blackness by well-meaning white liberals like Gretchen, the daughter of a "famed ban-the-bomb curmudgeon of the Penn history department" (54) for whom "Negroes are the tragic figures of America" and who asks Sarah, who is devoid of a sense of traumatized black subjectivity, "Isn't it exciting to be a tragic figure? It's a kind of destiny!" (55). Despite her parents' insistence that

> the perilous region below the Mason-Dixon Line . . . held a sad and violent heritage for little girls like me . . . , I had little idea of what they meant. For as long as I could remember, the civil rights movement had been unrolling like a dim frieze behind the small pleasures and defeats of my childhood; it seemed dull, a necessary burden on my conscience, like good grades or hungry people in India. My occasional hair-raising reveries of venturing into the netherworld of Mississippi or Alabama only added to a voluptuous edge to the pleasure of eating an ice-cream cone while seated on a shady curb of Franklin Place. (39–40)

Because this movement is widely considered to have taken place in distant states "below the Mason-Dixon Line"[9] to which it is doubtful Sarah has journeyed since her mother is dreadfully worried about "exposure," she lacks the racial consciousness and sense of "linked fate" across class divisions that Michael Dawson describes so persuasively. Sarah has never felt the natal connections of black community that Avey experienced both as a culturally immersed youth and as a recovering senior citizen on board ships whose passengers are predominantly black, and hence does not recognize such cultural contexts as personally constitutive. So when, in response to Henri's racism and the challenges of her ties to her family, race, and nation, she equates her Parisian experience with "the experimental naughtiness of children reacting against their training," we remain unconvinced that her "complicated return" (15) will enable deep or lasting racial immersion of a sort that Avey achieves at the end of *Praisesong for the Widow*.

Unlike Avey, she has no mentors on whom she can rely to aid her efforts at cultural return or immersion. In contrast to Marshall's protagonist, who dreams of her forebear's plaintive plea for her psychic return and meets the incomparable cultural guide, Lebert Joseph, Sarah has access only to cultural instructors who are or whom she perceives as ill-suited to those roles. Sarah's epic nocturnal battle with her former babysitter, Bessie, like Avey's dream, inspires in her a compulsion to return home, but it contains none of the reevaluative elements that would suggest that such a "complicated" return would be anything but fruitless. As a representative of an element within the race that is seen as marginal by the Phillipses and others of their ilk, Bessie is linked to Mrs. Jeller, a parishioner who greets the Phillips women who visit her convalescent home with a blues tale of coming "up the hard way"—a tale that includes rape, pregnancy, teenage marriage, motherhood, and almost unbearable loss. According to the protagonist, she responded to Mrs. Jeller's tale and her "bare legs and shamelessly tossing breasts [which] both disgusted and fascinated" her "in a curiously intimate way, like learning a terrifying secret about myself" (Lee [1984] 1993, 83). Aware of Sarah's willing service as exotic plaything for racist Europeans in the novel's opening chapter, we recognize that Mrs. Phillips's silence and subsequent evasion of the responsibility for mentorship for her daughter in her response to Mrs. Jeller's story contribute to her susceptibility to sexual abuse. Like Sarah, who sees no connection between herself and slaves, her mother refuses to push past her own bourgeois discomfort to compel her daughter to consider the cautionary possibilities of the aging parishioner's blues narrative of youthful exploitation.

Mrs. Jeller's narrative does lead Sarah to become aware "for the first time" of "the complicated possibilities of my own flesh—possibilities of corruption, confused pleasure, even death," but even more tellingly, it silences her guests and inspires the Phillips mother and daughter to feel "disinclined" to look at one another. In response, Mrs. Phillips defensively dismisses and seeks to contain the potentially harmful effects of their "exposure" to the narrative by calling into question its veracity and its teller's mental faculties: "Poor old thing, she's gotten senile" (Lee [1984] 1993, 86). Instead of using Mrs. Jeller's recollections as an occasion to caution her maturing daughter about the perils of growing up in the perplexing era of free love and continued female objectification, Mrs. Phillips reacts with a fear and loathing of displays of "funk" that cause the minister's wife and her sisters to respond to New African parishioner Miss Middleton's loosened tongue and "rapturous shrieks" with an exchange of "grimaces, . . . as if confronted by incomprehensibly barbarous behavior" (23). In an act of parental irresponsibility with potentially devastating consequences, she capitulates to her daughter's desire for bourgeois consumption, concluding that "she guessed I was old enough to make any mistake I chose" (86). Resisting the sense in Mrs. Jeller's tale—and in narratives of black and women's lives more generally—that people who possess personal and institutional power routinely abuse that power, Mrs. Phillips refuses to confront the complexities of oppression and the possibilities of Sarah's situational powerlessness. Instead, she posits a strategically simplistic view that her sixteen-year-old daughter has reached the stage where she can determine the direction of her own life, thus relieving herself of the burden of having to explain—and confront—the contemporary resonance of Mrs. Jeller's blues narrative. Just as she does with Aunt Bessie, whom she confines to an "archaic" past, Mrs. Phillips emphasizes Mrs. Jeller's belatedness, rendering her poor, old, and senile.

Similarly, Sarah's descriptions of her father emphasize his limitations as a mentor or, perhaps more accurate, her limitations as a student. Those limitations are most clearly manifested after his funeral, when she

> dreamed about him. In the dream he had fallen overboard from a whaling ship—like the one in *Two Years before the Mast*—and had come up from the ocean still alive but encased in a piece of iceberg. Through the ice I could see his big hands gesturing in a friendly, instructive manner while he looked straight at me and said something inaudible. It was the same word or syllable I had wanted to say in answer to Stuart Penn [a family friend who spoke at Reverend Phillips's funeral and requested that Sarah and her brother Matthew "try to do something out of the ordinary with your lives" (Lee [1984] 1993, 113)], and I couldn't figure out what it was. (114–115)

Just as when Sarah is confounded by her father's critiques of his people, she is unable to make out the precise meaning of his gesture and "inaudible" "word or syllable," for they are elements of signifying systems in which she is not versed. While she is able to recognize them as "friendly" and "instructive," she cannot gauge the precise meanings of his communicative efforts in her dream.

Having recognized that she cannot escape the deleterious effects of American formulations of blackness, even in a country like France, which is renowned for its gracious embrace of U.S. blacks and especially their expressive culture, Sarah still seems ill-equipped to develop an invigorating racial consciousness. Like Ibo Landing, the site of Sarah's imagined struggles is sacred cultural ground, "a marvelous private domain, a richly decorated and infinitely suggestive playground," but the exodus of New African's members from Philadelphia and to the suburbs left the church isolated "like a dreadful old relative in the city, one who forced us into tedious visits and who linked us to a past that came to seem embarrassingly primitive" (Lee [1984] 1993, 18). Undoubtedly increasing Sarah's sense of alienation from the church were the "bottles and papers and loungers" that desecrated the sacred, history-laden black Philadelphian cityscape and whose presence recalls the terrifying inner-city blues spaces described in the previous chapter in reference to the Temptations' song "Masterpiece." The church, situated on deteriorating streets and whose structural and economic survival is largely dependent on municipal, state, and federal governmental intervention, inspires in Sarah no sense of binding connection. Because of both the dilapidation surrounding the historic religious structure and its prescientific epistemology, the church stands with an "archaic" Bessie as a symbol of black American backwardness whose perspectives she soundly rejects. Unlike Avey, whose mother names her daughter in accord with Aunt Cuney's wishes, thus "saddl[ing] her with the name of someone people had sworn was crazy, and then as soon as she turned seven had ordered her father to bring and deposit her every August in Tatem" (Paule Marshall 1983, 42), Sarah is never compelled by her immediate family to absorb clarifyingly restrictive ontology. As Marshall writes, "In instilling the story of the Ibos in her child's mind, the old woman had entrusted her with a mission she couldn't even name yet had felt duty-bound to fulfill" (42). Avey is taught to marvel at the resilience and cultural power of her slave forebears and to adopt as her worldview her namesake's reading of the meanings of the Ibos' escape; as Aunt Cuney repeatedly relates to her successor at the conclusion of her narratives, "Her body she always usta say might be in Tatem but her mind, her mind was long gone with the Ibos" (39). In a national setting in which her people have been subjected to brutal oppression, Avey's forebear recognizes the necessity of adopting a strategic duplicity, a self-protective split between mind and body.

By contrast, Sarah inhabits an environment where she witnesses intense battles to determine the precise contours of blackness and where, as a consequence, she learns not to see herself as culturally, psychologically, or otherwise connected to the traumas and triumphs of her racial predecessors. Sarah's lengthy representation of the choir's contributions to the New African "prelude to the ceremony of baptism," "the moment that fascinated and disturbed me more than anything else at church" (Lee [1984] 1993, 23) culminates in her struggles with Bessie, who wants her to be a participant in this ritual. This passage portrays both the contestation between Afrocentric tradition and assimilation-related emergence endemic to her black environs and her resultant, individualistic responses:

> In spite of Jordan Grimes's efforts [to compel from it a classical performance], the choir swayed like a gospel chorus as it sang this spiritual; the result was to add an eerie jazz beat to the minor chords. The music gave me goose-flesh. Daddy had told me that this was the same song that the slaves had sung long ago in the South, when they gathered to be baptized in rivers and streams. Although I cared little about history, and found it hard to picture the slaves as being any ancestors of mine, I could clearly imagine them coming together beside a broad muddy river that wound away between trees drooping with strange vegetation. They walked silently in lines, their faces very black against their white clothes, leading their children. The whole scene was bathed in the heavy golden light that meant age and solemnity, the same light that seemed to weigh down the Israelites in illustrated volumes of Bible stories, and that shone now from the baptismal pool, giving the ceremony the air of a spectacle staged in a dream. (25–26)

This passage comments on and represents an instance of black American cultural creation. Beginning with a struggle for power between advocates of classical and gospel styles that results in their jazzy commingling, Sarah's representation of this evocative moment emphasizes disparate cultural levels: music ("an eerie jazz beat"), visual art, physiology ("goose-flesh"), and history (recreations of black rituals of baptism during slavery). At the very least, the text represents the commingled music, jazz, as the actualization of the Du Boisian ideal of a merged, African American self, and the scene's general exploration of polarities in terms that suggest Marshall's and Morrison's formulations of tangible connections between past and present, slave and freed man and woman, black American tradition and New World cultural reconfigurations.

However, Lee signals the limitations and repressions characteristic of Sarah's vision of merged sensibility. In her responses to the baptismal atmosphere created from a resolution of contested cultural styles, Sarah denies feeling any connection to the slaves whose ceremonies she imagines. That sense of disconnection enables her to conjure up trite images—most specifically, the "heavy golden light" of represented holiness—to approximate the complexities of her predecessors' collective decision to wade in sanctified waters. But Sarah speaks even of this romanticized light as oppressive, as "weigh[ing] down" the Israelites, who are connected both to slaves who embrace Christianity despite its use by U.S. slave masters to justify their enslavement and to the New African preparation for the symbolic cleansing of baptism. If there is a configuration of human connection here, that connection exists not between Sarah and her formerly enslaved racial forebears, whom she denies the status of ancestors, but between Israelites, slaves, and New African participants in the ritual of baptism, all of whom are subject to the restrictions of Judeo-Christian traditions.

Sarah's status as the minister's daughter exposes what is "hidden, encrypted, repressed, or unspoken" in the church, a dissociation of sensibility on which the capacity to see space as themed relies. If, indeed, the scene of worship that the Northeastern woodcut visualizes can be said to constitute "themed space," its theme is the inescapability of Christianity's violence-enforced truths. The church is represented as a site of repression, a place where its members are willing to resort to whatever means necessary—including entrapment and the threats of social, spiritual, and physical death—to ensure that nonbelievers will hear and heed the terms of order according to which the space is literally and symbolically structured.

In his essay "Presenting the Unpresentable: The Sublime," Jean-François Lyotard discusses painting's "impossibility" in a modern age dominated visually by photographic technologies that so effectively reproduce the physical surfaces on which cameras are trained that the painter is forced to re-imagine his or her form's aesthetics and responsibilities. Those artistic souls who want to participate at the highest levels of this venerable tradition must discover technocultural answers to increasingly complex questions with thoroughly (post)modern awareness. As Lyotard suggests, instead of continuing to aim for mimetic representation,

> those painters who persisted had to confront photography's challenge, and so they engaged in the dialectic of the avant-garde which had at stake the question "What is Painting?" Painting became a philosophical activity: previously defined rules governing the formation of pictorial images were not enunciated and applied automatically. Rather, painting's rule became the re-evaluation of those pictorial rules. (1982, 65)

According to Lyotard, modern painters had to represent realms of feeling, thought, and spirituality to which technologically sophisticated media such as photography and film had no easy access by "alluding to the nondemonstrable" (69). Rejecting representational precision and social responsibility as goals in favor of the pursuit of "the nondemonstrable," the painters Lyotard has in mind sought to produce an art that positioned itself self-consciously within modern representational parameters.

Lyotard is useful for the present discussion because of his concern with the challenges of representation at the precise moment when the social, ideological, and philosophical meanings of objects under artistic scrutiny were seen as utterly self-evident. *Sarah Phillips* is a provocative text precisely because, like experimental painting, it constitutes a compelling response to an emerging orthodoxy, in this case, of black and female representation. The issue of orthodoxy or "linked fate"—of thematic connections, similarities, or intertextualities—is raised in the first paragraph of the novel. Here, Sarah speaks of feeling like "a kind of sister or alter ego" to "Kate the Lake Forest debutante" who, according to rumors, "was being held prisoner in her apartment by her present lover and an ex-boyfriend, who were collecting her allowance and had bought a luxurious Fiat—the same model the Pope drove—with the profits" (Lee [1984] 1993, 3). This sense of connection arises despite the fact that "she was white and I was black," and that "back in the States I'd undergone a rush of belated social fury at girls like Kate" (4). Beyond setting up highly politicized racial and gendered connections between the young women which the novel ultimately abandons (we never, for example, see narrative evidence of this fury), Sarah's concern with Kate centers largely on their shared susceptibility to dominant social hierarchies—in Kate's case, class and gender, and in Sarah's, class, race, and gender—under whose strictures women and blacks are systematically victimized.

But Sarah also feels linked to Kate because of the latter's specialty within her chosen mode of artistic self-expression, photography: "making nudes look like vegetables" (Lee [1984] 1993, 3). If modernist photography offers access to an almost effortless mimesis that compels those artists who constitute the avant-garde to inquire, "What is painting?" one might argue that Kate's aesthetic is driven by the query "What is photography?" at a historical moment when the mere reproduction of reality has ceased to be artistically stimulating or pleasing. Indeed, Kate seeks to expand the boundaries of her art form, an act of transgression for which she is, in effect, punished by men committed to preserving the gender hierarchy. Her artistic manipulation of human subjectivity, in other words, leaves Kate subject to masculine formulations of themed space. To Sarah, who struggles to liberate herself from the social, cultural, and ideological limitations imposed on her because of her race, Kate's bold play with the meanings and structures of human nature is sufficiently compelling to allow her to bracket the racial differences between them.

But Kate's profession connects her not merely with Sarah, but also with the protagonist's childhood acquaintance, Curry Daniels, a "wonderful photographer" with whom Sarah becomes friends when both matriculate at Harvard in the early 1970s. Sarah describes Curry's work in ways that recall the novel's introductory formulations of Kate's transgressive project, even though the outcome of his efforts is vastly different:

> In his pictures pretty girls perched in fey poses in the branches of trees in Radcliffe Yard, or trailing Indian dresses, lounged against tombstones in Christ Church cemetery. Sometimes he photographed them nude, with contemplative expressions on their faces as they crouched inside cardboard boxes or huddled among heaps of crumpled newspaper. He was so successful at all this that he had already published several pictures—notably "Monica with Onionskin"—in photography magazines, and his telephone line . . . was murmurous with female voices. (Lee [1984] 1993, 90–91)

Like Kate, Curry is an "arty" photographer whose work helps determine his place in the gender economy. But while Kate's art, financed, like her "apartment near the Bois de Boulogne," by her "immense allowance," leads—if rumors surrounding her disappearance can be believed—to her being imprisoned by "her present lover and an ex-boyfriend," whose "hostile male voice[s]" (3) constrain her self-expression in traditional patriarchal ways, Curry's nudes enable him, despite his race, to increase his cultural capital, transforming his room into a multiracial heterosexual space "murmurous with female voices." To emphasize their similar artistic concerns and their vastly different outcomes, Lee invests Curry's "notabl[e]" picture, "Monica with Onionskin," with the sort of transgressive qualities that characterize Kate's work (91).

In her discussion of her own connections with Curry, Sarah casts their platonic relationship within the realm of the familial. For example, their mothers "were distant cousins and had been best friends at Philadelphia's Girls' High School," and Curry had grown up "in the same kind of surrounding I did in Philadelphia: a comfortable, insular, middle-class black neighborhood swathed in billiard-green lawns" (Lee [1984] 1993, 87). Curry, Sarah recognizes, looks "a bit like me, in fact, with his lean face that showed an almost evenly balanced mixture of black, white, and Indian blood" (88). Having on one occasion playfully suggested to him that he'd "better find a black girlfriend before you get yourself thrown out of that Frantz Fanon study group," Sarah "wondered briefly and coldly why Curry and I had never become lovers. The answer was fairly clear, as we stared at each other with eyes almost alike enough to be those of siblings, into faces that for each of us symbolized the unbearably familiar things of life" (94). In the estimation of both Sarah and Curry, their socioeconomic advantages over the black masses, whose struggles for justice dominated the political, legislative, and imaginative discourses of the nation in the 1960s, limited the amount of attention that was paid to children like themselves, the offspring of educationally and economically successful blacks. Rather than consider seriously the struggles of such children who were thrust unto racial fault lines of elite institutions such as Prescott and Harvard, their parents and the society at large positioned them not in the role of traumatized racial sufferer but as refutation of segregationists' claims of inherent black inferiority: "We spent a lot of time talking about what it meant to come from the kind of earnest, prosperous black family in which civil rights and concern for the underprivileged are served up, so to speak, at breakfast, lunch, and dinner. 'It made us naughty and perverse,' insisted Curry" (89).

Like numerous middle-class (and poor)[10] black children, Sarah and Curry were thrust into institutions that were unprepared to receive them; they exhibit a "naughty" perversity through their rejection of social constructions of blackness that limit, among other things, their capacity to view each other or, for that matter, other inhabitants of "the hermetic world of the old-fashioned black bourgeoisie" as potential mates. While they are capable of a purely "ascetic" (Larsen [1928] 1986, 94) appreciation of one another—for example, when Sarah appears naked before Curry just before he photographs her, he says, in a dispassionate, "dry voice, 'How perfect you are'" (Lee [1984] 1993, 93)—they cannot overcome their sense that a romantic union between them would satisfy their parents' "indiscreet eagerness" for a narcissistic self-perpetuation of the "almost evenly balanced mixture of black, white, and Indian blood" that causes Curry to look "a bit like me" (95, 88).

The most significant manifestations of their resistance to such parental desires are the products of their photo session. Curry demonstrated during earlier shoots witnessed by Sarah his enthusiasm for offering "fraternity-style appraisal of [his subjects'] measurements" (Lee [1984] 1993, 91)—behavior that recalls Henri's and his European friends' appraisals of her nude body—and ability to animate even his "faded and monotone" girlfriend, Phillipa, through his art. Consequently, it is telling that his photographs of

Sarah fail to display her "frisky excitement" (93). As Sarah insists, "The pictures were all horrible. After my first shriek I was able to observe, objectively, that while the body of the girl in the photographs looked relaxed and normal, her face was subtly distorted and her neck strained, as if an invisible halter were dragging her backward" (93). Clearly, Lee references Sarah's battles with Bessie here, suggesting that, like submitting to an archaic ritual like baptism, a near-incestuous union with her male double would constitute being "dragg[ed] backward" into an unchanging sameness. But this depiction of representational similarity and difference also echoes, in interesting ways, Helga's portrait by her European suitor, Axel Olsen, in *Quicksand*, one of the texts to which Mary Helen Washington believes Lee's novel can be profitably compared.

Indeed, a comparison of these novels' scenes of black female representation through and as art invites us to recall Lyotard, whose notion that photography forced painters to confront the ontological boundaries of their art presupposes that premodernist painters were compelled generally by mimetic impulses and photographers were not as capable as their painterly counterparts of inscribing the "undemonstrable" through formal manipulations of reality. These presuppositions are effectively challenged in these scenes, which foreground the protagonists' desires to disguise states of being that the novels clearly display—an exotically garbed and bedazzled Helga's sensuality, and Sarah's fear that a relationship with Curry could pull her "backward" into prefabricated constructions of normative bourgeois black behavior. Still, we are struck as readers by an intriguing interpretive conundrum: Ought our primary critical response be to minimize the import of the racist and phallocentric presuppositions that determine the outcome of Axel Olsen's gaze and of Helga's willing participation in her own exoticism, or to emphasize the distorting consequences of social conditions that cause Larsen's protagonist to repress an essential aspect of her humanity? While marrying Olsen would leave Helga with little hope of resolving the tension that results from a particularly pernicious combination of racism and sexism, one that, as Henri's racist comments about Sarah's heritage suggest, continued to manifest itself more than a half century later, her insistence that Olsen's portrait distorts her seems patently unsatisfying considering her sexualized self-presentation throughout her stay in Copenhagen. If this scene's astute interpretation requires that the reader choose between Olsen's and Helga's visions, that reader, I believe, must concede that such a choice is virtually impossible.

In fact, all of the works that emerge as significant intertexts within *Sarah Phillips* either endeavor unsuccessfully to codify essential features of blackness or explore the utter futility of such efforts. Indeed, these novels share with Lee's a concern with the social, spiritual, and philosophical conse-quences of embracing a view that black Americans can be said to constitute a "cohesive whole" because of and despite their traumatized subjectivities. Given the cultural fragmentation, contestation, and erasures that were the consequence of the United States' participation in a slave trade whose victims were inhabitants of a variety of West African regions and tribes, no cultural cohesiveness could be presupposed as a condition that slavery ruptured in the first place.

If, as Morrison theorizes in a 1984 piece, the ancestor is indeed a foun-dational figure in much black American literature, Lee's novel is marked by the Phillips family's condemnation of Southern-inflected ancestral presences such as an "embarrassingly primitive" Bessie (Lee [1984] 1993, 18). The Phil-lips family members lack a Morrisonian sense of black American cultural "rootedness," a fact that is particularly evident in scenes that are achingly familiar to readers of this body of literature, which causes them essentially to view (white) middle-class values as normative. For Sarah, who emerges from such a background, constituting a (racial) self means taking up the thankless task of positioning one's self fruitfully—either as an act of self-differentiation or of self-affirmation—with regard to the nation's governing narrative of black American deficiency, on the one hand, and, on the other, a notion emerging from within the race of black American authenticity as impoverished, long-suffering, victimized, and generally traumatized.

Sarah's father manifests a richly bifurcated identity that reflects his ca-pacities to engage—and speak powerfully of and to—the complexities of his American heritage. He possesses experiential connections both to a racial group and to a transracial class position, the latter of which enables him to navigate prestigious social and educational institutions. During a tour of Harlem, for example, when Sarah's father and Uncle Freddy speak in high, affected tones of "the tenements and the trash" their perpetually "Happy People" live in and among, Matthew has to explain to Sarah, "they're joking, silly—pretending to be white" (Lee [1984] 1993, 48). "Wondering at the com-plicated twists in grownup funny bones," a view that links her with scores of other children, Sarah "peered at the ruinous streets around us" (47–48), unsure of what to make of these insulting perspectives. Sarah is not a trau-matized black American discursively linked to signifying—to funky black speech and bluesy self-mockery—as either a native speaker or a listener.

Because she is consistently positioned as an outsider with regard to ritu-als of blackness that Helga sees as "indigenous to all Negro environments" (Larsen [1928] 1986, 92), Sarah's return to the United States to embrace the responsibilities attendant to her recognition of linked fate appears doomed.

Unable after his death to understand her father's sociopolitical mission or the friendly gesture he makes in one of her dreams, Sarah cannot accommodate funk, the "primitive," the lowdown folk whom Langston Hughes and others celebrate in response to pervasive black middle-class condemnation of their music, dress, and other modes of self-presentation. While the author of *Sarah Phillips* tellingly participates, in ways that are often quite inventive and illuminating, in an expressive cultural intertextuality, Lee's willfully oblivious character never manages to embrace the responsibilities of linked racial fate, which would require her to see her plight as being of a kind with other traumatized descendants of slavery.

In fact, Lee seems quite self-consciously to insist that knowing readers interrogate her novel in light of its echoes of works like *Quicksand*. If it is indeed the case, as Sarah posits in the novel's opening, that she seeks to escape racial imperatives by relocating in Europe, her motivations are strikingly similar to those that drive Helga from Harlem to Copenhagen. Yet, unlike Larsen's protagonist, Sarah seeks to distance herself from notions of a constitutively black essential identity. According to Sarah's formulation, class perspectives are invariably at the foreground in scenes of contestation that feature both the black bourgeoisie and the black poor. Note, for instance, her discussion of

> the hermetic world of the old-fashioned black bourgeoisie—a group largely unknown to other Americans, which has carried on with cautious pomp for years in eastern cities and suburbs, using its considerable funds to attempt poignant imitations of high society, acting with genuine gallantry in the struggle for civil rights, and finally producing a generation of children educated in newly integrated schools and impatient to escape the outworn rituals of their parents. (Lee [1984] 1993, 1)

Despite the novel's initial launching in the *New Yorker*, its appearance during a boon in black American women's writing, and Lee's forceful grappling with class issues that, by the mid-1980s, had emerged as dominant concerns in social science and humanistic research on black American life and expressive culture, *Sarah Phillips* remains, at best, a marginal, even unpopular, novel.[11] That lack of popularity is not necessarily because of the novel's artistic limitations or its failure to engage matters with which texts that have been more widely embraced within black American literary-critical circles are concerned. Rather, Lee's novel is unpopular, I believe, because it chronicles the challenges—and, sometimes, the utter impossibility—of assuming traumatized black subjectivity as one's own governing perspective when one's own life experiences render such a worldview largely unconnected to one's sense of self. Andrea Lee manifests a great deal of authorial control over a usable past of black expressive cultural formulations of blackness, but her protagonist remains so hopelessly disconnected from that culture that she cannot herself recognize her experiences as instantiations of earlier black American textual scenes and self-determining dramas. That is, Lee's protagonist remains unwilling or unable to see herself as psychically connected to slaves and their victimized descendants.

Being a contemporary black female subject, for Sarah, involves not the transcendence of class, racial, and gendered categorization, but a willed, individuating ignorance of their impact in one's own social interactions. What is most impressive about Lee's maligned and too-often ignored novel, for me, is that it offers an astute reading of black American class differences while at the same time manifesting an authorial claim to black textual linkages. *Sarah Phillips* is especially appealing because of its participation in debates about literary intertextuality, constitutive blackness, and the impact of racial, gender, and class hierarchies as a function of its protagonist's troubled rejections of the efficacy, in the (post)modern West generally and a post–civil rights America in particular, of such debates.

Notwithstanding claims such as that of the gifted artist Sherley Anne Williams that Lee's novel holds black expressive cultural traditions up to sustained mockery, *Sarah Phillips* succeeds as a contribution to contemporary black American expressive culture precisely because of its concern with exploring the origins of its bourgeois character's limited ability to embrace dominant social constructions of blackness. At the same time, it refuses to insist that such difficulties are the prevailing perspectives that animate the novel itself. The pains it takes to distinguish authorial and characters' perspectives on the representations of traumatized black subjectivity render it a work that offers what, following King, we might consider a thoroughly hybrid post–civil rights outlook (or, better, outlooks). *Sarah Phillips* is too tellingly a product of the conditions of blackness of its time to remain condemned to the margins of a black American literary tradition to which it contributes so knowingly.

4

Screening the (Beloved) Novel

On Oprah Winfrey and the Protocols
of Adaptation

*Toni Morrison and Oprah Winfrey, enjoying the festivities before a boisterous pre-
miere of the film adaptation of* Beloved. (Photo by Marion Curtis/DMI/Time Life Pic-
tures/Getty Images.)

D uring her whirlwind promotion of Disney's $65 million adaptation of Beloved, *the film's star and driving force, Oprah Winfrey, spoke frequently of her difficulty contacting Toni Morrison to secure the movie rights to the harrowing tale and, subsequently, getting the film made. As Winfrey writes in* Journey to Beloved, *a physically striking phototext that contains her ruminations on the making of this adaptation, on the day she finished the novel, she was overcome by the eerie feeling that the travails of the infanticidal Sethe were "my own remembering" (Winfrey and Regan 1998, 18). Feeling the need to speak to the author immediately, she dialed the fire department in Morrison's town and convinced its dispatcher to provide her with the novelist's unlisted telephone number. When she reached her, Winfrey informed her that "the world needed to hear this story, and the way to do it was through film," a comment in response to which Morrison "laughed and said, 'How can you be serious? How could this ever be a movie?'" (18).*

Readers aware that a December 1993 fire damaged Morrison's home may find elements of the talk-show host's anecdote—including the fire company being called on to aid in the possible destruction of the Nobel Prize winner's art—grossly insensitive. Having avoided the fate that befell Ralph Ellison, drafts of whose second novel were destroyed in a house fire a quarter century earlier, Morrison nonetheless faced the pressures of film adaptation that have confounded numerous authors who enter into such extraliterary bargains. The benefit of having one of her novels adapted into film, presented to her by a cultural force capable of persuading a civil servant trained to display grace under the pressure of life-and-death scenarios of the urgency of her desire to speak to the town's famous resident, made Morrison's accession to Winfrey's request unsurprising. But I imagine that her laughter was inspired by something other than her skepticism about Winfrey's ability to adapt her traumatic story and image-rich prose. Instead, I suspect that it was the nervous response of a masterful artist to the naïve formulations of a powerful talk show host (then popularly known as the "Queen of Trash") and part-time actress who assumed that Morrison could possibly deem the cultural resonance of her widely read, frequently taught narrative—recognized by the New York Times Book Review *subsequently as the best American novel of the last quarter of the twentieth century ("What Is the Best Work" 2006)—insufficient.*

What seems to have motivated this emergency call to Morrison, in fact, was not the need to retell an already masterfully told—and widely read—story but Winfrey's desire to relive her consumption of and by Beloved. *Winfrey insists that she was "absorbed by it" to such an extent that she*

> *felt I was in the interior of the words. The world resonated with me in a way that doesn't often happen. There's a difference between reading a*

> *book and enjoying—even loving—the story, and having the feeling that
> the words are somehow connected to some part of you, and that then
> becomes your story. (Winfrey and Regan 1998, 18)*

*Winfrey, the protocols of whose book club centered on readers' capacity to
see their own struggles reflected in contemporary fiction,*[1] *longed to enact the
drama of narrative possession on the screen. Interestingly, the anxiety she records during the making of* Beloved *centered on the challenges of manifesting
her enthrallment sufficiently to demonstrate that the matricidal Sethe's story
was or had, indeed, become hers.*

*More than half a decade before filming on the adaptation began, I was in
Morrison's presence when she expressed reservations about Winfrey's capacity
to adapt her masterwork. I was dining in a swanky restaurant in New Jersey
roughly fifty miles from Philadelphia, with Morrison—then a distinguished
professor at Princeton—two other members of the Princeton faculty, a book
editor from Oxford University Press, and Houston Baker, my dissertation ad-
visor, who had delivered a lecture earlier in the day. In town for a semester as
a postdoctoral fellow in Princeton's Program in Afro-American Studies, I was
close enough to home to visit my family relatively frequently but far enough
away from its distractions that I was able to have had a remarkably productive
five months of writing. Consequently, I worked diligently and still enjoyed my
occasional encounters with celebrated Princeton faculty members such as Morrison. Most mornings when I drove to campus listening to Philly's leading R&B
station, WDAS-FM, I searched out her well-worn Jaguar, which I parked next
to whenever I could. Eventually, I became comfortable enough in her presence
to engage her in collegial chitchat, but I was thrilled every time I saw her in
and around Dickinson Hall. Determined to take advantage of this rare opportunity, I finagled from her an invitation to the book party for her fifth novel,*
Jazz, *at Manhattan's Four Seasons, which I attended despite the fact that my
oldest child—who had almost been named Antonia, a combination of my
mother's and Morrison's names—had a fever of 104.1 when I left her with her
mother.*

*In the Princeton restaurant, I felt a bit overwhelmed to be breaking bread
at the same table as the author whose first novel,* The Bluest Eye, *had motivated me to see the study of black American literature as something close to a
spiritual calling.*[2] *Because I was anxious about the etiquette of sophisticated
dining, I processed few of the details of the experience and recall little about
the general drift of the conversation. I do remember watching with trepidation
while one of her colleagues tried to figure out how to dry off the front of Morrison's blouse after he accidentally spilled a glass of water on her. Also, I remember bringing up the work of Gayl Jones—a superb writer, a former professor of*

English at the University of Michigan, and a notoriously troubled person after whom I later named my chaired professorship[3]—because I knew that Morrison had been her editor when her first two novels were published. Mostly, however, I recall her mentioning that she had sold the movie rights to Beloved to Winfrey and her trepidation about how her novel would be adapted. Having, I suspected, seen Harpo Studios' pedantic adaptation of Gloria Naylor's The Women of Brewster Place (1992), Morrison admitted to being afraid that Winfrey was incapable of creating a film like Daughters of the Dust with the visual splendor, psychosocial depth, narrative daring, and technical dexterity that her material demanded.

By the time the film appeared, I was again living near Philadelphia, this time just outside the city's northern limits and teaching at the University of Pennsylvania, where I had written a dissertation on four black American women's novels. (Eventually, all of these novels—Their Eyes Were Watching God, The Bluest Eye, The Women of Brewster Place, and The Color Purple—became attached to Winfrey either via her acting in their movie adaptations or, in the case of Morrison's first novel, her book club.) Bolstered by ubiquitous advertising that emphasized its First City connections, the movie premiered in Philadelphia with great fanfare, an event graced by the presence of local and national dignitaries, including Winfrey herself. I attended the premiere, Morrison's concern reverberating in my head. Not wanting to miss a minute of a relatively long film whose tickets cost $250, I left my seat during the introductions—actually, just after the incomparable Patti La Belle waved to her hometown crowd—to empty my bladder.

As I made my way to the bathroom, the hallway was virtually empty until a phalanx of dark-suited men large enough to block out the sun or to pick up the most furious linebacker blitz approached me at a determined pace. Enthralled by their threatening synchronicity, I kept moving even when I spied Winfrey positioned at the exact center of this organized mass. Shorter and thinner than I had imagined, her fabulous hair bouncing, behaving, and shimmering in concert with her gown and jewelry, she walked gingerly, as if her high-heeled feet were killing her. Perhaps because there was nothing else in the hallway for her to focus on, for a second or two, she looked directly at me as I passed the beefy procession. Not knowing whether to speak or to leave her to her concern about blisters and bunions, I resorted to scholarly self-protection, recalling a paragraph about Winfrey I had read that week in an essay by Michele Wallace. Watching Oprah watch me—perhaps expecting me to display some excitement over seeing her or fearing that I was a crazy misogynist bold enough to try to harm her—I thrust Wallace's skepticism metaphorically between us like an ornate shield:

Most of us became familiar with the name Oprah Winfrey when she appeared in the role of Sofia in the movie The Color Purple, which was adapted from the black feminist novel by the author Alice Walker, but which became, under the guidance and supervision of Hollywood director Steven Spielberg, a sentimental tale which had little to do with . . . changing the status and condition of black women as a group. As the most successful daytime television talkshow host the networks have ever seen and as the first black female to ever own a prosperous TV and film production company, Oprah Winfrey is buying up all the "black feminist" literature she can lay her hands on. (1992, 657)

Instead of echoing Wallace's dismay during this encounter in the neon-lit hallway of Philly's Riverview Cineplex, I managed a shy half smile, at which point Winfrey's head turned, and she continued to move straight ahead with the sore-footed but determined gait of a long-marching protester during the civil rights movement. Finally, buoyed by Morrison's and Wallace's words, yet frankly pleased to be less than ten feet from this famous black American woman, I stopped to marvel again at the choreography of the megastar enwrapped by four beefy men. And perhaps because we were in my city, less than a mile away from the playground where as a child I had learned to curse and to disrespect authority, as she made her well-protected retreat, I whispered, "I hope you didn't fuck up Toni's book, Oprah."

We live in a land where the past is always erased and America is the innocent future in which immigrants can come and start over, where the slate is clean. The past is absent or it's romanticized. This culture doesn't encourage dwelling on, let alone coming to terms with, the truth about the past.

  —Toni Morrison, quoted in Paul Gilroy, "Living Memory"

I must remember that a movie is a movie, and a book is something different. . . .

  My problem is, and has been, feeling that I have to remain so true to the words of the book. Jonathan [Demme, the director of *Beloved*] says, "Your preparation is excellent. But you're being harnessed by the book." I used to walk around with the book, constantly referring to it. Now I've finally let it go.

  —Oprah Winfrey, *Journey to Beloved*

> [B]eing faithful to . . . the "spirit" or "essence" of the work . . .
> involves not merely a parallelism between novel and film but
> between two or more readings of a novel, since any given film
> version is able only to aim at reproducing the filmmaker's reading
> of the original and to hope that it will coincide with that of many
> other readers/viewers. Since such coincidence is unlikely . . . , the
> critic who quibbles at failures of fidelity is really saying no more
> than: "This reading of the original does not tally with mine in
> these and these ways."
>
> —Brian McFarlane, *Novel to Film*

In December 1998, holiday shoppers browsing the Barnes and Noble bookstore in the Philadelphia suburb of Abington confronted an irrefutable sign of the box office and ancillary product failure of the $65 million Touchstone film *Beloved*. Featured prominently on a display table in the store's middle aisle, in close proximity to contemporary novels whose covers were adorned by Oprah Book Club insignias, were roughly a hundred copies of Oprah Winfrey's *Journey to Beloved*, its 50 percent markdown reflecting a difficulty of selling this relatively new title that neither its parent company nor Hyperion, the book's publisher, had anticipated.

The book's commercial failure was surprising given the identity of its author and the voluminous, largely fawning attention the film received before its opening from some of the nation's most influential periodicals. While the film, shot in and around Philadelphia during the summer of 1997, adapted the Pulitzer Prize–winning novel by Nobel laureate Toni Morrison and was directed by Oscar winner Jonathan Demme, its prerelease media attention was due almost exclusively to Winfrey's participation as an actress and producer. A logical culmination of her work as a television movie actress and producer following *The Color Purple*, *Beloved* can also be seen as an energetic reaction on her part—not unlike her book club—to vituperative critiques of the daytime talk-show genre inspired by Vicki Abt and Mel Seesholtz's 1994 essay, "The Shameless World of Phil, Sally, and Oprah: Television Talk Shows and the Deconstruction of Society." Following its generally austere beginnings with the professorial Phil Donahue, the genre's entries, by the 1990s, were foible-obsessed freak shows hosted by Sally Jessy Raphael, Jerry Springer, Montel Williams, Jenny Jones, Ricki Lake, and rating leader Winfrey. Rather than continue to exploit the moral laxity, sexual perversion, and psychosocial maladjustment of its often defiantly twisted guests and voyeuristic audience, Winfrey transformed the tone and intention of her show following the 1994–1995 season, shedding the label of "Queen of Trash" and beginning a lengthy reign as the nation's arbiter of cultural tastes, fictional narratives, and appropriate modes of empathic self-inquiry.[4]

The commercial failure of *Beloved* engendered quizzical articles assessing why this obvious labor of love had become a colossal commercial flop. In little over a month, then, like the film it was produced to promote, the attractively packaged musings of Winfrey, the United States' book salesperson par excellence, had been roundly rejected by the general public. Still, *Journey to Beloved* offers compelling documentation of Winfrey's concerns about her acting, the film's intended meanings and potential impact on the lives of the descendants of slaves, and her waning commitment to her talk show, whose psychological and emotional rewards were dwarfed by the pleasures she received making films. Her musings are supplemented by Ken Regan's magnificent location photographs and by comments praising the film, the novel, Demme, and Winfrey herself, that are written almost exclusively by its actors, including Danny Glover, Thandie Newton, Beah Richards, and Kimberly Elise.

During Winfrey's summer 1997 residency in Philadelphia while *Beloved* was being filmed, Winfrey sightings—her comings and goings from the Rittenhouse Square hotel in which she stayed and where she ate, exercised, and shopped, and with whom—became big news in *Philadelphia* magazine and the city's daily newspapers. The local media, starved for confirmation of the city's contemporary significance, was more than happy to add Winfrey and Glover to the roster of A-list celebrities—including Denzel Washington, Samuel L. Jackson, Bruce Willis, Brad Pitt, and Glover's *Lethal Weapon* series costar, Mel Gibson—who had resided in the city while making movies. And because of these stars' presence, the result of the efforts of Sharon Pinkenson, executive director of the Greater Philadelphia Film Office,[5] that have generated well over a billion dollars for the local economy, the City of Brotherly Love was deemed desirable by participants in television and movie industry insiders. Having filmed his previous movie, *Philadelphia*, in the area, Demme clearly had developed enough of a sense of the city's lush bucolic surroundings, old-city charms, and relative inexpensiveness to regard it as an ideal place to shoot the project Winfrey had offered him whose script, he insists, "dealt with subject matter and themes—including this country's legacy of slavery—that I'd been wanting to work with for years" (Winfrey and Regan 1998, 7).

The October 9, 1998, premiere of the film was held at the Riverview, a multiplex located roughly a mile from the well-preserved structures and cobblestone streets that were transformed by Demme's crew into Cincinnati of the 1870s. Annually traversed by millions of U.S. and international

tourists, the Old City neighborhood featured in the market scenes of *Beloved*
had been the stomping grounds of the nation's first president, George Washington; Thomas Jefferson, who penned the Declaration of Independence in
a small house within walking distance of Independence Hall; and Benjamin
Franklin, the city's favorite son. The *Philadelphia Inquirer*'s Karen Heller vividly positions the Riverview, a cookie-cutter modern structure, "in a strip
mall . . . past the Staples, before the Wal-Mart" (1998, A1). More than five
hundred ticket holders—myself included—paid $250 to preview *Beloved* and
experience the excitement generated by the presence of Winfrey, who "threw
back her exquisitely tressed head" as she entered the theater "attired in a
Calvin Klein scoop-necked, chocolate silk jersey gown and safe deposit-size
diamonds" and proclaimed, "The reason I'm here . . . is because I love Philadelphia" (Heller 1998, A1).

Following brief remarks by Pinkenson; Demme; Mayor Ed Rendell, who
announced that Winfrey had agreed to participate in the Greater Philadelphia Tourism Marketing Corporation's "This Is My Philadelphia" campaign;[6]
and Winfrey herself, the hushed audience witnessed the adaptation of Morrison's depiction of the post-traumatic stress endured by survivors of Sweet
Home plantation and their descendants. Later than night, Winfrey attended
the local NAACP chapter's Freedom Fund Banquet where, "plugging *Beloved*
six times in twenty minutes . . . , the saleswoman went into overdrive. 'If
any film needs it, this movie—which opens October 16—needs all of our
support'" (Heller 1998, A1). Heller ends her article by noting that Winfrey,
the self-described Philadelphia enthusiast who had dieted "madly from
210 pounds to a size 10 to make *Beloved*," vowed to participate in the time-
honored ritual of consuming the local cuisine used by politicians and visiting
dignitaries to establish their bona fides with the natives: "I'm going to have
me a cheesesteak this time" (A1).

Neither the hushed awe of the audience within the theater watching the
film nor, before that, the excitement registered on the faces of hundreds of
onlookers braving a steady downpour to catch a brief glimpse of *Beloved*'s
star from behind long yellow police barricades prophesied hefty box office
receipts. But if the novel's vast readership and the star's popularity failed
to translate into commercial success, the comments made by one audience
member before she entered the Riverview attest to the enormous impact
Winfrey has had in the realm of television.

> "She really changed my life," said Linda Schutzer, a 49-year old edu-
> cator, who added that watching Winfrey encouraged her to seek ther-
> apy several years ago.

"I would have paid $5,000 to be here tonight. I'd rather see her than Moses, Jesus or Buddha. She has made that difference in my life." (Pendleton 1998, 5)

Though I had not experienced a similar type of transformation in response to Winfrey's endeavors, I purchased an undiscounted copy of *Journey to Beloved* at the Abington Barnes and Noble on the day after the Philadelphia premiere. My purchase was a reflection not only of my long-standing fascination with Morrison's fiction and my deep admiration for her fifth novel but of my apprehension about the adaptation that I had viewed while in a state of celebrity-induced mesmerism that largely disabled critical reflection. I purchased *Journey to Beloved*, in other words, largely because I was concerned about how the heavy-handed doyenne of self-liberating confession would describe the challenges presented both by a complex novel and by her roles as producer and actor. I wondered how this novel would survive its encounter with Winfrey, whose work as an actress and a filmmaker I generally found unremarkable.

Memories of Harpo Studio's adaptation of Gloria Naylor's *The Women of Brewster Place*, which initially aired during the week following the novelist's visit to the University of Michigan to meet my graduate class on black American women novelists and lecture on the influence of *Their Eyes Were Watching God* on her novel *Mama Day*, led me to feel an almost proprietary sense of dread. I worried about how she would adapt a novel designed, as Morrison indicates in the widely cited essay "The Site of Memory," to reveal the interior lives of former slaves that were edited out of their written accounts of their experiences. Morrison says about the genre of the slave narrative whose significance had been persuasively established during the 1970s and 1980s as a result of scholarly acts of careful critical archaeology and close reading:

Popular taste discouraged the writers [of slave narratives] from dwelling too long or too carefully on the more sordid details of their experience. Whenever there was an unusually violent incident, or a scatological one, or something "excessive," one finds the writer taking refuge in the literary conventions of the day. "I was left in a state of distraction not to be described." . . .

Over and over, the writers pull the narrative up short with a phrase like, "But let us drop a veil over these proceedings too terrible to relate." In shaping the experience to make it palatable to those who were in a position to alleviate it, they were silent about many things, and they "forgot" many other things. (1990, 301)

Discussing her efforts in *Beloved* to supplement these strategic accounts by representing what she believed was slavery's largely unspoken psychological and emotional impact, Morrison, whose fiction might best be described as beautifully rendered examinations of "sordid details," attempts to convey the psychological consequences for blacks of well-organized efforts to delegitimize, compel forgetfulness of, and, hence, effectively silence protest against such oppressive acts. As she explains, "For me—a writer in the last quarter of the twentieth century, not much more than a hundred years after Emancipation, a writer who is black and a woman—. . . [m]y job becomes how to rip that veil drawn over 'proceedings too terrible to relate'" (302).

In this essay, composed as she was writing *Beloved*, Morrison insists that fidelity to the craft of fiction and to her own authorial promptings requires judicious engagement with retrievable remnants of history if she is to offer plausible representations of the otherwise unrecoverable truth of that experience. That truth, as she conceives of it, is

> the product of imagination—invention—and it claims the freedom to dispense with "what really happened," or where it really happened, or when it really happened, and nothing in it needs to be publicly verifiable, although much of it can be verified. By contrast, the scholarship of the biographer and the literary critic seems to us only trustworthy when the events of fiction can be traced to some publicly verifiable fact. (1990, 302)

Interestingly, as we will see, Morrison's views of historical invention and verification are fundamentally at odds with those of Winfrey, the commanding cultural force behind her novel's adaptation. Winfrey's reimagining of *Beloved*, like the pursuit of moral, emotional, psychological, and physical wellbeing that is her show's hallmark, is informed by her notion that products of the imagination are trustworthy *only* if they can be made to confirm her notions of self-improvement and transcendence.

Morrison states that she is driven artistically by the mystery of "how I gain access to that interior life." As part of her preparation to write *Beloved*, she examined slave narratives and other remnants of historical moments to ascertain both what they readily communicate and the strategically hidden truths that can be revealed through informed acts of the imagination. She describes her encounters with history as "a kind of literary archeology" that enables her to "journey to the site to see what remains were left behind and to reconstruct the world that these remains imply" (1990, 302). Insisting that "no matter how 'fictional' the account . . . , the act of imagination is bound up with memory" (305), Morrison emphasizes the significance, particularly for a writer concerned with the emotional and psychological impact of traumatic events, of drawing on informed assumptions about the past both to witness and to "reconstruct the world" of meaningful events that concern her.

Like "The Site of Memory," which offers readers access to a noted figure's authorial processes and engagement with history in anticipation of a forthcoming work, *Journey to Beloved* records Winfrey's ruminations on her efforts to "reconstruct the world" of slavery to communicate its otherwise inaccessible truths. But instead of relying, like the self-assured novelist, on acts of imaginative reconstruction, Winfrey, the apprehensive part-time actress, seeks to lose herself to discover precisely how slavery felt.

> When I was preparing for the role of Sethe, I read an article in Smithsonian Magazine about a man who had done a trek a year previously . . . , shipping himself in a box from one state to the next. . . . I had him on my show and asked him to create a day so that I could feel what it would be like to go through that journey. So he took me into the woods, blindfolded me, sat me on a bench under a tree, and said, "We're going to regress you." . . . We started in 1997 and tried to push back the memories from that year, went back through the decades until he said to me, "Now we're in 1861. And when the blindfold is taken off, everyone you see will be representative of that period. Your name is Rebecca, and your story is that you live in Baltimore as a free woman. You were captured overnight and brought to this place. Men broke into your home, they brought you here, and now this is where you live. And just like every other slave, it's up to you to take from this what you believe to be true of yourself and let go of that which you think is not." (Winfrey and Regan 1998, 26)

During her time as Rebecca, a blindfolded Winfrey is verbally accosted by a slave master who informs her that she's "a nigger gal" and that, if she "learned to obey . . . , maybe he and I could get along and I could come and visit him sometime in the big house—that whole sexual stuff." Following this experience, evidence to her "that slavery prohibited your thinking and your *ability to act* on your thoughts," the talk-show host, who suffered repeated acts of sexual abuse as a child, "started to weep uncontrollably":

> [I was] absolutely hysterical, saying to myself: *I know I'm Oprah Winfrey, I know that's who I am, let's just take the blindfold off, this is making me nauseated, sick.* I felt an indescribable pain. . . . [W]hat it

felt like was death with no salvation. And that became my definition of slavery: Death with no salvation on a daily basis. . . . And I also remember thinking: *I couldn't feel this if I didn't know what freedom was.* I went to the place inside myself that knew what freedom was like and was then told that I no longer had it. That was my biggest connection to understanding why Sethe [committed infanticide]. . . . She . . . refused to be a slave [again]. And the experience didn't leave me bitter, it left me with the greatest sense of light and hope. Because I knew I'd been there: I came from there, from that hole of nothingness in a world where every moment told you that you were less than nothing. (Winfrey and Regan 1998, 27)

Winfrey's preparations and their resultant discomfort call to mind the controversial staging during October 1994 of mock slave auctions that, according to the Colonial Williamsburg's African-American Interpretation and Presentations unit, were intended "to re-create life" in antebellum Virginia to "educate visitors about a brutal yet important part of black American history" (Janofsky 1994). While Christy S. Coleman, the unit's director, "recognize[d] that this is a very, very sensitive and emotional issue," she was distressed to discover that "there are those who would have us hide this [very real history] or keep it under the rug." Discussing her own willingness to take on the role of "a slave offered at auction," Coleman insists that

only by open display and discussion can people understand the degradation and humiliation that blacks felt as chattel. She compared the pain of the slave auctions for blacks to that of the Holocaust for Jews and said if museums are built to illustrate the horrors of one, why should not attempts be made to illustrate the other.

"The legacy of slavery in this country is racism," Ms. Coleman said. "Until we begin to understand the horrors that took place, the survival techniques enslaved Africans used, people will never come to understand what's happening in our society today." (Janofsky 1994)

Coleman then challenges the view of the NAACP's local chapter, whose spokesperson

said that many callers to the NAACP office say that the [proposed mock slave] auctions represented such a wrenching chapter in black history that "they don't want to see it rehashed again." He also said that many people expressed alarm that the event might be inaccurate or sensationalized for entertainment. . . .

"Blacks around here don't want to be reminded," [a bricklayer who refused to give his name because he said he feared retribution] said. "It bothers people. People think it's very insensitive to dig it all up again." (Janofsky 1994)

This desire not "to be reminded" of the forms of humiliation American slavery commonly assumed is at odds not only with Coleman's and her foundation's restorative project but with both Morrison's desire "to rip that veil drawn over 'proceedings too terrible to relate'" and Winfrey's faith in the reparative potential of shedding light on traumatic chapters of our personal and collective experiences.

Still, there are huge differences between the attitudes of these part-time thespians preparing to portray slaves in the service of their larger cultural missions. According to Coleman, the Williamsburg reenactment enabled observers to witness *similarities* between the contemporary and antebellum status of blacks that necessitate their use of core racial survival techniques in response to "proceedings" that both slave narrators and protesters of the mock slave auction deemed "too terrible to relate." Conversely, Winfrey insists that slavery's thoughtful reenactment should lead blacks to recognize the *differences* between their ancestors' degradations and their own felicitous historical place in which their racial traumas have largely healed because of the freedom struggles led by Martin Luther King, Jr. and others.

In other words, Winfrey believes that slavery can be reconstituted as a narrative of the "strength and courage" of a people who, despite significant obstacles, "helped to create the entire country having lived our lives day by day—giving our services and ourselves, carrying the strength of our Ancestors" (Winfrey and Regan 1998, 22–23). The message of the slave past and its effective representation that Winfrey wants "to share with every African-American" is "don't let slavery embitter you but let it truly free you, because you have been through and survived the worst. So, my God, look at what you can do now. You have all that behind you" (24). She goes on to say:

We don't need to live our lives in bitterness and anger now, consumed by hatred and fear because of what happened then. Now we truly are liberated to create the highest vision for our lives that is possible. Each of us . . . , particularly those of us who are descendants of slaves, is living the vision the Ancestors had for us and for themselves. We are the manifestation of their vision. And we have an obligation and responsibility to carry that on. It should be the foundation of strength and peace and courage and honor and reverence. That's what the legacy of slavery can mean for us today. (24)

For Winfrey, then, the history of slavery can be reimagined as a mythic tale of a people's resilience, one whose inspirational lessons "*need*" to be used by blacks to move beyond the sense of perpetual disenfranchisement that hinders their capacity to recognize their social, economic, and political potential in the nation that has positioned her as its floating signifier of culture, taste, morality, and spirituality.

In a profile of Winfrey whose aim was to publicize the release of *Beloved*, *Philadelphia Inquirer* movie critic Carrie Rickey writes, "Because Harpo Productions has a deal with ABC, which is owned by Disney, the doyenne of daytime went to Disney production chief Joe Roth in 1995 and told him, '*Beloved* is my *Schindler's List*,' [a comparison that] . . . got Roth's attention" (1998b, F1). Later in this chapter, I discuss several films to which Winfrey's 1998 production might be compared fruitfully because they demonstrate the ongoing concern of *Beloved*'s director, Jonathan Demme, with how to depict essential connections between the past and the present. At this point, however, it is important to note comparisons Winfrey herself offers to Rickey between the themes of the novel and of her talk show:

> What drew Winfrey to *Beloved* was that it is a story of a woman who could [escape the traps set for her by her historical situation]. It reminds her of one of her scenes with costar Danny Glover.
> "When Danny's character [Paul D] says to me, 'You're your own best thing, Sethe,' that was epiphanal. That's what I try to do on my show. So you were abused? Who wasn't? You are also respected. I get to say in this movie what I've been trying on the TV show for years." (1998b, F1)

Looked at in light of her comments about the need for blacks to overcome "bitterness and anger," her "epiphanal" remarks about oppression—the enslavement of her people and systemic mistreatment suffered by members of her primarily female audience—level and universalize abuse ("Who wasn't?"). Further, they suggest that oppression, in all of its manifestations, can be overcome when abused people can recognize that they are that "also respected." Unlike the Williamsburg protesters, who object to slavery's depiction because of their sense of the systemic affinities between it and contemporary manifestations of racism, Winfrey wants its stark recreation to inspire appreciation of post–civil rights freedoms and a transcendence of pain.

Positing that the phrase "you're your own best thing" encapsulates the essence of Morrison's *Beloved*, Winfrey suggests that her film and talk show are similarly designed to offer hope to traumatized black Americans. This perspective, which connects their survival of the peculiar institution with avenues to improved self-esteem available to respect-hungry victims of all races who have suffered rape, domestic abuse, and other types of gendered oppression, fails sufficiently to anticipate the responses of at least two groups as invested as she is in contesting received notions of the relationship of the past to the present. These groups, which intersect in some respects, are (1) blacks who, like Coleman, conceive of black American history as an unending series of demoralizing events, and (2) people motivated by unshakably male-centered beliefs about how black heroism and racial empowerment should be represented.

Numerous observers connected to one or both of the aforementioned groups were troubled by what they saw as *Beloved*'s recapitulation of Hollywood's enduring vision of ceaseless black American suffering, raising questions for them about whether slaves' pain that was not heroically avenged should be represented at all. In an article that explores "what becalmed *Beloved*," Rickey, returning to the subject of Winfrey's film, interviews black industry insiders about its lackluster box office receipts. As she reports, "the Oprah Winfrey epic" that was "launched with galas and cover stories and borderline-reverent reviews" and "arrived wrapped in Oscar predictions has been anything but beloved at the box office. In the five weeks since its October 16 release, the $65 million picture . . . has earned a disappointing $22.5 million. Its failure . . . has prompted a rethinking of the market for prestigious, black-themed films" (1998a, D5). The industry insiders with whom Rickey spoke insisted that *Beloved*'s poor performance was not indicative of—in the words of George Mansour, a consultant to Philadelphia's Ritz chain—"a backlash against black films." Instead, they saw its failure as both a cautionary tale and "an example of how [and why some types of] serious films about blacks don't make it" commercially (D5).

Mansour's views are echoed by Kenneth Lombard, president of Magic Johnson Theaters, who characterized African Americans as "a sophisticated audience" that "support[s] serious black-themed films like *Eve's Bayou* and *Soul Food*" and identifies the crucial difference between Winfrey's film and these more profitable movies in the following way: "Though they [also] deal with family tragedy, those films offer black heroes and heroines who emerge positively, unlike the victim protagonists of *Beloved* and [Steven Spielberg's] *Amistad*" (Rickey 1998a, D9). And Warrington Hudlin, president of the Black Filmmakers Foundation, while also concerned with issues of characterization, speaks of *Beloved* (whose commercial failure he insists "should not be a referendum on African American cinema") as evidence of Hollywood's insatiable desire to depict blacks as "victim protagonists" (D9).

> Why is it, Hudlin asks, "that when Hollywood thinks about black experience, it so often thinks in terms of misery and suffering?
>
> "For the psychic needs of African American audiences—which are no different from the needs of Americans across the board—if we're going to talk about that period [of slavery], we don't need *Beloved* or *Amistad*, we need *Spartacus*," says Hudlin, referring to the 1960 classic about a slave revolt in the Roman Empire. (D9)

Yet another knowledgeable figure, Robert L. Johnson, then chairman and CEO of Black Entertainment Television, references the Kirk Douglas movie: "In *Beloved* there are victims; in *Spartacus* there are heroes" (Rickey 1998a, D9). Despite what Winfrey describes as the arduous task of getting her film made, these commentators imply a connection between its representation of black victimization and Hollywood's willingness to fund the project. As Rickey writes, "Johnson isn't alone in wondering why *Beloved* and *Amistad* got major financing, while more positive black-themed films never get the green light" (D9).

> "It's not coincidental that the stories of slave heroes aren't made and the stories of slave victims are," Hudlin suggests. "Because if they satisfy the psychic needs of black Americans, these stories might scare white Americans."
>
> He'd love to see the story of Nat Turner, the Spartacus of American slavery, made into a movie. But Hudlin thinks that Turner, who led an 1831 uprising that left 55 white people dead, is too hot a subject for the studios to handle. (D9)

Rickey goes on to cite factors such as "its running time" and the difficulty of adapting "a dense, non-linear literary novel" (D5) as potentially contributing to *Beloved*'s box office failure. The impression left by the collective weight of her experts' opinions, however, is that Winfrey's film was a bloated, poorly told, victim-centered disaster that did not sufficiently "satisfy the psychic needs of black Americans" or "scare white Americans" (D5).

Calculations of the "psychic needs" of audiences are inevitably subjective, as are evaluations of Hudlin's and Winfrey's competing ideas about how best to represent slave heroism, since these ideas reflect, among other things, their largely gendered beliefs about felicitous black behavior and its representation in an imperfect democracy. Like Johnson, Hudlin sees slave heroism—the only thematic emphasis worth pursuing—as constituted as, and resulting in, the dramatic murder of enemies on racial battlegrounds. For Winfrey, conversely, heroism is manifested in the "strength and courage" it took for blacks to help to create the progressively more egalitarian United States that those who endured its degradations have bequeathed their descendants. In other words, black American heroism for Winfrey can be discovered not in the muscular exertions of exceptional blacks like Nat Turner but in a quiet resilience that enabled slaves to lay "the foundation of strength and peace and courage and honor and reverence" on which subsequent generations can build as they strive to "to create the highest vision for our lives that is possible."[7] From Winfrey's perspective, then, Hudlin's discussion of psychic needs is flawed because it suggests that blacks remain (1) filled with "bitterness and anger," (2) "consumed by hatred and fear because of" historical oppression, and (3) unable to achieve a state of true freedom that would enable them to recognize—and revel in the fact—that they "have been through and survived the worst."

While the film's paltry box office has not diminished the stature of its source—in a 2006 *New York Times Book Review* poll of prominent writers and scholars, *Beloved* was named the best novel of the final quarter of the twentieth century ("What Is the Best Work" 2006)—it validates the skepticism of some observers about the efficacy of Winfrey's ownership of the film rights for and participation in the adaptations of black women's literary texts. Concerns within the black scholar community about this subject predated the appearance of the film adaptation, as evinced in the remarks from Michele Wallace's 1992 essay "Towards a Black Feminist Cultural Criticism," which I reference in the preface to this chapter.

Because of its source's acclaim, any hope that the film adaptation of *Beloved* would be viewed as a significant achievement depends on the ability of viewers to see it as either a compelling reflection of or departure from general perceptions of slavery's traumatic legacy and of the worldviews of Morrison and Winfrey. Also, because its characters continue to be measured against extant and emerging notions of black heroism and "psychic needs," expanding the meanings of these concepts and their applications to filmic representation may prove necessary if we are to assess the film's strengths and limitations. Given both the fortitude Sethe displays in *Beloved* when she escapes further violations at Sweet Home and—to address the critique of Spielberg's film attached by Rickey's experts to *Beloved*'s postmortem—the graphic depictions of Cinque's mutiny and continued resistance in *Amistad*, her experts appear not to have attended closely to the films they place in a continuum of representations of black victimization palatable to an undifferentiated white mass that both controls and is the primary intended audience of Hollywood cinema, a mass whose willful evasion of American racial oppression means that a major Hollywood studio will never fund a film about vengeful slavery resistance.

Rather than launch here a sustained critique of the critiques of *Beloved*, a film whose limitations generally are, in my view, the result of the timidity of its depictions of its traumatized characters' memories of slavery, I first consider the implications of Winfrey's position as omnipotent cinematic interpreter of "'black feminist' literature." As I have indicated, Winfrey has been involved in adaptations of a number of well-known black novels; in addition to her roles on the screen or behind the scenes of film versions of novels by Naylor, Hurston, Walker, Morrison, and Dorothy West, she appeared as Bigger Thomas's mother in the *American Playhouse* adaptation of Richard Wright's *Native Son*, which graphically depicts what numerous scholars view as misogynistic violence against women.[8] Considering some of these adaptations in the context of her talk show, including Winfrey's book club, enables us to explore tensions between her mission to improve the lives of her viewers and her engagement with literature that generally resists the desires it acknowledges to reward readers with therapeutically happy endings on which her film and talk-show narratives consistently rely.

As the nation's preeminent salesperson of books and interpretive approaches via her book club, which Cecilia Farr describes as "a cultural phenomenon of amazing vitality . . . and unprecedented economic reach in the literary world" (2004, ix), Winfrey is concerned with the transformative effects of reading U.S. fictional and, to a much lesser extent, autobiographical narratives. While I am generally—and genuinely—agonistic about the book club itself, I believe that, in her role as adapter of black American women's novels, Winfrey has participated in and, in fact, overseen their thematic and formal bludgeoning to fit her notions of textual inspiration. In an astute analysis, Malin Pereira emphasizes the impact on the host's investigation of books of the tension inherent in the *Oprah Winfrey Show* between the exposure of "the failures and limitations of the American Dream for women and African Americans," on the one hand, and on the other, the show's investment in this "classic mythology . . . that self-actualization is indeed the key to social and economic success" and that this dream "is accessible to everyone, regardless of the social forces governing their lives" (2007, 191). When she engages literary texts that depict debilitating structural forces that "refuse to endorse the American Dream in any version," their discussion seems "deliberately framed to assert the primacy of individual agency," since the "belief that the American Dream is accessible to everyone, regardless of the social forces governing their lives, dominates the narrative of the show" (193, 192). Whatever other benefits her promotion of reading have produced, Winfrey's discussions of narratives that are often highly critical of the American Dream—Pereira foregrounds in her analysis of another Morrison novel, her mock-epic *Song of Solomon*, for example, "the disfiguring effects of American materialism on three generations of an African American family" (193)—undercut such critiques in favor of what another scholar who has written on Oprah's Book Club speaks of as an overemphasis on purportedly "happy endings."

Entertainment Weekly's Ken Tucker states that Winfrey "undermines the good work she does in promoting reading on her show by clinging to the belief that fiction, nonfiction, or memoir should be useful and uplifting," and by not recognizing that "healing—the reader's self-improvement—is irrelevant to real artists" (Tucker 2004). According to Tucker, Winfrey's "literary criticism"—whose primary concern is whether a text "hold[s] up as a work of the imagination"—emphasizes the capacity of readers not only to be "swept along [and] moved" (2004) but also positively changed and therapeutically healed by their interactions. Her notions of textual engagement, which reduce literature to the status of self-help manuals, equate the fictional and autobiographical narratives she endorses—many of them highly critical of U.S. society—with the fairy-tale plot elements and cathartic ending of *The Color Purple*, whose adaptation helped both to move Winfrey to the forefront of America's consciousness and to legitimize her subsequent acting, film production, and book club endeavors. And if, as Demme insisted, her performance in *Beloved* initially suffered because she was "being harnessed by the book," in her role as the contemporary novel's most powerful advocate, she harnesses texts to a simplistic, pro–American Dream formula, and in the process manifests an inability or refusal to recognize and respect the non-altruistic priorities of "real artists."

Interestingly, *Beloved*, which Winfrey promotes in conjunction with her "change your life" prescription even if the film itself reflects enough of Morrison's worldview to resist such reductive efforts, fails to engage many of its source's central themes and illuminating images. This failure is in large part the consequence of the time limitations confronting filmmakers adapting this capacious narrative on the one hand and, on the other, their apparent capitulation to national strictures against engaging the traumatic implications of U.S. slavery. Much of Winfrey's mainstream appeal stems from her promotion of jingoistic formulations such as the American Dream, and the intergenerational racial trauma that is the focus of *Beloved* cannot easily be made to conform to her notion that, by force of will alone, empowered individuals can overcome constricting social forces. The best evidence of the extent to which Winfrey is beholden to nationalist ideology, which Pereira argues informs her textual readings, are her adaptations of black American women's novels.

Consider *Oprah Winfrey Presents: Their Eyes Were Watching God*, which aired on ABC in March 2005. Winfrey operates as a largely unchecked evaluative force in a culture that is so enthralled with her celebrity and her infectious passion for reading that the *quality* of her analyses is subjected to little serious scrutiny. Consequently, when she introduces her adaptation of Zora Neale Hurston's provocative novel by discussing her reading experience with the film's viewers, she expects to influence her audience's views of an artistic project that is the direct result of those experiences and analyses:

> I remember when I first read this book, I fell in love with the story. It was one of the most beautiful, poignant love stories I'd ever read. This is a story about a woman allowing herself to be a full woman, and not subjected to the definition or identity that others have carved out for her.
> The first time Janie and Tea Cake kiss reinvents the whole idea and notion of kissing. I would have to say that if you can get a kiss like that, you can die a happy woman.
> When this movie airs, Zora Neale Hurston, wherever she is, is going to give a shout. (*Oprah Winfrey Presents* 2005)

From the vantage point of professional critics and laypeople alike who have thought carefully about *Their Eyes Were Watching God*, Winfrey's prefatory comments appear at best sophomoric and at worst ill-informed. For example, her view that Janie escapes "the definition or identity that others have carved out for her" is highly debatable if, as Mary Helen Washington argues in her introduction to the novel, "Janie's voice is dominated by men even in passages that are about her own inner growth" (Washington 1998, xiii–xiv). But even more problematic is Winfrey's assessment of *Their Eyes Were Watching God* as an uncomplicated love story.

That assessment drains the novel of many of the qualities that have fueled its recovery, popularity, and analysis since the 1970s. These analyses addressed such topics as its narrative voice's movement between Standard English and black vernacular modes of speech; its investigation of gender and racial politics, including formulations that insist that, irrespective of her "interior life," Janie's light complexion makes her an ideal object of black male desire; its presentation of the legacies of slavery and their impact on post-Reconstruction visions of black socioeconomic progress; whether Janie and Tea Cake's relationship is a "beautiful, poignant love story" or merely the most successful of her efforts, as a woman in a male-dominated community whose members compel what Washington calls the novel's "uncritical depiction of violence toward women," to make "the dream . . . the truth" (Washington 1998, xiii–xiv, 1). In the intellectual communities that recovered *Their Eyes Were Watching God* from the dustbins of U.S. literary history and positioned it as a previous unappreciated treasure for Winfrey to discover, the talk-show host's conclusions—that Janie achieves "full woman[hood]," a "definition or identity that others have [not] carved out for her," a near-perfect relationship with Tea Cake, and the ability to "die a happy woman" because she has experienced both romantic fulfillment and self-actualization—have been the subjects of careful analysis and heated debate.[9] Having entered the arena of literary interpretation, Winfrey's claims invite—but do not stand up well to—careful scrutiny.

Her reading, as well as the adaptation it spawns and to which it attempts to harness Hurston, necessitates the erasure of, among other things, the subject of U.S. racism. Specifically, the adaptation excises Nanny's discussion of her experiences as the sexual partner of her slave master, Mrs. Turner's hierarchical notions of racial worth, and the trial scene in which Janie—confronted by the "killing thoughts" of blacks who believe that she is structurally allied with white emasculators of black men—focuses on convincing white middle-class female spectators that she murdered a rabid Tea Cake in self-defense.[10] Given these and other excisions, along with the visually striking but otherwise inexplicable sight of Janie (Halle Berry) floating on beautiful bodies of water declaring that she is "watching God," I suspect that if the Hurston I have encountered in her autobiography, *Dust Tracks on a Road* ([1942] 2010), and in Robert Hemenway's illuminating biography (1980) were indeed able to "shout" at Winfrey, she would be driven by something other than the thrill of recognition. Indeed, I imagine that the Barnard-trained anthropologist would improvise a blues song bemoaning "what she done to my book," hop a plane to Chicago, make her way to Harpo Studios, and lay a profanity-laced verbal whupping on its CEO.

My own objection to Winfrey's formulations is not a function of its failure to recreate *my* vision of Hurston's novel. Indeed, I am fully aware that this manner of reductive critique stems from the naïve but persistent desire of viewers for a type of fidelity that, as film and literature scholar Brian McFarlane explains, rests on "a notion of the text as having and rendering up to the (intelligent) reader a single, correct 'meaning' which the filmmaker has either adhered to or in some sense violated or tampered with" (1996, 9). Filmmakers, like all interpreters, ruminate on textual moments that compel them imaginatively and thrust to the background or altogether ignore elements by which they are confounded or that they find inessential. Despite the overwhelming agreement of scholars such as McFarlane about the flaws inherent in viewers' demands for textual fidelity, however, films continue to be seen by moviegoers, television viewers, and professional critics alike as introducing inexcusable discrepancies between source and adaptation.

Take, for example, Alynda Wheat's review of *Oprah Winfrey Presents: Their Eyes Were Watching God*, which argues that the adaptation is flawed precisely because it fails to engage several of what she perceives as the novel's unavoidable concerns:

> Hurston's novel is about impurity at its most complex. Janie is the inevitable mélange of sex and slavery; a child so racially confused she believes she's white until almost age 6. Pages are devoted to the strain her ethnic ambiguity puts on her relationships—nearly a whole chapter given over to a black friend's [Mrs. Turner's] vicious rant against darker African Americans. It's the inheritance of slavery's color-coded caste system, a shameful chapter in African-American history. (2005)

If objections to adaptations reflect desires on the part of viewers for fidelity to their perceptions of texts, they often arise, as in Wheat's analysis, when the resultant work fails to address issues (including, in this case, racial "impurity") that interpreters believe are central to the narrative power and thematic thrust of the source. In such cases, interpreters tend not to see their own necessarily limited analyses (i.e., Wheat's view that "Hurston's novel is about impurity at its most complex," as opposed to Winfrey's that it is "a romance, pure and simple" [2005]) as constituting a similar sort of violation. But if, like literary criticism, adaptations are interpretations that attempt to bring thematic coherence to selected parts of their sources, when filmmakers like Demme, who implored Winfrey to remember that "a book is something different" from a movie, acknowledge their own necessarily revisionist designs, they enhance our ability to move beyond notions of adaptations as unfaithful violations.

However, in *presenting* the novel to a television audience, Winfrey claims that her own reading experience—and the interpretation it spawns—yields the "single, correct meaning" to be derived from it by suggesting that Hurston herself would affirm the film as a faithful adaptation of her novel rather than as a markedly divergent work that uses its title and strategically selected aspects of its narrative. Considering *Their Eyes Were Watching God* as Winfrey would have us do—as an escapist romance verifying the genre's governing belief that true love conquers all—I am struck less by the limitations of her interpretation than by the unabashed hucksterism that informs it. In promoting her reinvention, Winfrey employs a shameless sales pitch to ensure that the size of the audience for this project is not limited by what "becalmed *Beloved*": narrative complexity, slavery's legacy, and a commitment to representing what Winfrey herself might call the "emotional truths" of the source. And if Wheat's objection stems from the adaptation's avoidance of the "mélange of sex and slavery," the film's excising of many of the novel's emphases can be said to reflect what Susan Sontag speaks of as the United States' general refusal to participate in a "perpetuation of memories" of its painful slave past:

There is no Museum of the History of Slavery—the whole story, starting with the slave trade in Africa itself, not just selected parts, such as the Underground Railroad—anywhere in the United States. This, it seems, is a memory judged too dangerous to social stability to activate and to create. The Holocaust Memorial Museum and the future Armenian Genocide Museum and Memorial are about what didn't happen in America. . . . To have a museum chronicling the great crime that was African slavery in the United States of America would be to acknowledge that the evil was *here*. Americans prefer to picture the evil that was *there*, and from which the United States—a unique nation, one without any certifiably wicked leaders throughout its entire history—is exempt. That this country, like every other country, has its tragic past does not sit well with the founding, and still all-powerful, belief in American exceptionalism. (2004, 87–88)

In a remark summarizing her reactions to the failure of *Beloved* that echoes Sontag's concerns and anticipates Wheat's objections to her adaptation of *Their Eyes Were Watching God*, Winfrey insists that she will "never do another film about slavery. I won't try to touch race again in this form, because people just aren't ready to hear it" (Lawrence 2005, 43). Looked at in this context, her description of Hurston's novel as a love story can be seen as an attempt to justify her evasion of issues she vows never again to explore. Certainly, her comment may help us to understand, if not necessarily to evaluate less critically, the film's avoidance of subjects directly connected to the thorny issue of slavery.

Winfrey's reading of Hurston's novel and her post-*Beloved* decision to avoid the subject of slavery, in other words, reflect the calculation of a successful businesswoman of the need to minimize or eliminate altogether from her adaptation those elements of another highly regarded novel authored by a black American woman that her core audience might find disquieting. Whatever service *Oprah Winfrey Presents: Their Eyes Were Watching God* performed for Hurston's reputation and estate—including pushing the novel onto the best-seller list and the novelist temporarily to the forefront of America's consciousness—the adaptation also enabled Winfrey, in the wake of *Beloved*'s disappointing reception, to be seen again as a commercially viable interpreter of black women's fiction. But ultimately, the success of every adaptation must be measured not in terms of how faithfully it recreates its source's essential elements but in terms of how successfully it brings its own aesthetic, ideological, and thematic coherence to the parts it selects from that source. For, as Christopher Orr asserts, "the issue is not whether the adapted film is faithful to its source, but rather how the choice of a specific source and how the approach to that source serve the film's ideology" (quoted in McFarlane 1996, 10).

Despite the obvious public synergy between Morrison and Winfrey—the Nobel laureate confers an element of high cultural legitimacy on Oprah's largely "middlebrow" book club (Farr 2004, 34–36) via her appearances on the talk show, which in turn multiplied the novelist's book sales—their work is compelled by starkly different worldviews. Time and time again, Winfrey has demonstrated her investment in happy narrative endings,[11] and the governing theme of her public endeavors at least since 1994 is that, by being receptive to uplifting, revelatory messages, including those found in works of literature, you can learn—as she herself claims she has—to "change your life" positively and to "live your best life." That perspective informs her promotion of her adaptation of Morrison's novel, whose most harrowing moments, Winfrey predicted while promoting the film in Philadelphia, would leave audiences "speechless" and so emotionally devastated that "you'll want to be going [to the movie theater] with someone to share" in "*Beloved* gatherings." According to Winfrey, the moviegoer willing to pay the necessary psychic, emotional, and monetary price would be compensated richly by her discovery of a theme, reduced, by the media-savvy entertainer, to an easily digested sound bite: "the essence of the film is what we all know—you are your best thing. . . . Triumph!" (Rickey 1998b, F1). Like her insistence that *Their Eyes Were Watching God* is a love story with an eminently saleable— and filmable—feature, a transcendent kiss shared by two beautiful people, her interpretation of *Beloved* does more than merely guide her viewers toward an uplifting concluding vision. Instead, it prescribes the arch of their viewing experience: shock, speechlessness, and therapeutic ending.

Discussing *Beloved*'s First City premiere, *Philadelphia Daily News* reporter Tonya Pendleton writes that Winfrey "proudly noted that Toni Morrison's Pulitzer Prize-winning novel . . . is climbing the best-seller list again" (1998, 5). Despite Winfrey's ability to cause this sales explosion, she does not possess the power to rewrite the rejuvenated novel so that it ends with "epiphanal" grandeur or "triumph." Neither the literary source nor the film, for that matter, both of which focus on the consequences of "thick" maternal love and the debilitating impact of horrific memories, invest Sethe with an "interior life" that is not wholly conditioned by these painful imperatives. Consequently, the reaction of readers and filmgoers to Paul D's assertion, "you your best thing," must necessarily be as quizzical as that of the character Winfrey portrays, who asks, in response to the long-absent man's utterance, "Me? Me?" (Morrison 1987, 273).

Precisely what, beyond a form of mother love shaped by debilitating oppression, is there in Sethe to cherish? What is she besides the consequences of the traumas of slavery, including her particular version of the perils of motherhood? When Paul D declares, "You your best thing," a physically weakened and emotionally bereft Sethe appears close to death, occupying the bed to which her mother-in-law, Baby Suggs, confined herself when she lost her will to live. Entombed in a deathbed, Sethe mentions her grief over *Beloved*'s departure as well as her own complicity in Sweet Home's degradation of blacks by preparing the ink that schoolteacher used in the plantation's official records to divide slaves' human and animal "characteristics" (Morrison 1987, 271). Hence, the encouraging words of Paul D are intended to empower a deeply traumatized Sethe. In this circumstance, truth is less important than providing the grieving woman with an alternate perspective on her circumstances, or what the trauma scholars Bessel van der Kolk and Onno van der Hart call "narrative flexibility."

The woman who precedes Sethe in the downstairs bed, Baby Suggs, the Ohio community's priestess who implores other blacks to honor those aspects of themselves that whites "do not love" (Morrison 1987, 88–89), is herself eventually so overwhelmed by long-standing anguish (from the sale of all but one of her children) and more recent agony (the result of losing both her "crawling already" granddaughter and her community's high regard) that her life is reduced to the painless exercise of contemplating unfamiliar colors. Consequently, there is little reason to believe that Sethe, still distraught over losses she can hardly bear—of breast milk stolen from her by schoolteacher's "mossy-toothed" nephews; of her husband, Halle, who Paul D informs her went mad after being unable to stop schoolteacher's nephews from violating her; of her sons, who cannot abide living in a house possessed by the spirit of their murdered sister; and of that daughter, whom she felt compelled to kill—could achieve "epiphanal" self-regard following her experiences with the figure she believed to be Beloved reincarnated. Paul D's words convey the governing theme of neither version of the narrative, which gives us no reason to assume that Sethe will affirm or absorb what might be seen in other circumstances as their commonsensical wisdom. Even if it is difficult to choose conclusively between the Sweet Home survivors' perspectives on the proper intensity and manifestations of black postbellum love—to decide, in other words, how to assess Sethe's choice to kill her children—the narratives undoubtedly place us at a sort of interpretive crossroads. In the face of that interpretive dilemma and moral conundrum—what should an otherwise powerless mother have done to protect her children—it is difficult to imagine how Winfrey's craving for narrative triumph is satisfied by *Beloved*. For Morrison represents slavery as an instrument of trauma that effectively destroyed black self-determination, one whose psychic escape, even years after its bloody termination, is virtually impossible.

We are left, then, not with "triumph," but with traumatized survivors longing to shield themselves from painful memories of what others have done to them and what harm their own restricted and restrictive worldviews have led them to inflict on others. And if, when we come to the end of the adaptation, we believe that Sethe's life will be saved because she will come to see herself as Paul D claims to view her—as her own "best thing"—that interpretation certainly is not one that flows organically from either a viewing of the film or a reading of the novel on which it is based. Rather, it is a manifestation of the triumph of the type of specious reading that motivates Winfrey to see *Their Eyes Were Watching God* simply as a "beautiful . . . love story."

Winfrey's appearance in *The Color Purple* coincided with her ascension to the position of the United States' most popular talk-show host and, later, the nation's most respected arbitrator of debates about the roots, manifestations, and consequences of corrosive, self-defeating, and malicious behavior. Coincidentally or not, striking similarities exist between that film's imposition of a conventionalizing conclusion and its breakout star's subsequent commitment to triumphant endings. Like Walker's novel, the film dramatizes Celie's reunion with her sister, Nettie, whom Celie's ex-husband Albert banished from his house for rejecting his sexual advances, and her own two children whom her stepfather and rapist refused to permit her to rear. However, perhaps because it is less committed than the novel to interrogating the socially imposed nature of gender identity, the adaptation expands the role Albert plays in enabling that reunion while prohibiting his active participation in the happy resolution.

Indeed, the conclusions of both *The Color Purple* and *The Women of Brewster Place*, the two foundational Winfrey films, deviate significantly from their fictional sources in order to offer happy endings. Looked at in light of her subsequent book club and "change your life" pronouncements, these adaptations represent templates for her endeavors in the service of which nothing—not interpretive complexity or artistic nuance, not calls for fidelity either to the depiction of Albert's earned inclusion in the reassembled community or to the skepticism of Naylor's novel about the ability of black sisterhood to improve "the status and condition of black women as a group" appreciably—supersedes Winfrey's commitment to investing stories with unambiguously transformative messages.

The conclusion of *The Color Purple* radically alters two of the concluding scenes of its source, forcing viewers who have also read the novel to consider the radical differences between Walker's and Spielberg's depictions of gender and religion. For example, Joan Digby asserts that the "painfully detailed," "visually triumphant" depiction of the dramatic castigation of Albert during Easter dinner "prevented the screenwriter from allowing Celie to be reconciled with Mr. _____ in the film as she is in the novel" (1993, 164). And John Peacock argues that while both versions "depict Albert, after Celie has left him, drunk and filthy in his messy house," and "Spielberg visually narrates the steps Albert takes to reunite Celie and Nettie" when he "realizes he needs to mend his ways," the film "grossly oversimplifies how Walker originally developed Albert's reconciliation with Celie: the estranged couple patch up their differences after Albert starts visiting Celie again in her new home where he finds her sewing pants" (1994, 123). Theorists of adaptation insist that such deviations are essential to the filmmaker's efforts to communicate his or her artistic vision. If we are to take their views seriously, it is essential that we consider precisely how its deviations enable Spielberg's film to replicate, critique, or distinguish itself from its source.

Besides providing him with an opportunity to include the sort of rousing gospel moment on which Hollywood has relied for decades, Spielberg's choice positions the resolution of Shug's fractured family plot as a major concern alongside that of Celie's banished family. This choice reestablishes the blues singer as a major focus after her sexual relationship with Celie had been severely truncated and her non-Christian perspectives had been excised. According to Digby, *The Color Purple*

> invents the minister-father . . . who finally throws his arms around her and accepts her appeal to understand that 'sinners have souls too.' . . . [W]hen, like the Pied Piper, she leads her audience out of the juke-joint and into the church he confers an embrace of implied absolution [which,] in the context of the film's ending, . . . defuses Shug's restless quest for love and releases her from the spell of her own sexual self-image. (1993, 164)

Unlike Peacock, who argues that "in adapting an African-American feminist novel, Spielberg failed to translate the very different folk traditions of that genre and ended up perpetuating Anglo-American stereotypes about blacks" (1994, 123), Digby concentrates on what and how the director's (and screenwriter's) additions contribute to the film's articulation of its distinctive thematic concerns. Hence, Peacock emphasizes the fact that

> the conclusion of Celie's odyssey as Walker wrote it is quite a bit different from the "visual and emotional marginalization of men" that Andrea Stuart admires at the end of Spielberg's film when she accurately describes the film's final scene: it "begins with a powerful shot of the three women [Celie, Sofia, and Shug] emerging from Celie's house . . . to welcome Nettie—their husbands all in the background, at the edges of the screen." (1994, 123–124)

Peacock goes on to argue that the film places Albert and Harpo "on the margin of the process of women's development, making men objects of it rather than participants in it. This is, in fact, what men sometimes do to women in failing to see them as subjective participants in men's own development" (124).

At this point, we would do well to recall Keith Cohen's influential view of textual infidelity, in which he states that the adaptation of novels into film

> is a truly artistic feat only when the new version carries with it a hidden criticism of its model, or at least render implicit . . . certain key

contradictions implanted or glossed over in the original. . . . The adaptation must subvert its original, perform a double and paradoxical job of masking and unveiling its source, or else the pleasure it provides will be nothing more than that of seeing words changed into images. (Quoted in Giddings, Selby, and Wensley 1990, 12)

Film adaptations, then, are no more than pictorial renderings of fiction writers' words if their creators fail discernibly to deconstruct their sources. In their pursuit of art, filmmakers who undertake adaptations must, according to Cohen, call attention to or probe what they perceive to be weaknesses in their sources. Accordingly, ambitious filmmakers must be compelled not only by a desire to render the most successful and distinctive aspects of their sources but by the challenge of devising intriguing ways to assemble the reconstructed parts of their subversive retellings to reflect their own, necessarily divergent points of view.

Consisting largely of letters written by two sisters separated by the malice of patriarchs, Walker's novel provides Spielberg with a major artistic challenge: figuring out how to deemphasize the written text's focus on writing and reading—letters addressed to God by Celie because her oppression is predicated on an enforced silence (her stepfather's insistence, after his rape of her, that she "better not tell nobody but God" [1992, 1], a deity whom Celie grows to feel is unresponsive, uncommunicative, and inattentive ["you must be sleep" (177)]) and letters written by Nettie to a sister that she believes never reads them because they are never answered—while depicting tales of sexual abuse, inescapable oppression, and compensatory female bonding recorded in these acts of interrupted communication. The film, then, is forced by its source's epistolary form to do more than simply provide viewers with what Cohen identifies as the "pleasure . . . of seeing words changed into images" (quoted in Giddings, Selby, and Wensley 1990, 12).

This adaptation's success is predicated in part, then, to echo Cohen's perspectives, on its ability to "subvert its original" by relegating the novel's concern with written modes of address to the narrative background. Spielberg introduces several significant changes, including the establishment of Charles Dickens's *Oliver Twist* as a precursor whose description of systematic oppression Celie reads at the precise point in the film when she is transformed visually from the little girl whom Pa rapes and Albert marries and into the woman whom Shug grows to love. Such changes enable the filmmaker to create continuity between aspects of the story he inherits, but on which he chooses not to dwell. For example, despite deemphasizing the contents of Nettie's letters written in and about Africa, Spielberg uses jump cuts, one of the medium's most effective means of making comparisons and building tension, to connect the scarification ceremony to which Celie's son and his African girlfriend submit and the preparations of an enraged Celie, who had recently discovered the stash of Nettie's letters of which Albert had deprived her, to kill him with the sharpened razor he has ordered her to use to shave him.

In addition, Shug's reconciliation with her father establishes other continuities: between gospel, whose overhearing draws her back to the bosom of her church and of grateful minister-father, and the blues, the devil's music whose performance had precipitated her exile, as well as between the God whom Celie comes to believe is unresponsive to her entreaties and the attentive deity who, according to the rousing song, "is trying to tell you something." However, the minister's embrace occurs not because he achieves a more sympathetic perspective on his daughter's blues life but when Shug acknowledges the Christian God's responsiveness to the human condition, an acknowledgment that validates her father's governing perspectives and expectations. In other words, Shug's tearful reunion with her father in the film is predicated on *her capitulation* to the will of the Father, whom she rejects in Walker's novel in favor of a notion of divinity uncorrupted by institutional forces. By reestablishing the law of the Father as the locus of familial and religious community, Spielberg's adaptation ultimately reconstructs Shug, turning her into someone bent on repentance and atonement so as to be granted a comforting paternal embrace. And if the reconstitution of the fractured black family—Celie's murdered, dispersed, diasporic bloodline—represents the triumphant dénouement of the story Spielberg receives from Walker, by aligning it with his interest in the fractured middle-class white American family as evinced in such films as *Close Encounters of the Third Kind*, *Minority Report*, and *A.I.*, he depicts its healing (Shug's reconciliation with her minister-father and, as we see later, of Celie's reunion with her sister and her own children) as the consequence of willing conformity to patriarchal law.

Looked at in light of Shug's embrace of familial and religious obligations in *The Color Purple*, Celie's tragic family plot is resolved happily following Albert's embrace of the traditional masculine role of father-provider. Having verbally and physically terrorized Celie, whom the widower marries solely because of his need for inexpensive domestic labor, Albert is nearly murdered and then is verbally chastised by her for withholding her sister's letters. Resisting the novel's feminizing modes of male transformation and restitution, which include Albert's embrace of sewing and bonding with Celie over a shared sense of the mysteries of human existence and heartache over the absence of Shug, Spielberg's Albert rectifies the wrongs and ends the separation he and other agents of patriarchy had imposed on the family. In the film he becomes, as a consequence, a patriarch whose benevolence leaves essentially intact the traditional notions of masculinity and femininity under whose regime he and Celie have suffered.

Whatever else we might say about Spielberg's film, it offers Winfrey a template for "epiphanal," "triumph[ant]" endings in which traditional narratives of gender are reinforced and serve as the impetus for the happy endings themselves. The status quo preserved, the characters learn neither to question nor to strive to overhaul the patriarchal regime under which they suffered. Instead, they become, as a consequence of their seduction by patriarchy, willing performers of the roles it assigns to them.

W infrey's comments about slavery's transcendence demonstrate her willingness to support, promote, and urge others to work within the firmly established parameters of an American ideology by which her people have been physically, economically, and emotionally scarred. She is an inspirational figure for a variety of people because of her remarkable rags-to-riches story; much of her success appears to result from her insistence that self-fulfillment for marginalized people results not from questioning or seeking to invalidate the governing principles of oppressive regimes but from discovering ways to make these principles work for them. For example, her talk-show viewers are often discouraged from challenging contemporary justifications of the objectification of women; instead, they are shown how to make themselves thinner and appear more attractive—including by means of Botox, collagen shots, and other less invasive procedures—without exceeding their financial means. And rather than challenge the romance narrative because of which so many of her viewers have been emotionally scarred and physically harmed, her preface to the adaptation of *Their Eyes Were Watching God* promotes its energetic pursuit and actualization in the form of a death-justifying kiss.

In an analysis of Winfrey that coincided with the release of *Beloved*, Ann Oldenburg and Kevin V. Johnson spoke in October 1998 of "the Oprah backlash" that was inevitable given her popularity and her show's changing emphases, both of which were the result of her unwavering opportunism. As they report, critics had begun to speak of Winfrey's talk show as "self-serving" and "oppressive":

> Dean Richards of Chicago's WGN [is] . . . tired of the "self-serving attitude on her show this year." "I admire what she's done professionally and personally," he says. But now, "everything has to go through the 'Oprah-me' filter. . . . It's Oprah-palooza."

> . . . Chicago Sun-Times columnist Richard Roeper lambasted her
> two weeks ago for her "new age nuttiness." And New York Post col-
> umnist Thelma Adams jumped on the bandwagon this week, saying,
> "Her overwhelmingly positive, you-can-do-it message-mongering
> has become too much to bear. As, I fear, has she."
>   And there's a Web site . . . , complete with Gripe of the Day, de-
> voted to ranting against Winfrey. . . . The intro says, "Join those of
> us who still eat hamburgers, think our lives are pretty OK, and are
> tired of watching virtual strangers weep out their innermost grief on
> national television." (1998, 4E)

Winfrey's emergence at the beginning of the 1998–1999 season as a secular
evangelist troubled critics in large part because of her seeming narcissistic
pursuit of multiple roles: movie star and producer, book club maven, *Vogue*
cover girl, and even vocally challenged singer of her show's theme song. The
criticism directed at her during this period was as venomous as it had been
before her denouncement of talk shows' degrading exploitations of human
weaknesses that led to her being dubbed the "Queen of Trash" a half decade
earlier. In response to the growing tide of criticism of her efforts to inspire
her viewers, Winfrey started a website on which, as Oldenburg and Johnson inform us, she offered the following statement: "It's a shame that we've
evolved into the kind of society where evangelical is considered negative.
I have come to believe that we are all, or at least most of us, searching for
the assurance that good exists in our world, even in the midst of evil and
abuse. . . . [S]ome people choose to call it evangelical, and that's fine with me"
(1998, 4E).

Considering this comment in light of her adaptations of black American
women's novels, we might say that, like her show's evangelicalism, triumphant
endings are marshaled to provide evidence "that good exists in our world,
even in the midst of evil and abuse." This evangelical turn, coupled with the
cloying terms in which it is delivered and its relationship to other manifestations of her uses of her enormous cultural power, triggered intense ridicule of
Winfrey. If *The Color Purple* represents a template for Winfrey's subsequent
narratives, bracketing her entertainment career as fledging actress and, in
the case of its Broadway revival, its over-the-title producer, we would do
well to return at this point to Spielberg's adaptations of his source's conclusion. As I've suggested, in the case of Celie's ex-husband, the abusive, father-
dominated, weak-willed Albert, Spielberg's film rejects Walker's representation of his moral and psychological growth whose trajectory is socially constructed as feminine. The film's Albert ends up a distanced, rehabilitated

patriarch who embodies enduring features of masculinity, particularly its exhibition of isolation, reticence, and physical strength (he tells no one of his role in reassembling his ex-wife's family; in the movie's conclusion, he observes the reunion he has enabled during a break from invigorating farmwork).

This happy ending, then, is achieved without reimagining the sociocultural systems that have historically sustained forms of U.S. racism and sexism. I am not implying that this adaptation is flawed because it alters Walker's source material where Albert is concerned but that the representations of the triumph of good over evil to which Winfrey attached herself are generally unconcerned with fidelity to the sorts of radical perspectives that animate the novel. Winfrey's cultural power as a populist, aggressively female-centered talk-show host was more a function of her ability to anticipate, address, and help shape her audience's extant concerns and curry its favor through the gifts of cars, beauty and weight-loss tips, interesting novels, and manifestations of deep concern than of her willingness to challenge the social structures that dominate their lives. Given its homeostatic impulses, Winfrey's projection of the triumph of good over evil must be achieved without, for example, Walker's disruptive vision of gender and of God, without the ambiguity of *Beloved*'s ending, and, following her adaptation's commercial failure, without depicting the legacies of slavery that have doubtlessly shaped black American formulations of romance in her reimagining of Hurston's novel.

If Christopher Orr is correct that "the issue is not whether the adapted film is faithful to its source, but rather how the choice of a specific source and how the approach to that source serve the film's ideology" (quoted in McFarlane 1996, 10), understanding Winfrey's ideology, her trumpeting of a good-over-evil secular evangelicalism, requires that we examine her interpretations of black American women's novels from the beginning of her career as a studio executive when she was seeking challenging acting vehicles for herself. In *The Women of Brewster Place*, her first major public engagement of a black woman's novel following *The Color Purple*, we are confronted, in its insistence on the corrective power of black sisterhood and reworking of the novel's conclusion, by perhaps the preeminent challenge facing viewers familiar with the novel: assessing the success of a film that uses its source's materials to arrive at an entirely contradictory conclusion. How fully do—and should—we engage perceptions like those of Orr and Keith Cohen, who holds that "adaptation is a truly artistic feat only when the new version carries with it a hidden criticism of its model, or at least renders implicit . . . certain key contradictions implanted or glossed over in the original" (quoted in Giddings, Selby, and Wensley 1990, 12)? Can we acknowledge the rights—perhaps even the responsibilities—of filmmakers to alter their source materials while contending that, in the case of *The Women of Brewster Place*, those alterations greatly diminish the power of the story?

In addition to presenting its adapters with many of the conventional dilemmas that filmmakers face "when a three-hundred-page novel is made into a two or three-hour movie" (Beja 1979, 84), *The Women of Brewster Place* compels Winfrey and others to consider an essential difference between film and literature pertaining to representations of temporality. In their overview of "the literature/screen debate," Robert Giddings, Keith Selby, and Chris Wensley describe challenges related to the fact that "the novel . . . has a whole gamut of grammatical tenses," while film—because "what we see on the screen is in the act of happening, [as] we are given the gesture itself, not an account of it"—essentially "has only one" (1990, 15). Particularly when compared to the novel, in other words, film cannot conclusively distinguish between past and present, dream and reality, the products of a character's imagination and hard narrative fact.

The narrative challenges with which Naylor is concerned involve the formal and thematic complexities of creating what her subtitle calls "a novel in seven stories." In the miniseries based on Naylor's novel, "the so-called 'grammar' of the screen," including techniques such as dissolves, sharp cuts, montages, and the rhythmic flow of images, is employed to depict, among other things, continuities within and between scenes from distinct stories. But if, in adapting literature, filmmakers confront "key contradictions implanted or glossed over in the original," Naylor's engagement with questions of form—especially how to achieve thematic coherence in a story collection that aspires to be seen as a novel—compels Winfrey's team to consider how most effectively to perform the "double and paradoxical job of masking and unveiling its source."

The novel's "key contradiction" is its designation of the destruction of the wall isolating Brewster Place—a wall that is the site of and a metaphor for much of the community's pain—as its means of achieving thematic and structural coalescence, even when it insists that its destruction occurs solely in the elaborate dream of Mattie Michael. If the novel as a form can more easily handle shifts in time and consciousness than film, the choice of the filmmakers to render the events that compose Mattie's dream as *narrative incidents* rather than nocturnal imaginings can perhaps be seen as a function of the form's propensity to represent that which it renders at any given moment as *reality*. The filmmakers appear to avoid the complications created by an awareness that the wall's destruction occurs only in Mattie's dream by presenting it as an incontrovertible fact. That intention is manifested most clearly in the screenwriters' insertion of the following sentiments, articulated in a voice-over by Winfrey's character, Mattie: "We learned that when we women came together, there was a power inside us that we never felt before." That sentiment, ultimately rejected in the novel, becomes the animating theme of the miniseries, dovetailing with the nascent female-centered "change your life" mission of *Oprah* and Winfrey's much-expressed desire to represent the triumph of good over evil.

Brian McFarlane argues that for a film adapted from a novel to "have any value of its own, it will need to have its own point of view, its own sense of the significance of what it is presenting." Conversely, George Linden insists that "for a film to be an adequate rendition of a novel, it must not only present the actions and events of the novel but also capture the attitudes and subjective tones toward those events" (McFarlane and Linden quoted in Giddings, Selby, and Wensley 1990, 14). Viewing *The Women of Brewster Place* in light of the seemingly competing perspectives of these critics, it is possible to suggest that the filmmakers' intention is not to replicate the novel but rather to draw from and supplement those aspects of it that enable them to articulate Winfrey's governing point of view. However, in drawing on the novel's emphasis on the significance of female coalescence and Winfrey's emerging "change-your-life" philosophy, the film ignores the tensions between that emphasis and its own representations of black female self-deception. For, as a consequence of their experiences with powerlessness and desire, the women at the outset of their stories generally behave as if they believe that "the dream is the truth," to cite Hurston's prefatory remarks in *Their Eyes Were Watching God*, and they "act and think accordingly" ([1937] 1998, 1). In replicating Naylor's depictions of the disastrous consequences of her characters' belief that they can actualize their desires despite overwhelming evidence to the contrary (i.e., Mattie's faith in her son Basil, Etta Mae's belief that her desperate flirtation with Reverend Woods will eventuate in marriage, and Ciel's contention that Eugene can be a loving father and supportive mate), the film, like its source, encourages skepticism about the women's abilities to understand and respond effectively to the challenges they face. And so as it reaches its conclusion, where Brewster's women achieve catharsis as they destroy the wall that has sapped the life of Mattie's plants, shielded drug dealers from detection, and served as the site both of Lorraine's rape and of Ben's murder, we are left to wonder: What, precisely, is the source of their sense of triumph?

What, indeed, do they feel will change? Certainly, the film offers us no reason to believe that the city officials who isolated Brewster Place from the rest of the city will embrace the visions of residents of this impoverished neighborhood or that the funds that the block party has raised will be sufficient to secure legal representation that will help the residents gain restitution from their neglectful landlords. While the scene of triumph is satisfying on visual and emotional levels, it contains no evidence of a radical change in circumstances. The problem with making Mattie's dream the truth in the miniseries, then, is not that that choice deviates from the facts of the novel, but that it is not accompanied by a radical rethinking of the baleful outcomes of the women's misplaced desires that the film draws from its source. No proclamation by Mattie concerning female empowerment can erase the viewers' skepticism owing to the film's failure to depict unambiguous manifestations of that power before its melodramatic ending.

If its characters indeed "learned that when we women came together, there was a power inside us that we never felt before," the adaptation fails to depict, before the final scene, the empowering consequences of their coalescence. To reference *Their Eyes Were Watching God* again, one of the works (along with Shakespeare's *A Midsummer Night's Dream* and Langston Hughes's "A Dream Deferred") to which Naylor's engagement of the subject of dreams refers, it is as though, like Janie confronting incontrovertible evidence that she has compromised her integrity in remaining with Joe Starks, the filmmakers believe that unless they can demonstrate the plausibility of Mattie's dream, the women's lives "won't be nothin'" (Hurston [1937] 1998, 72). Simply voicing the opinion that Brewster's women are empowered by their unity does not alter the film's presentation of them, especially when the actualization of that power is unconnected to its scenes and is represented by the tearing down of a wall that city officials can have replaced within a week. Faith is a good thing, but in instances of storytelling as well as in the realm of interpretation, it must be securely grounded in evidence.

A daptations provide filmmakers with the opportunity to deconstruct available narratives and to reimagine them in ways that reflect their own abiding perspectives. In the case of *Beloved*, the challenges are related to adapting omnisciently narrated, thought-driven, and memory-obsessed fiction, and producing a compelling representation of aspects of the traumas of slavery for a nation generally committed to its evasion. David Denby's *New Yorker* review insists that Demme was perplexed by these challenges:

> The book [*Beloved*] poses a trap for adaptors, and the screenwriters . . . fell into it. Most of the emotionally significant events take place in the past; the present is a shuddering remnant, struggling to exist. Yet the filmmakers have tipped the balance toward the present. We

are in the Ohio farmhouse, a gray and featureless place, and when we are shown a past event—say, an ex-slave's memory of being whipped or shackled—the image flares luridly on the screen for an instant and disappears. Many of these flashbacks will mean nothing to the uninitiated, while those who have read the book may be shocked by the blunt stupidity of mere illustration—shocked by the stupidity of movies. What is before us is either commonplace or sensational, and unsatisfactory either way. (1998, 249–250)

While recognizing the media's essential differences, Denby argues that emphasizing, and lingering on, "emotionally significant events" of the slave past might have enabled Demme to create a more impressive adaptation. For Denby, these shortcomings are especially evident when the film moves from the past, whose terrors are effectively communicated by "Lisa Gay Hamilton, the actress who plays the young Sethe in a series of tumultuous flashbacks," to the present, where Winfrey's and Danny Glover's faces, voices, and mannerisms fail to convey "the sense of incomparable experience, of terrors confronted and mastered" (1998, 250). Attempting to account for a talented director's failure to make sound artistic choices, Denby writes:

> In a novel, one can dramatize the act of telling, but in a movie something must be told, and in "Beloved" almost every possibility of narrative excitement and moral exploration has been ignored. If Sethe's mental activity is impossible to re-create in a movie, then surely her slave past has to be re-created—the life that brings her to the point of murdering her children. For it is the moral condition of the murderess which fascinates us, not the admittedly pressing domestic problem of how to live with a ghost. (1998, 250)

To constitute an effective adaptation, given the difficulty for Winfrey and Glover of communicating via necessarily measured responses the enduring impact of Sweet Home degradations, *Beloved* needed to have depicted their experiences as slaves much more thoroughly.

Owen Gleiberman's review echoes Denby's contentions about the implications of the film's general evasion of slavery:

> Hollywood has yet to deliver the movie we so desperately need about slavery, the one that will plunge us . . . into a newly intimate and terrifying contemplation of the obscenity of the African-American holocaust. There are moments in *Beloved*, the somberly forbidding, nearly

three-hour adaptation of Toni Morrison's novel, in which I imagined what that movie might look like. . . .

For *Beloved* to work, we need to understand how a mother could . . . [resolve to kill her children and herself rather than allow them to be enslaved]—and in our heads, at least, we do. But I'm not sure the film makes the case in our hearts. (1998, 45)

Like Denby, Gleiberman suggests that the film needed to have rendered the slave past so as to contextualize Sethe's choice to murder her child by offering illuminating representations of some of the traumatic events she experienced. Denby goes so far as to imply that the film's failure to contextualize Sethe's decision results from Winfrey assuming greater control over the production than the renowned filmmaker she handpicked. Clearly both critics feel that Demme's work suffers as a consequence of his self-recriminations for "the gruesome, sensationally effective 'Silence of the Lambs,' and the somber AIDS melodrama 'Philadelphia'" (Denby 1998, 250).

Taking such comments seriously, in the next section, I look at other Demme films in order to explore a nagging question that connects them with *Beloved*: How does film, a medium of "presentness," reference and engage the past? Instances in which the past is rendered in—and in relation to—the present in *The Silence of the Lambs, Philadelphia,* and *The Manchurian Candidate* demonstrate that Demme possesses the requisite temperament to have been compelled artistically and emotionally by the issue of how memories of slavery bleed into, animate, and disrupt the lives of Sweet Home's survivors. Still, acceding, intentionally or not, to the long-standing national desire to ignore its devastating impact, Demme offers a notably truncated representation of the slave past in *Beloved*. Instead of effectively depicting specific degradations to which Sethe was subjected as a slave, the film itself evades what Morrison refers to in "The Site of Memory" as their "sordid details." That evasion may have been motivated by desires that are startlingly similar to those of slave narrators: not wanting to offend popular taste. In its refusal to "dwell . . . too long or too carefully on the more sordid details of" Morrison's representations of slavery, the film indisputably "pull[s] the narrative up short" (Morrison 1990, 301). And "in shaping" *Beloved* "to make it palatable to those who were in a position," finally, to confront slavery's "rememory," the filmmakers "were silent about many things, and they 'forgot' many other things" (301). Certainly, it is curious that the film's limitations are said to relate precisely to its refusal to depict slavery when it was the novel's powerful rendering of its degradations that inspired both Winfrey's and Demme's desire to work on its adaptation in the first place.

The Oscar-winning psychological thriller *The Silence of the Lambs* (1991) is the story of the FBI's dogged search for a serial killer. The film is dominated by notions of the childhood roots of adult behavior espoused by the two masculine authority figures to whom the neophyte FBI agent Clarice Starling (Jodie Foster) reports in the course of learning to deal with mutilated bodies, gruesome crime scenes, and her own deep-seated fears. As a consequence of her interactions with the dour FBI administrator, Jack Crawford (Scott Glenn), and the charming sociopath, Dr. Hannibal Lecter (Anthony Hopkins), both of whom urge her to recognize crime solving as a forensically enhanced form of psychoanalysis, Clarice is able to track down the villainous serial killer, free his terrified captive, and transcend the childhood traumas that led her to pursue a career in law enforcement.

The film's central figures are obsessed with issues of character motivation, desperate to discover, for example, why the serial killer captures "big girls," cuts off sections of their flesh, and sticks exotic moths in their throats, as well as how trauma shapes the behavior both of psychopaths and of law enforcement officers. Given the characters' shared belief that detailed accounts of painful events reveal human motivation, Lecter's fascination with Clarice's childhood and her motives for joining the FBI is not surprising. Recognizing in her signs of acute psychological damage, Lecter gets Clarice to agree to an information-sharing arrangement: in exchange for providing her with his knowledge about his former patient, Billy, he demands a detailed account of the painful events from her childhood: "I tell you things, you tell me things. Not about this case though. About yourself. Quid pro quo." If the gruesome behavior of his former patient is the result of "years of systematic abuse," so, too, Lecter posits, are Clarice's law enforcement ambitions.

The film focuses on Clarice's attempts to follow the investigative trail from "a fledgling killer's [Billy's] first efforts at transformation," through his subsequent acts of mutilation and murder, and to his current location, where he has imprisoned a senator's daughter. During her investigation, she learns of Billy's use of a rare mutating insect to symbolize his period of gestation and the resultant achievement of what he hopes will be a less conflicted transgender identity. Billy, it could be argued, shares with Clarice a desire for transformation—in her case, from traumatized rural West Virginia orphan, to vulnerable raw trainee, to skilled investigator who kills the criminal and frees his captive despite the house's blinding darkness.

During her conversations with Lecter, Clarice describes two events that traumatized her when she was ten: (1) burglars' murder of her father, a town marshal and a widower who "had become the whole world to me," and (2) her own failed attempt two months later, as an orphan living on a "sheep and horse ranch in Montana" with relatives, to save lambs about to be slaughtered. Recollection is established as a major issue in their initial meeting, when, upon seeing Lecter's skillful recreations of picturesque locations in Europe, Clarice marvels at his ability to record "all that detail just from memory." In response to her crude attempts at flattery, Lecter replies, "Memory, Agent Starling, is what I have instead of a view." To become a great agent, she needs to understand the psyches of criminals, Lecter insists, which requires from the clearly unsettled Clarice not only the methodical study of case files but also learning to "listen carefully, [and] look deep within yourself." In other words, successfully tracking down the serial killer who is tormenting vulnerable young women requires that she mine the experiences that shaped her worldview, including—especially—her own "worst memory." According to Lecter, then, Clarice's self-revelation and careful listening will enable her to connect the past and present, herself and her prey. Her professional ambitions are inspired by her small-town West Virginia father's commitment to criminal apprehension; the film presents Clarice's memory of her father's body in a casket, a memory inspired by her seeing a dead man in a coffin at the funeral home she has entered to examine the corpse of one of Billy's victims. Metaphorically connecting her father, the man in the coffin, and the dead girl's body, as well as petty crime and pathology, Clarice makes a correlation between her father and Billy's victims, one that is later exploited by Lecter during exchanges with the agent that take the form of psychotherapy.

After discovering the origins of the exotic moth lodged in the victim's throat, Clarice goes again to question Lecter, who demands that she share with him her "worst memory of childhood" before he agrees to divulge additional information. In response, she discusses her father's murder and during a subsequent interview speaks of running away from the Montana ranch where she lived for two months with a relative and her husband when she was orphaned. Silencing Lecter's sexually sadistic line of questioning—"Did the rancher make you perform fellatio? Did he sodomize you?"—by insisting that the rancher "was a very decent man," Clarice acknowledges being traumatized by her father's murder and by her experiences on the ranch, where she was awakened one night by the screams of lambs being prepared for slaughter that sounded "like a child's voice." The then-ten-year-old Clarice "crept up into the barn. I was too scared to look inside but I had to." After failing to free the herd, she "took one lamb, and I ran away as fast as I could." Eventually found shivering by a sheriff "a few miles" away from the ranch, she was returned to the home of the rancher, who "was so angry that he sent me to live in an orphanage." Utterly unable to free the herd and to save the heavy lamb with which she escaped, she admits to Lecter the lingering impact of this event:

> Lecter: You still wake up sometimes, don't you, wake up in the dark and hear the screaming of the lambs?
>
> Clarice: Yes.
>
> Lecter: And you think if you save poor Catherine you can make them stop, don't you? You think if Catherine lives you won't wake up in the dark ever again to that awful screaming of the lambs.
>
> Clarice: I don't know. I don't know.
>
> Lecter: Thank you, Clarice. Thank you. . . . Brave Clarice, you will let me know when those lambs stop screaming, won't you?

If "what we see on the screen is in the act of happening," if film generally represents "the gesture itself, not an account of it," then these references to Clarice's past exemplify what it means to render the past as "gesture," or action represented, and "account," or what one character tells either another character or the viewer via the device of voice-over. In *The Silence of the Lambs*, these distinctive types of references to the past possess a clearly complementary, even interdependent, relationship. The film's brief scenes depicting, on the one hand, playful banter between a ten-year-old Clarice and her father and, on the other, her shocked expression as she approaches her dead father in his coffin, offer the viewer a context through which to register what Denby calls a "consciousness of suffering" that he claims is absent in *Beloved*'s blank present. Foster's communication of her character's painful memories—her harrowed expression, halting speech, and darting, tear-filled eyes—manifest anguish that establishes the memories' "presentness" as tangibly as its brief recreations of her father's return from failed efforts to catch criminals and her hesitant approach of his casket after he had himself become their victim. Having witnessed Clarice's account, Lecter surmises the nature of the novice agent's investment in this case: by rescuing Billy's captive, she hopes to "silence . . . the screaming . . . lambs" that haunt her troubled dreams and "wake [her] up in the dark."

Law enforcement, then, offers her a way to begin to resolve her childhood pain that leads her to connect her father's violent death to her inability to save lambs about to be slaughtered. Her accounts of these experiences to Lecter, along with the glimpses the film provides of her father and his funeral, enable the audience to comprehend Clarice's implication in the gruesome particulars of the serial killer's maladjusted self-transformation, and precisely why she is willing to risk life and limb both to end Billy's reign of terror and to rescue Catherine. This Demme film, then, successfully connects memory and crime detection, past and present, the traumatic pasts of the pursuer and the pursued in ways that create a compelling, cohesive narrative.

Demme's first post-*Lambs* release, *Philadelphia* (1993), is similarly focused on a unlikely association: between Andy Becker (Tom Hanks), a white gay male junior associate with a high-powered law firm whose partners fire him because they suspect he has AIDS, and Joe Miller (Denzel Washington), a proudly heterosexist, ambulance-chasing personal injury attorney who takes on Becker's discrimination suit after a number of more reputable lawyers refuse to represent him. As a consequence of Joe's eventual recognition of the fundamental decency of his client and his friends, lover, and family and of the anti-American nature of his own prejudices and biases, he is able to transcend his own and his heterosexual community's AIDS hysteria and rampant homophobia. Two scenes in particular, emphasizing the preservation of family history, challenge the rationality of homophobia and the AIDS hysteria of the 1980s and early 1990s, advancing a political agenda whose pursuit critics assert caused Demme to fail in *Beloved* to achieve a level of skillful storytelling that had previously distinguished his work.

In the first scene in question, Andrew and his lover Miguel (Antonio Banderas) have traveled to a family gathering that is being held in Andrew's childhood home in the Philadelphia suburb of Lower Merion. After using a minicam to record his lover's recollections of youthful play outside his home, Miguel films Andy embracing relatives, exchanges intended in this didactic film to waylay fears that the virus can be spread by casual contact. Andy then embraces his mother (Joanne Woodward), informing her that he's having "a good day" despite suffering from what we have learned is full-blown AIDS. When Andy leaves her to greet another family member, his mother's mask of joviality slips, an indication of the psychological burdens his medical condition has caused his family. The black-and-white video then pans from Mrs. Becker's pained expression to Andy's excitement when he learns of his sister's pregnancy from his young niece.

Challenging preconceptions that gay Americans necessarily experience painful childhoods and bitter homecomings, the amateur film's heartwarming images of familial love are followed by a meeting instigated by Andy, who warns his family members that his upcoming trial may be especially difficult for them because it will include lurid details of his personal life. Concerned about the possible negative ramifications of such exposure, he is willing to withdraw the lawsuit to spare his family's feelings. To a man and woman, they voice their staunch support, and when his pregnant sister articulates her concern over the emotional costs of the lawsuit on their parents, Mrs. Becker (Joanne Woodward) says that she has not raised her children "to sit in the back of the bus."

Mrs. Becker's phrase references the King-led Montgomery, Alabama, boycott that marshaled in the modern civil rights movement, from which images were widely disseminated, clarifying the urgency of black Americans' struggles. As Washington's character reminds the press at the start of Andy's trial, the United States' promises of life, liberty, and the pursuit of happiness for all of its citizens were authored in the City of Brotherly Love. At this and other moments in the film, Philadelphia is positioned as the mythic First City, the enduring symbol of democratic ideals and the nation's most resonant site of memory. Consequently, when its mayor, Ed Rendell, appears on screen to proclaim the city's commitment to work only with businesses that do not engage in discriminatory employment practices, the film's title, location, and subject matter cohere effectively. In Mrs. Beckett's reference to the Montgomery bus boycott, then, black and homosexual rights are analogized in such a way that audiences are compelled to assess their own willingness to abide un-American forms of discrimination against figures such as an extremely affable, self-effacing, self-described nonpolitical man like Andy. Indeed, the film encourages viewers to empathize with Andy, to whom virtually no homosexual male stereotype—effeminacy, promiscuity, far-leftist politics, familial alienation, heterophobia, and so on—applies. A fundamentally decent man blessed with an admirable family, an accomplished Ivy League–educated lawyer, Andy struggles at the end of his life to be afforded the rights that, less than a mile from City Hall, where his trial takes place, the Founding Fathers guaranteed him and all other tax-paying, law-abiding citizens.

This family gathering, then, takes on strong nationalist undertones, and the audience members are asked either to preserve the principles of America's grand experiment or to acknowledge that we possess the "caveman" attitudes of Joe's drinking buddies who harass him for defending a "tutti-frutti." Are we ideologically in cahoots with the law librarian who seeks to confine a clearly infirm Andy to a private room during his examination of documents concerning AIDS discrimination because the lawyer's appearance and fits of coughing disturb patrons, who are clearly worried about being contaminated? Or do we, like Joe, come to recognize the undemocratic illogic of our prejudices? Are we, like Joe, ultimately willing to challenge discriminatory practices both in public buildings and in our private lives? Joe's enlightenment is enabled, of course, by the fact that he is a member of a race that had itself been treated as if it were a threat to contaminate members of the dominant group—what other justification could there have been for "Whites Only" water foundations and lavatories?—and in need of constant surveillance. Indeed, Joe, initially afraid that the plastic-covered cigars he purchased to celebrate his daughter's birth are infected by Andy's touch, ultimately is able to adjust his client's oxygen mask and sit with him on what is clearly his deathbed.

In the second scene with which I am concerned, which also takes place in Becker's suburban Philadelphia home, Andy's friends and family gather to mark his passing and celebrate his life. The members of this eclectic group interact without the sense of the tensions between homosexual and heterosexual, black and white, AIDS-infected and uncontaminated that was prominent earlier in the film. They act, instead, as a grieving community, gathered to remember the life of a gifted, remarkably likable, fundamentally decent young man. This final gathering of otherwise disparate Philadelphians whose somber visages contrast with the joyful faces of racially and ethnically diverse residents in the film's opening montage that complements Bruce Springsteen's Oscar-winning song "The Streets of Philadelphia." Representing the city's various neighborhoods, like the eclectic group gathered in Lower Merion, any and all of these happy citizens may, as a consequence of the disease's rampant spread, be stricken or be called on to mourn the death of a ravaged loved one. The incorporation of Joe into Andy's beloved community is particularly noteworthy, given that he was plucked from a neighborhood quite distinct from Lower Merion and was initially hostile to defining aspects of Andy's life. But, the film insists, these characters are linked by what binds all Americans: a devotion to seeing the principles of the nation's founding documents applied to their loved ones and themselves.

As Andy's beloved community members interact, recorded images of his childhood flicker on the living room television. Featuring Andy as a boy surrounded and clearly nurtured by his adoring family—at the beach, dressed as a cowboy on Halloween and struggling with a huge jack-o'-lantern, and playing baseball—they show us a sweet, slightly reserved boy pursuing aspects of the quintessential middle-class white American boyhood as he is showered with familial love. Having seen him endure great physical pain because of his illness and inhumane treatment at the hands of his law firm's AIDS-phobic senior partners, having glimpsed the wonderful family from which he has sprung, the audience, which has been brought along with Joe into his inner circle, mourns his passing. Invited to join his beloved community and compelled, like Joe, the (black) American everyman, to question our prejudices and transcend our fears; watching scenes of Andy's earlier life, we aspire to be worthy of literal or figurative citizenship in the City of Brotherly Love, to be Americans who recognize connections between black struggles for civil rights and the ongoing struggle of gay and lesbian fellow citizens to be granted full brotherly and sisterly rights.

If *Beloved*'s failure prompted the end of Winfrey's acting career and discouraged her from investigating the legacy of slavery publicly, it also negatively affected the career of Jonathan Demme, whom Will Joyner speculated "has the most to lose" if the adaptation "ends up being considered an artistic failure" (1998, 13). If not widely recognized as a return to form, Demme's remake of *The Manchurian Candidate* (2003), the John Frankenheimer–directed 1962 film starring Frank Sinatra and Angela Lansbury, further demonstrates his investment in stories that interrogate the relationship between the present and the past. The remake stars Denzel Washington as Louis Marko, a traumatized Gulf War veteran; Liev Schreiber as Raymond Prentiss Shaw, his socially insecure former sergeant; and Meryl Streep as Shaw's manipulative mother, a long-time U.S. senator who browbeats her party's leaders into nominating her son, a congressman whose fabricated Gulf War heroism was literally implanted in his memory and those of his troop members, as its vice presidential candidate. Detailing an elaborate plan to corrupt the American democratic process that involves assassinating the party's presidential nominee before his victory speech so that the brainwashed Raymond can step into the most powerful office in the world, the film is deeply concerned with the uses of technology to enhance the malleability of memory.

If collective memory can be said to constitute coherent, strategically constructed, and thematically related narratives of the past around which members of a community structure crucial aspects of their lives, Demme's political thriller takes that concept a terrifying step further. Marko's military unit, the lives of whose members literally depend on each soldier's fulfillment of his assigned roles, is brainwashed by a sinister Manchurian Industries scientist to believe that Raymond single-handedly defeated a large contingent of Iraqi fighters and saved most of his troop from certain death. After memorizing this script, the survivors are implanted with microchips that reinforce the memory-distorting effects of the brainwashing. These soldiers' collective memory, then, does not preserve aspects of the group's past, but is invented by Manchurian business interests to propel Raymond's political career. Allowed no deviation from the implanted script, Corporal Al Melvin (Jeffrey Wright), who attends Marko's presentation to Boy Scouts about the Congressional Medal of Honor, recites verbatim the story they have been programmed to remember of Raymond's "reckless disregard for his own safety." Moreover, the scientist intervenes whenever Marko and Melvin exhibit what becomes dis-ease about incompatibilities between their waking recollections of Raymond's heroism and their vividly detailed nightmares of an ordeal that included torture, brainwashing, and intratroop murder.

The Manchurian Candidate critiques both the avarice of big business and the United States' lengthy military involvement in the Middle East. In addition, it is a cautionary tale about the manipulability of national memory. Demme's film concludes with Marko and Raymond, having gained some control over their memories and their actions, foiling the cartel's efforts to effect a coup by resisting commands that they eliminate the victorious presidential candidate. Marko, a skilled marksman, uses a single rifle shot to kill both Raymond, who seems unable to survive the shame he feels when he becomes aware of his behavior, and his politically and sexually manipulative mother, who accedes to Manchurian desires to alter her son's mind ("just a little bit," she rationalizes).

Like *Beloved*, then, *The Manchurian Candidate* is concerned with memory, repression, trauma, and the complexities of responding effectively to the return of the repressed. If Denby is correct that *Philadelphia* constitutes Demme's "penance for the gruesome, sensationally effective 'Silence of the Lambs,'" and if *Beloved* can also be seen as penance for an allegedly sordid blockbuster that takes "the form of a renunciation of storytelling itself" (Denby 1998, 250), *The Manchurian Candidate* might be characterized as an act of contrition. The film uses Demme's narrative strengths in the service of a subject—traumatic haunting—that is also at the center of Morrison's novel, which he fails to adapt successfully in large part because of his inability or refusal to depict the horrors of slavery sufficiently to illuminate what motivates Sethe's act of infanticide. The meanings and facts of the past in the latter film—in Corporal Melvin's obsessive records of his dreams; in lengthy flashbacks to scenes of both implanted memory and the troop's helplessness in the face of scientific reprogramming—are wholly subject to manipulation. However, the past cannot be erased permanently or reconstructed in the minds of those who have lived through it. Ultimately, authentic memory triumphs, as do the deep fraternal bonds between military men taught to protect the nation from threats such as the diabolic Manchurian plot to its democratic way of life.

Beloved's failure to grapple more effectively with the presence of the past is the result neither of Demme's being harnessed to the book, as the director accused Winfrey of being, nor of his inability to devise a compelling manner of depicting how the traumatic past affects the present. For the horrors of slavery that compel Sethe to murder her child to be felt deeply by a U.S. film audience, its members must be able to witness those horrors in illuminating detail. It is not enough to see the wound on Sethe's back. We must be shown its infliction if we are to comprehend the psychic pain she experienced during and as a consequence of her beating. It is not enough for Sethe to mention or even for the film to depict briefly the theft of her milk. We must be allowed to feel what that theft means to her, what precisely the milk represents within the structures both of her thinking about her slave experiences and of the film. Because *Beloved* fails at crucial points to provide such information, it does not allow its audiences to begin to understand the postemancipation sections that Demme's film preserves from Morrison's novel or to care as fully as they might about the strange occurrences that literally rock 124 Bluestone Road. Because the film leaves us barely cognizant of Sweet Home's horrors and because we cannot fully gauge the significance of the theft of Sethe's milk for her, like Paul D, we are forced to wonder why she resorted to infanticide and whether there was not, indeed, "some other way" for her to have protected her children. Thus, *Beloved* fails to become the film about slavery that Gleiberman believes America needs and that Winfrey claims she wanted to produce.

In *Journey to Beloved*, Winfrey emphasizes her intention to link her film and its source in terms of the quality of feeling they communicate. Morrison's novel, she felt, "allows you to feel what slavery was like; it doesn't just intellectually show you the picture. It puts a human face on it and makes it so personal you feel the pain. When I finish reading the book I felt I'd been into the interior of what it is like to have endured and come out of slavery" (Winfrey and Regan 1998, 19). If her "original intention in making BELOVED was that people would be able to feel deeply on a very personal level what it meant to be a slave, what slavery did to a people, and also to be liberated by that knowledge" (29), her film failed to reflect what Winfrey calls "the purest of my intentions, but not the only one" (29). While the film's ninety-five-day shoot was, according to Winfrey, "one of the best times of my life" (Heller 1998, A1), and while it brought in $15.5 million in revenue to the Philadelphia area and helped legitimize a film renaissance that began in 1992 when Mayor Rendell appointed Sharon Pinkenson as executive director of the Greater Philadelphia Film Office, it did not communicate "what it meant to be a slave, [and] what slavery did to a people."

At *Beloved*'s Philadelphia premiere, Winfrey talked about how warmly the city had embraced her, and she emphasized her connections in her ad for the Office of Tourism, in which she claims to have fallen "in love [with the city] when I was making a movie" (Von Bergen 1998). But certainly in May 2011, when she ended *The Oprah Winfrey Show* to devote her attention to the

Oprah Winfrey Network (OWN), her connections to Philadelphia, where her show aired at 4:00 P.M. on the local ABC affiliate, WPVI, seemed no more significant than those to numerous other major cities for whose residents she had been a daily late-afternoon presence. It is no coincidence, I believe, that she proclaimed a deep affinity with "her Philadelphia" at a time when she seemed to be actively pursuing multimedia ubiquity.

Perhaps the backlash of which I spoke earlier was a response to Winfrey's brazen empire building, which resulted in the birth of OWN. The critiques of such impulses perhaps reached their zenith in Jeff MacGregor's snarky *New York Times* article "Inner Peace, Empowerment and Host Worship." Characterizing the show as "a psychospiritual Reformation really, in which any attempt to entertain has been abandoned in favor of a search for Truth, Wellness and Reduced-Fat Snacks That Still Satisfy," he says of its most troubling aspects, whose emergence coincides with the release of *Beloved*:

> Gamely (if immodestly) titled "change your life TV," the show is devoted solely to the mind-numbing clichés of personal improvement. It is a self-help anthology, presented with the missionary zeal of someone who's already got hers. Thus it is about nothing so much as Ms. Winfrey herself, and her pilgrimage toward a more rewarding state of Oprahness. . . .
>
> Her regular appearances in the financial monthlies as one of the highest paid/most powerful people in entertainment are based on more than her performance as television's most beloved ubiquitous empath. She is a shrewd businesswoman too. Thus, like many gurus and circuit riders before her, Oprah has found a way to shamelessly market the history of her own misery and confusion as a form of worship.
>
> . . . Oprah cuts out the middleman and dispenses advice like a vending machine. . . . In fact, the entire show has become completely self-referential. (1998, 30)

After discussing Winfrey's "desultory" performance of her theme song, MacGregor distinguishes between two traits he believes were in evidence during the show's thirteenth season:

> The show has more in common these days with an Al-Anon meeting . . . than it does with any recognizable form of television talk show. Rather it is an hourlong interpretation of the Gospel According to Oprah. Shot through with the usual platitudes of New Age

unmeaning, there is talk of "empowerment" and "gratitude" and "getting to a better place." Homage is paid and prayers are offered to the "greater spirit." . . . Parables are told and conversions witnessed and the liturgy of ritualized victimization is pronounced. (1998, 30)

Aspiring to intellectual profundity and spiritual enlightenment, the show instead, in MacGregor's view, devolved into a quasi-religious revival whose essential message to its viewers is that they should emulate Oprah:

> Oprah's shows . . . encourage [us] . . . to relax like Oprah, to be good to ourselves like Oprah, to "journal our gratitude" like Oprah. . . .
>
> Oprah's solipsistic approach [results in] . . . a cryptoreligion of self, a systematized fixation on personal entitlement. Conveniently ignored is the fact that Oprah's self-examination is the product of her success, not vice versa.
>
> Mostly, though, this kind of navel-gazing seems to result in a myopic national selfishness wherein we trade our commonly agreed upon moral imperatives for the short-term comforts of our now in-contestable individual emotions. (I feel, therefore I am.) We want to feel good about ourselves, or at least better, sometimes at the cost of our best collective interests. (1998, 30)

For MacGregor, "the secret of her real success" is that "she was and is . . . a sly avatar of the holy possibilities of personal reinvention" (1998, 30). Many observers of the Oprah celebrity machine were skeptical of her efforts to help us "change our lives" and feel good about ourselves, points that were made over and over again on her show, on which she incessantly prodded her audience to embrace the host's perspectives.

Could her goal of teaching members of her talk-show audience to actualize their "best selves" have been achieved at the same time that her film asked Americans to imagine the horrors of slavery and their contemporary implications? In a nation whose citizens generally refuse to consider troubling aspects of its past, the subject was bound to force to the surface rifts even more profound than the ones Williamsburg experienced during its debates about reenactments of the auctioning of black bodies. Unlike her talk-show exhortations to discover and embrace the good, confronting slavery via her film meant awakening slumbering ghosts, acknowledging sins that the nation has categorically refused to repent, and fingering the jagged grain along America's racial divide. Engaging slavery seriously, in other words, invited us to feel bad about ourselves and our nation.

During the first months of the 1998–1999 television season, Winfrey, promoting painless healing in welcoming households and engaging her people's bottomless pain in mostly empty movie theaters, appeared to have been at a professional crossroads. *Journey to Beloved* indicates that she had contemplated ending her talk show when her contract expired in 1999 but concludes that she "would be a fool to give up the *Oprah Winfrey Show*" (Winfrey and Regan 1998, 68), which had proven unsatisfying to her in ways she does not articulate clearly. While speaking of turning "the remaining 2 years [of her contractual obligations to do the show] . . . into something special with enhanced leadership" (68), she later acknowledges that "before I started this movie I felt strongly that I could end the show" (148). And after citing a passage from Maya Angelou on slavery that insists that "we may yet survive our grotesque history," Winfrey writes, "So this is where I've come from. How dare I even think of quitting. Now I have a voice that can be heard around the world. I must find a way to say what needs to be heard" (119–120). At the very least, her comments—and her show's evangelical turn—suggest that, compared to the historical resonance and thematic weightiness of the film, *The Oprah Winfrey Show* had come to seem essentially frivolous.

But as sincere as Winfrey appeared to be about the evangelical mission of her talk show, it is fruitful to consider it in the context of her discussions of her "original intention in making *Beloved*." After insisting that she wanted viewers to understand "on a very personal level what it meant to be a slave, what slavery did to a people, and also to be liberated by that knowledge" (Winfrey and Regan 1998, 29), she acknowledges a less "pure," less altruistic motivation that she does not spell out. And following her claim that "most people are unaware of their intentions" because "they live subconsciously" and that she tries "to live consciously and to be aware of my intentions" (29), Winfrey avoids what "others around" her apparently saw: *Beloved* was the culmination of a ten-year process to manufacture "the right conditions" for her to play the sort of transcendent part that positions film actresses to receive Oscar nominations and other engaging roles.

The closest she comes in *Journey to Beloved* to addressing these motives is in her comparison of the joy she felt while making *Beloved* and *The Color Purple*. Clearly, there is a major difference between being a relative unknown working on her first movie set under the watchful eye of the most commercially successful director in film history and being, while she was making *Beloved*, "on the cover of *Life* magazine with a title that says I'm the most powerful person" (Winfrey and Regan 1998, 134). Her own vision and determination inspired the adaptation of Morrison's novel, and her own cultural capital helped her both to persuade the author to sell her the film rights and to secure a $65 million budget for a movie whose commercial potential was at best questionable. Despite the resultant pressures, Winfrey insists that she had "never felt so joyful as when I was working on BELOVED. The only time I've experienced this joy and challenge was during the making of *The Color Purple*. And during that time I felt, how could I top that dream! Then this happened" (29–30).

Beloved, then, enabled her to experience the sort of "joy and challenge" that no other professional endeavor—including her talk show—had offered her. Indeed, as she acknowledged while she was promoting *Beloved*, she had tried, with disastrous results, to use her show as a springboard to a successful acting career. Referencing her exhausting experience of acting in and executive-producing the short-lived weekly television series into which *The Women of Brewster Place* morphed at the same time that she was hosting her talk show, she admits, "I bought the [Harpo Films] studio with the idea that I'd finish the talk show, go to the next [sound] stage and put on the Brewster Place character's clothes" (Lawrence 2005, 50). If we consider *Beloved* as an opportunity for her to experience the joy that her participation in Spielberg's film engendered, we might be as skeptical as her employees of her proclamation that she considered *Beloved* a "on[c]e in a lifetime" experience that she had no intention of trying to repeat. Had this film been as commercially successfully and critically acclaimed as *The Color Purple*, Winfrey knew that she would have to choose between perfecting an evangelical talk show and pursuing a high-profile acting career. Her abandonment of the incomparable "joy and challenge" of acting following *Beloved* seemed also to have resulted from an astute calculation on her part of the vast discrepancy between her talk show's consistently high ratings and her film's anemic box office.[12]

In her review of *Journey to Beloved*, Lisa Schwarzbaum situates Winfrey in terms of history, race, geography, gender, and the enabling American myth of self-reinvention: "135 years after Abraham Lincoln signed the Emancipation Proclamation, Oprah Winfrey, a black woman from Kosciusko, Miss., reigns as one of the richest, most influential women in American popular culture" (1998). Insisting that Winfrey inspired the making of a film "that would not [otherwise] have been made," Schwarzbaum argues that her "astronomical American success" is "built on a public persona that extols such virtues of empathy, altruism, luck, introspection, common sense, savvy, honesty, believability, and hard work" (1998). But if Schwarzbaum concedes that Winfrey's is an American success story par excellence, she is also acutely aware that her endeavors often suffer because of her insistence on taking on a number of conflicting roles—"Oprah the mogul becomes Oprah the author" (1998)—and, hence, to occupy two or more distinct cultural roles simultaneously. The tensions between these roles are manifested in her self-consciousness throughout a book which is largely "about being Oprah Winfrey, that most empowered of free Americans, playing a slave" (1998). In addition, while Winfrey has proven to be a "compelling talker," her writing manifests that she is "hamstrung by the printed word" (1998). One way Winfrey might have approached the demands of her multiple roles, Schwarzbaum implies, was to have brought to them a core consistency. The roles she adopts in support of *Beloved*, and of her empire generally—"role model, business leader, tastemaker, regular woman fretting about her weight" (1998)—are daunting. And in *Journey to Beloved*, her efforts are not wholly successful because Winfrey does not assume that her readers, like her millions of regular talk-show viewers, "are already in her corner," and hence, she fails to "talk to [them in the comfortable, confident] . . . way she talks on TV" (1998).

But if P. David Marshall's formulations in *Celebrity and Power: Fame in Contemporary Culture* are persuasive, occupying prominent positions in various media—in this case, primarily television and film, as Winfrey does during October 1998—is inherently difficult, given the contrasting means of gaining, maintaining, and registering cultural capital in varied media. Whereas film celebrity, according to Marshall, "plays with aura through the construction of distance" from audiences, "the television celebrity is configured around conceptions of familiarity" (1997, 119):

> The television personality is surrounded by other messages that are unconnected to the narrative focus of his or her program. These disjunctures are normalized into the flow of television. The film star's filmic text is relatively integral, uninterrupted by other messages, other images. The film star maintains an integrity of being; the television star is pulled out of an aesthetic into the bare economics of production and consumption. Whereas the film celebrity maintains an aura of distinction, the television celebrity's aura of distinction is continually broken by the myriad messages and products that surround any television text. (121)

If Winfrey represents the quintessence of television celebrity "knowability" as opposed to movie star "mystery," the conflicts between the celebrity roles she attempted to occupy in 1998 are readily apparent. As Marshall notes, her "status as celebrity is connected to her continual presence on her eponymous daily nationally syndicated talk show," a fact that has significant consequences in terms of how she is perceived:

The television star who emerges as host and interpreter of the culture for the audience is treated as someone everyone has a right to know fully.... The talk-show host's opinions are obvious and forthright.... Where the film celebrity projects a number of public images through performances as an actor, the television talk-show host, though constructing a public persona, is also constructed as clearly presenting him- or herself.... The construction of sincerity and conviction is supposed to be part of the authentic host.... [T]he talk-show host is an example par excellence of the form of familiarized subjectivity that television constructs for its audience. (1997, 131–132)

By October 1998, what was familiar about Winfrey's "alluring, exciting personality," which is "structured to envelop the treatment of any issue" (133), was solutions-oriented certainty, best represented by the smile plastered on her face on the cover of every edition of the magazine *O*. The contemporary embodiment of the Horatio Alger myth, Winfrey performed a cultural role that was intricately connected to her promise to help us achieve the sorts of good feelings she appears to have achieved despite and because of myriad obstacles. Her certainty that good feelings can come out of trying experiences stands in stark contrast to the uncertainty, indeterminacy, unrelieved pain, and unmitigated suffering of the slave experiences she brought to the screen and attempted to embody in the form of *Beloved*. Positioning herself as indistinguishable, because of her hard-won knowledge, from the expert witnesses that her show continued to book (albeit more sporadically than before), her essential narrative, her cultural role, is to model pain's transcendence. But Morrisonian formulations of slavery's "rememory" offer a quite different challenge, one that is bound to leave unsatisfied those people Winfrey has inspired to seek quick fixes and to discourage pain-adverse viewers from following that sort of cultural work from the boob tube to the movie theaters.

Winfrey's is, in Marshall's words, "a personality that emerged from the more common people and maintained a sensitivity to their needs," and she has become "the channeling device for providing the form of dramatic tensions and resolutions between persons and issues" (1997, 143). However, slavery in Morrison's text and for a nation that has never confronted the still-festering wounds it created does not enable such "resolutions," and, hence, is not easily transformed into Winfrey's narrative of empowerment. In essence, it leaves U.S. citizens in a position of ultimate vulnerability because it exposes, and forces us to confront, the model democracy's unthinkable sin; its politically expedient Founding Fathers' complicity and cowardice; its white inhabitants' unchecked avarice and their descendants' creation of Jim Crow, a *de facto* second-class black citizenry; blacks' bafflement and rage at their shameful treatment largely because of the color of their skin; and whites' halting efforts to determine how they should feel about black American historical pain.

Ultimately, Winfrey was not able to promote good feeling and to exhibit enduring trauma simultaneously. If it is indeed the case, as Marshall argues, that "her reason for possessing an exalted status . . . is never secure and is always the subject of debate and inquiry" (P. David Marshall 1997, 143), it is not surprising that Winfrey chose talk-show platitudes over the challenges of an acting career. Following the major failure of her career as a national entertainer before her establishment of OWN, and her inability to seduce Americans to enter movie theaters to witness in *Beloved* the piecemeal representations of the lingering pain of slavery that survive the unavoidable violence of literary adaptation, Winfrey opted for the "blockbuster," "mainstream-pack-'em-in," feel-good format of her talk show. Just as her adaptation of *Their Eyes Were Watching God* excised Mrs. Turner's rants against dark-skinned blacks, Tea Cake's massive insecurity, and telling distinctions between "the dream" and "the truth," Winfrey banished the traumas of the slave past and the stain they left on the national consciousness from her evangelical mission. In her reconstituted vision, as carefully controlled as the Manchurian scientist's implantation of false memory, the dream and the truth appear to be virtually indistinguishable, even if, in time, the differences between them may become readily available and, moreover, painfully obvious.

Interestingly, the commercial and artistic failure of *Beloved*—the disappointment of which caused Winfrey, by her own admission, to eat thirty pounds of macaroni and cheese prepared by her private chef—is used as a reference point in analyses of the struggles faced by OWN, Winfrey's cable network that was launched during the last months of *Oprah*'s twenty-five-year run. For example, in an article about the network's sagging ratings, Javier David reminds us that "the accolades that followed her movie and television roles were no help to her movie adaptation of Beloved, which crashed and burned upon lift-off from the box-office" (2012). Indeed, according to Meagan Murphy, its wreckage continues to reverberate throughout her empire, where "the unspoken word . . . was 'Beloved,'" and "the big fear is that OWN is the new 'Beloved'" (2011). It is ironic that a project driven by Winfrey's (and, of course, Morrison's) need to uncover slavery's heretofore unspeakable horrors is now itself unspeakable in Winfrey's presence. Like the unsealed traumatic memories Paul D carries with him, *Beloved* is deemed a story not to pass on by her protective employees, even though, like slavery itself, signs of its haunting presence are, irrefutably, everywhere.

Conclusion

No Longer at Home?

In "A More Perfect Union," a March 18, 2008, speech delivered in the National Constitution Center, Barack Obama sought to quell concerns that his racial politics were shaped by the controversial views of his minister, Philadelphia native Jeremiah Wright. (Photo by Mike Mergen/Bloomberg via Getty Images.)

In an interdisciplinary collection focused on "the ambiguity of mourning and memory at century's end," James E. Young, a prominent figure in Holocaust studies, asks, "Just how does a city 'house' the memory of a people no longer at 'home' there?" (2000, 131). Recognizing the psychic challenges attendant to adding an extension to the Berlin Museum to showcase a people and a culture purged from a vital German city during the Holocaust—the extension would offer "no mere reintroduction of Jewish memory into Berlin's civic landscape but an excavation of memory already there but long suppressed" (131)—this question might also be asked in response to efforts of major U.S. cities and small towns following the civil rights movement to come to grips with their infamous historical contributions to black oppression. Philadelphia, an aggressive peddler of an inspiriting discourse of individual freedom, stands as a prominent physical and psychic site where the traumatic effects of racism on blacks who were never permitted to feel fully there at home are particularly acute.

Seeking a suitable way to describe "the free-floating anxiety that seems to accompany every act of Jewish memorialization in Germany today," Young settles on Freud's notion of the uncanny: "something which is familiar and old-established in the mind and which has become alienated from it only through the process of repression . . . ; something which ought to have remained hidden but has come to light" (130). What we might call the American racial uncanny inevitably accompanies anxious moments of national remembrance in the City of Brotherly Love such as the National Park Service's turn-of-the-century plans to build a new pavilion for the Liberty Bell in close proximity to the fabled Independence Hall. In January 2002, following years of Park Service planning of new lodgings for the bell, historian Edward Lawler, Jr. threw a wrench in the proceedings when his article "The President's House in Philadelphia: The Rediscovery of a Lost Landmark" (2002) was published in the *Pennsylvania Magazine of History and Biography*. Lawler unearthed evidence that the pavilion was scheduled to be built on the site of George Washington's presidential residence, whose slave quarters were positioned directly below its envisioned entrance. If Park Service plans for a new Liberty Bell enclosure were not altered, millions of unsuspecting tourists, traveling to the First City to reckon with its well-preserved structures and other artifacts of national freedom, would trample on willfully concealed evidence that while Washington struggled to actualize nascent dreams of representative government, his home was the site of a dramatic denial of liberty, legal personhood, and political standing.

In response to the controversy generated by Lawler's discovery, the agency initially insisted that, the grounds' historic significance notwithstanding, it intended to proceed with its plan to use them to provide "interpretation of the Liberty Bell," hoping, in the words of the *Philadelphia Inquirer*'s Stephan Salisbury, "literally [to] bury . . . an unpleasant past by not allowing an archaeological dig of the area" (2002, 1). Ultimately lost on no one, however, were the moral, historical, and political implications of concealing Washington's participation in the young nation's peculiar institution in order to house a bell that had been appropriated as the antislavery movement's most resonant symbol. Faced with challenges such as Mayor John Street's call for "earnest dialogue with the Park Service about how to address the issue of slavery on Independence Mall" and declarations from local, state, and national politicians urging it to recognize formally what historian Randall Miller called "the endless contradictions embedded in this site" (Salisbury and Saffon 2002, 1), a suitably chastened Park Service decided to find another location for the bell and to highlight the newly discovered house's uncanny historical complexity.

In the summer of 2011, when I visited the site with my wife, LaSonia, a Detroit native with an intense interest in black American historical suffering, I got to see firsthand the impact of the revised commemoration. The Liberty Bell has been moved southeast from its intended corner location, and the first president's former residence is recognized in an architecturally striking house without walls replete with weatherproof displays of slavery's cruel presence. Reckoning with the freedom dreams of both the father of our country and heretofore anonymous black aspirants, I looked cursorily at the exhibit, overwhelmed by memory and mixed emotion. I recalled the public restrooms that occupied this corner of Sixth and Market Street when I was a child, a corner that now rivals Logan Square, whose Art Museum's steps Rocky Balboa used to test his fitness, as the city's most visually appealing location. Looking briefly at LaSonia, I wondered how it might feel to experience this unparalleled site of national self-making as a tourist rather than as a grizzled veteran of anxious homecomings and welcomed departures.

Just minutes after we arrived at the President's House, my wife informed me that she could not stand anymore to be in such close proximity to the disquieting place where Washington's slaves had been forced to live. Perhaps because, for me, the city, ghost- and graveyard-filled, is a realm of vast commemoration for the illustrious, defamed, and anonymous alike, I am largely immune to the specific kind of psychic pain she experienced. As she stood, bewildered, within the open spaces of a disinterred house from which one could see both the fabled hall where U.S. independence had been theorized and the cramped, subterranean cells where it was denied, I focused on improvements to the cityscape and the willingness of officials finally to place the region's slave past front and center for tourists and passing citizens to ponder. I was impressed by the striking amalgam of new and old architecture, and native pride allowed me momentarily to ignore the pain of subjugated forebears and the incongruous, dishonorable fact of the First Father's slaveholding. And so, even as I fulfilled my marital and tribal obligations, expressing concern about my wife's indignation about Washington's ability to exalt (white immigrant) freedom while denying it to familiar black aspirants, I experienced a deep sense of regional and national pride in which I knew it was unwise to luxuriate.

As we walked away from the President's House, whose history substantiates Baby Suggs's claim in *Beloved* that "not a house in the country ain't packed to its rafters with some dead Negro's grief" (Morrison 1987, 5), La-Sonia confessed that she had felt as if she could touch, taste, and smell the residue of black people's lack of freedom. So I was hardly surprised that when we reached the Constitution Center, her mood became even more somber as we encountered a calligraphic inscription of the document's first three words, "We the People," etched ten times the size of the rest of the Preamble on the building's exterior. The stark juxtaposition of the Preamble's claims of national unity and Washington's exclusion of blacks moved her to tears. "We weren't 'the people' they had in mind," she sobbed, the ideal so painfully at odds with the first president's illiberal use of black bodies that she reacted as if the protective scab covering her soul's instantiation of our people's collective wound were being peeled slowly, methodically away. "We weren't the people they had in mind," she repeated, considering the rhetorical perversions of white men who excluded us from an imagined national community by inscribing black identity as permanently fractionated. After paying the steep entrance fee, we meandered through the center, marveling at descriptions of multiracial ingenuity and patriotism elucidating stunning photographs, statues, and film images, some of them records of familiar faces mouthing utterly familiar words. Still, we both felt a bit out of place. And I found myself wondering, in this space as devoted as the President's House to coming to terms with the American racial uncanny, just how does a city house the memory of a people *never* at home there?

The primary reason we visited the center was to see the site where Barack Obama's celebrated 2008 presidential campaign speech on race, "A More Perfect Union," had been delivered. Among other things, the then presidential candidate, exploiting Philadelphia's incomparable significance, insisted that the contemporary United States was indeed a welcoming home for black Americans. Having avoided making the subject of race a major focus of his campaign, Obama found himself forced to respond to assertions that his candidacy was untenable because of his association with Reverend Jeremiah Wright, who invoked scripture to support his claim that God damned the United States for its immoral treatment of nonwhite people. Obama also proposed felicitous future possibilities for "we the people" in light of the troubled racial history of an otherwise spectacularly successful nation. His choice of Philadelphia as the location placed him on the native grounds of his minister and acknowledged father figure. Curiously, while partaking of the city's symbolism, Obama ignores Wright's Philadelphia childhood as the scion of well-educated parents, including a father who, as the longtime pastor of Germantown's Hope Baptist Church, bequeathed to him a progressive religious mission. Thus, an oft-uprooted Obama transforms the minister into an estranged black everyman whose critique of the United States is a function of misplaced personal bitterness in order to demonstrate that his own unconventional identity and personal history are quintessentially American.

In describing the source of Wright's disappointment with the United States, "A More Perfect Union" asserts that the minister's invective underscores the importance for blacks of acknowledging "the burdens of our past without becoming victims of our past" (Obama 2009, 246). Compelling us to instruct "our children . . . that while they may face challenges and discrimination in their own lives, they must never succumb to despair or cynicism" and "that they can write their own destiny" (247)—the very message, I imagine, that parents imparted to a young Jeremiah, who shares a name with the biblical prophet whom God warned, "Attack you they will, overcome you they can't"—the speech argues that the minister's concern with placing contemporary black American challenges into an exclusively racial context leads him to ignore how these challenges are shared by nonblacks. That failure, for Obama, is the result of Wright's view that the United States still manifested the racism of its "tragic past":

> The profound mistake of Reverend Wright's sermons is not that he spoke about racism in our society. It's that he spoke as if our society was static; as if no progress has been made; as if this country—a country that has made it possible for one of his own members to run for the highest office in the land and build a coalition of white and black; Latino and Asian, rich and poor, young and old—is still irrevocably bound to a tragic past. But what we know—what we have seen—is that America can change. That is the true genius of this nation. What we have already achieved gives us hope—the audacity to hope—for what we can and must achieve tomorrow. (Obama 2009, 247)

Digging deeply into the nation's store of governing formulations, Obama references its founding motto, *E pluribus unum*, insisting that Americans "cannot solve the challenges of our time unless . . . we perfect our union by understanding that we may have different stories, but we hold common hopes" (238).

Ultimately, however, Obama expresses a faith in the American narrative of progress that his own wife suggested a month before her husband's Philadelphia speech that she has not always shared. According to Michelle Obama, who carries "within her the blood of slaves and slaveowners" (Obama 2009, 238), her husband's initial presidential campaign marked the first time in her adult life that she was "proud of my country because it feels like hope is finally making a comeback" (Thomas 2008). Characterizing the period covered in this study, the racially divisive post–civil rights era, as singularly uninspiring, she admits that she had "been desperate to see our country moving in that direction [of progressive change that her husband's campaign promised] and just not feeling so alone in my frustration and disappointment" (Thomas 2008). Of course, she knew full well that she was not alone in that desperation, having heard similar sentiments concerning the impoverishment, hopelessness, and damnable aspects of U.S. political and social life articulated by Wright, her longtime minister, as she sat next to her husband in the pews of Chicago's Trinity United Church of Christ.

Taken together, these varied statements concerning the nation's commitment to its ideals reflect the persistent dilemma at the heart of black American identity. Its inherent contradictions are evident, for example, in Obama's claim that race is "an issue . . . this nation cannot afford to ignore" (Obama 2009, 242) before his first term as president. Once in that office, however, he seemed to ignore the politics of race except when he chastised the Congressional Black Caucus for critiquing his commitments, and when news coverage of controversies associated with Harvard's Henry Louis Gates, Jr. and the USDA's Shirley Sherrod compelled him into an embarrassing Beer Summit and an excruciating apology, respectively. Faced with challenges such as a disastrous economy, massive military involvement in the Middle East, health care, Tea Party intransigence, and a Gulf Coast natural disaster, perhaps President Obama felt he had no choice during his first term but to ignore what candidate Obama had deemed the United States' desperate need for racial healing.

Ultimately, Wright's and Obama's rancorous disagreement is focused on the precise nature of the contemporary United States' racial dilemma and how the blood-soaked past shapes—or ought to shape—black American perspectives in the present. Scholars encourage us to consider this dilemma as at least partly a function of the traumatic black American cultural past whose psychic scars cannot be wholly and definitively healed, continuing to shape our responses to and relationship with the Land of Opportunity that has also been the cause of our racial nightmares. Unable at times to distinguish between remembered and imagined danger, black Americans often seem to experience the altered reality of which Obama is justly proud as indistinguishable from the brutal, murderous past when our people could be and were maimed with impunity. As a result, even the suggestion of racial animus sometimes operates as a trigger for black Americans, who remain susceptible to perceiving slight or nonexistent threats as soul-shatteringly dangerous.

My own twenty-first-century encounter with the American racial uncanny as exhibited in Colonial and contemporary Philadelphia suggests that—to invoke Obama's paraphrasing of Faulkner—"the [racial] past isn't dead and buried" (Obama 2009, 243). But what, precisely, ought we make of perceived connections between what Obama speaks of as "the history of racial injustice in this country" and the continuing "disparities that exist in the African-American community today [that] can be directly traced to inequalities passed on from an earlier generation that suffered under the brutal legacy of slavery and Jim Crow" (243)? According to Obama, Wright's caustic assessments demonstrate that he has not learned—as Ralph Ellison urges in his compelling definition of the blues—to transcend his and his race's black-and-blue experiences, which remain too "alive in [his] achieving consciousness . . . to finger the jagged grain" (Ellison 1964, 91) of the contemporary racial landscape lyrically, as it were.

Wright's vision might accurately be viewed as traumatic, a blues note without resolution. Still, Obama's calls for both the explorations of the vagrancies of what Ellison terms our "brutal experience" (91) and efforts to rise above the resultant pain may seem premature, particularly since his own administration, like those of his predecessors, has failed to meet the challenges presented by our racial history. According to Roy Brooks's *Atonement and Forgiveness: A New Model for Black Reparations*, black American forgiveness of the United States for its racial sins "is morally objectionable" (2004, 168) unless and until the nation atones for the nightmare it created, turned a blind eye to, and justified using racist scientific and religious perspectives. Its historic importance and symbolic hold on the contemporary imagination position Philadelphia as a site where democratic promises are proffered, contextualized, mythologized, tested, resisted, rejected, and wholeheartedly embraced. The 2012 Republican presidential primary season yielded a motley band of candidates who confirm the view offered in "A More Perfect Union" of the persistence of white "anger over [urban crime,] welfare and affirmative action [that] helped forge the Reagan Coalition" (Obama 2009, 245). This anger is exemplified by the reactions of conservative debate audiences in response to former Speaker of the House Newt Gingrich, who employed racially incendiary language in characterizing Obama as the "food stamp president" (Bjerga and Oldham 2012).

As I write this Conclusion, after Obama has served three years in office but before his own reelection campaign is set to begin in earnest, I do not know if President Obama will refrain, as he did in his 2008 Philadelphia speech, from calling such sentiments "misguided or even racist" or if he will continue to insist that "they are grounded in legitimate concerns" (Obama 2009, 246). If he responds, he will certainly have in mind stirring words composed in Philadelphia that wrote a democratic nation into being. When he campaigns in my hometown, I hope that, before his obligatory exodus to the Italian Market to sample Pat's or Geno's cheesesteaks, he will consider Washington's slaves and the choice of the city's third black mayor, Michael Nutter, to put a $20,000 bounty on the heads of violent offenders and to employ law-and-order rhetoric reminiscent of Frank Rizzo in a desperate attempt to curb the early 2012 black-on-black homicide epidemic that has returned Philadelphia criminality to the national news. Recognizing that he is seen alternatively as the actualization of prophetic civil rights vision and as evil incarnate for those afflicted by white fear of black American difference, perhaps the president's sojourn to the City of Brotherly Love will inspire from him a candid assessment of the willingness of Gingrich and his ilk to expose their lack of deep compassion for the suffering of black Americans, compassion that nominally is a governing feature of Philadelphia's—and the nation's—character.

Notes

PREFACE

1. See Matthew Countryman's *Up South* (2007) for an excellent discussion of black Philadelphians' participation in civil rights struggles in the City of Brotherly Love.

2. My description of black Americans echoes "Streets of Philadelphia," Bruce Springsteen's transfixing contribution to the soundtrack to the Jonathan Demme film *Philadelphia*.

INTRODUCTION

1. Similar accounts appear, for example, in Sylvia Winter's and Houston Baker's contributions to *A Companion to African-American Studies* (2006).

2. For more extensive discussions of the implications of the Rodney King video and verdicts, see Gooding-Williams 1993 and Anna Smith 2002.

3. For an earlier discussion of Erikson and black American cultural trauma, see Awkward 2009, 37–46.

4. One of the most provocative discussions of American cultural or collective memory is offered by Marita Sturken (1997).

5. The profound hold this murder has had on the U.S. psyche is perhaps best evinced in Christopher Metress's riveting documentary history *The Lynching of Emmett Till* (2002).

CHAPTER 1

1. The list includes, in addition to King and the Kennedy brothers, Medgar Evers, Malcolm X, Patrice Lumumba, and two prominent white racists—George Lincoln Rockwell, the leader of the American Nazi Party, and Hendrik Verwoerd, the prime minister of South Africa and a major architect of apartheid.

2. For a riveting account of Atlanta's—and the nation's—commemoration of King, see Burns 2011.

3. A particularly revealing account of the life and career of this athlete and social activist is found in Rampersad 1998.

4. In 2012, after thirty years of eligibility, Walker was inducted into the Basketball Hall of Fame, voted in by the Springfield, Massachusetts, shrine's Veteran's Committee. He joins the other key contributors to the transcendent 1966–1967 championship 76er team: Wilt Chamberlain, Billy Cunningham, and Hal Greer.

5. For an entertaining take on the upstart ABA, which the NBA later absorbed after years of bitter rivalry, see Pluto 1991.

6. See also Connery 1968.

7. For example, in *Hole in Our Soul*, Martha Bayles cites Peter Guralnick's discussion of "why Southern soul broke up in 1968: It was in April of that year that Martin Luther King, Jr., was assassinated—in Memphis. As Guralnick reports, the event was traumatic for everyone at Stax. For example, the black songwriter Isaac Hayes told him: 'I couldn't write for about a year—I was filled with so much bitterness and anguish'" (1994, 265).

CHAPTER 2

1. For an excellent study of the burdens and benefits of this visionary program, see Zweigenhalf and Domhoff 1991.

2. Another nostalgic Philadelphia mother song from the period is the Spinners' "Sadie." Insisting that self-negating maternal sacrifice has become rare, it is "dedicated to those who cherish that memory" of devoted young mothers who sacrificed their dreams so that their children would have a chance to thrive—children whose difficult adulthoods compel them to yearn for those sweet but trying times when their mothers absorbed all their aches and pains.

3. In R&B music, the idea of domestic imprisonment drives Laura Lee's hypnotic minor 1971 hit that claims that often, for women, "wedlock is a padlock."

4. This historical turn is evident in literature (best represented, perhaps, by Toni Morrison's first three novels, *The Bluest Eye* [(1970) 1994], *Sula* [1973], and *Song of Solomon* [1977]), in filmic depictions of earlier eras (*Sounder* [1972], *Roots* [1977], *Cooley High* [1975], and *Lady Sings the Blues* [1972]), and in back-to-nature songs by urban-centered groups (including two Philadelphia songs, the Ebonys' "Life in the Country" and the Stylistics' "Country Living," along with War's instrumental "City, Country, City").

5. Darlene's recognition of her limited "part of the drama" confirms Easthope's belief that often, in the performance of masculinity, "men are really more concerned about other men than about women at all" (Easthope 1990, 6).

6. One feature of this "New Land" may be that it is a place where black masculinity can assert itself or, at the very least, not feel confined within a social space, domestic or otherwise (A. Wilson 1986, 51, 50). And while black paternal desertion may have significant economic and especially psychological costs for family members, including the abandoned son, these literary explorations suggest some of the risks that accompany the decision of the "free" black man to remain within familial spaces. In the case of Wilson's drama, that decision leads to the psychological and/or physical abuse of

two generations of sons, among other things; in Cholly's case, it leads, most tragically, to his sexual abuse of his daughter, Pecola, whom he "love[d] . . . enough to touch . . . , envelop . . . , give something of himself to" and whose "matrix of . . . agony" he "filled . . . with death" (Morrison [1970] 1994, 163).

7. I reference here the title of famed Stax producer David Porter's 1971 concept album that stages the beginning, end, and possible resumption of a couple's pain-filled love affair. The album cover features the performer seated on a drum and dressed in a red and purple clown suit. As we see later, the notion of the male lover as clown recurs frequently in these songs of heartbreak.

8. Such sentiments also appear in Marvin Gaye's "Heard It through the Grapevine," in which the cuckolded protagonist insists, "I know a man ain't supposed to cry," and the Temptations' "I Wish It Would Rain," in which the deserted male lover describes his "tear-stained face pressed against the windowpane," searching the skies for rain that will "hide [his] teardrops."

9. As is the case in the fabled deathbed scene in Ralph Ellison's Invisible Man, Patches is offered by his male progenitor instructions for living that amount to a curse, even if it is not clear that his selfless devotion to his father allows him to experience them as such. And though dissemblance figures prominently in both instances, in "Patches," it serves not as a treacherous act in an undeclared war against one's oppressors, as in the case of the novel's patriarch, but as part of an arsenal of impoverished gendered behavior, the most logical outcome of which is one's own self-destruction. Notice the truly defensive elements of the grandfather's practice that have no equivalent in Carter's song:

> Our life is a war and I have been a traitor all my born days, a spy in the enemy's country ever since I give up my gun back in the Reconstruction. Live with your head in the lion's mouth. I want you to overcome 'em with yeses, undermine 'em with grins, agree 'em to death and destruction, let 'em swoller you till they vomit or bust wide open. (Ellison [1952] 1995, 16)

In effect, the grandfather pursues social advancement through a form of black masculine dissemblance that we can connect to folkloric trickster figures—to black minstrel performers who before World War II dominated popular perception of Afro-American theatricality, turning what may have been well-disguised racial animus into profitable art—and to R&B music's miraculous male clowns who roam love's bloody battlefields. There is a sense of playfulness in the grandfather's description of disguise that is virtually absent from the deadly serious gendered practices and generational instructions of "Patches."

10. In a book that serves as both autobiography and group history, Otis Williams speaks suggestively about the power of the pop producer during this period to determine the direction of the musical output of even very successful acts like the Temptations. The cowriter and producer of both "Rolling Stone" and "Masterpiece" was Norman Whitfield, who created songs for the group such as "Cloud Nine," "Runaway Child, Running Wild," and "Ball of Confusion," which placed the quintet at the forefront of popular artists who were engaged in socially conscious musical expression. However, tensions between the group and the producer emerged in part because the members quickly became "so damned sick of this kind of song. We begged to go back to ballads" (Williams and Romanowski 1989, 158). And if such comments help us recognize the

limitations of social protest in the views of pop acts like the Temptations, Williams's comments about lead singer Dennis Edwards's resistance to "Rolling Stone" offer some perspective on the challenges of performing others' words. Williams tells us:

> Adding the icing to the cake were the opening lyrics—"It was the third of September, the day I'll always remember, 'cause that was the day when my daddy died." They didn't sit too well with Dennis, since his father had died on the third of September. The whole time we were recording it, we were five very angry guys, and Dennis sang it through clenched teeth. We walked out of the studio that night furious and certain that "Papa" wasn't going to do anything. Once it flopped, we figured, they'd have to let us go back to singing about romance. (158)

11. In June 2009, led by Tom Harkin, the U.S. Senate passed a nonbinding but highly symbolic resolution acknowledging the nation's historic wrongs against black Americans. It read in part:

> An apology for centuries of brutal dehumanization and injustices cannot erase the past, but confession of the wrongs committed and a formal apology to African-Americans will help bind the wounds of the Nation that are rooted in slavery and can speed racial healing and reconciliation and help the people of the United States understand the past and honor the history of all people of the United States. (Fears 2008)

CHAPTER 3

1. See, for example, Anderson and Hevenor 1990 and Harry 1987.

2. One sign of the attitudinal divide between the black center and its more affluent margin is the embrace by young inner-city residents of what, following the lead of the influential rap group N.W.A, among others, we could term "gangsta, gangsta" cultural politics. In *Am I Black Enough for You?* Todd Boyd argues that the thematic concerns of gangsta cinema like *Boyz n the Hood* and *Menace II Society* are largely derived from the dominant filmic representations of white gangsters. These gangsters, who have emerged as romantic figures in American popular culture, are depicted as self-empowered social outsiders who embrace organized crime in part because of the difficulties they confront as members of marginalized groups in accessing legitimate means of achieving the dream of American material success. According to Boyd, the most accomplished and influential of these films for gangsta cinema, the first two installments of the *Godfather* trilogy, suggest that

> oppression forced these Italian immigrants into a subversive lifestyle and economy much like that practiced throughout southern Italy, especially in Sicily. Borrowing from their own cultural tradition, some of these new Americans used the underground economy as a vital means of sustenance in the face of ethnic, religious, and cultural oppression. And though their desire, being heavily influenced by the discourse of an "American dream," was to ultimately be fully assimilated into American society, the achievement of this desire was revealed to be at the cost of losing their ethnic and cultural heritage. (1997, 84–85)

Unlike the assimilationist trajectories Boyd witnesses in these films, full social incorporation is represented as neither desirable nor possible in gangsta cinema. In John Singleton's and the Hughes brothers' debut works, for example, much of the thematic power derives from the directors' reliance on juxtapositions of the 'hood and its spatial and cultural obverse, the white man's land, suggesting that the antisocial rituals that dominate both gangsta and middle-class imaginings of ghetto spaces—including theft, drugs, and murder—have a seductive charm in part because of these citizens' keen awareness of mainstream social, educational, and workplace Afrophilia. In such films, efforts to embrace mainstream values signal a naïveté about the realities of urban, lower-class black life, as in the case of *Menace II Society*, or a manifestation of racial betrayal, as in the case of *Boyz n the Hood*. The pursuit of mainstream success, in other words, brings along with it the potential loss of (black American) place.

3. Writing perceptively of the difficulty of dealing "with the devilish impenetrability of social space, with our bodies' temptation to misremember the categorical struggles that have founded our world," Yaeger speaks of "the additional pressure of what is hidden, encrypted, repressed, or unspoken in global and local histories" (1996, 25). If social space "attempt[s] to be thematic or real, to convince us of its solidity or authenticity" (25), it is, as a consequence of the interpretive efforts of those who have sought to delimit its character, occupied, as it were, by a plethora of competing inscriptions of its constitutive meanings. While we may become aware of as many of a themed space's clearly mapped and "encrypted" meanings as possible, we are obligated by our acknowledgment of that space's conceptual power to recognize that once we have chosen to embrace one set of group qualities over its competitors, we have settled, at least temporarily, the matter of the meaning of (national, racial, gendered, class, etc.) identity. For, as Yaeger states, "to treat something as real is to endorse it" (25).

4. Lee's novel was published three years after Toni Morrison appeared on the cover of *Newsweek* in anticipation of the publication of her fourth novel, *Tar Baby*; two years after the publication of *The Color Purple*, the Pulitzer Prize–winning epistolary narrative by Alice Walker that sold millions of copies and engendered a controversial Steven Spielberg film, which I discuss in Chapter 4; and just after the publication of Barbara Christian's *Black Women Novelists*, the first book devoted to the subject of a black woman's literary tradition. In addition, Lee's novel appeared just after Mary Helen Washington's canon-establishing anthologies of black women's writing, *Black-Eyed Susans* and *Midnight Birds*; *Conjuring*, the essay collection coedited by Hortense Spillers and Marjorie Pryse that explores the nuances of black women's literary traditions; and Claudia Tate's indispensable "conversations," *Black Women Writers at Work*, and in the same year as Mari Evans's important collection, *Black Women Writers (1950–1980)*.

5. I have much more to say later in the chapter about the use of photography in particular and of visual representation generally as thematic and marketing features of *Sarah Phillips*.

6. For an extensive discussion of these matters, see Gates 1984, 3.

7. As we see later, in the estimation of postmodernist theorist Jean-François Lyotard (1982), these advances challenge painting's status as a representational art, creating the conditions for a lengthy, mesmerizing swerve away from thematic and formal decipherability.

8. See Reinhold 1971.

9. For a compelling analysis of Philadelphia as an active site of civil rights agitation, see Countryman 2007.

10. See Zweigenhalf and Domhoff 1991.

11. The novel, however, has been the subject of several interesting analyses during the last few years. See, for example, Hogue 1994, McCormick 2004, and Thompson 2009.

CHAPTER 4

1. For an engaging discussion of this issue, see Wu 2008.

2. I discuss this calling in *Scenes of Instruction* (Awkward 2000, 9–12), and I analyze *The Bluest Eye* at length in *Inspiriting Influences* (Awkward 1989, 57–96).

3. See, for example, Manso 1998.

4. Vicki Abt and Leonard Mustazza's *Coming after Oprah* (1997) offers the most extensive discussion of the freak-show nature of the genre of the talk show both before and after Winfrey's adoption of a quasi-messianic agenda in the mid-1990s.

5. The mission of the Greater Philadelphia Film Office (GPFO), according to its website, involves working "to attract film & video production to the region, including everything from feature films to TV commercials to music videos and industrial films," "cutting [through] red tape" for the companies who choose to film in the city, and expanding "the local film and video industry in every way possible, recognizing its huge economic impact in job creation and its unparalleled public relations effects for the region" (Greater Philadelphia Film Office, n.d.).

6. According to its website, the Greater Philadelphia Tourism Marketing Corporation (GPTMC) celebrated its fifteenth anniversary in 2011. "Since GPTMC began promoting Philadelphia and The Countryside® as a premier leisure destination in 1996, the region now welcomes 10 million more leisure travelers a year than it did before the organization launched its first campaign. This boost in visitation has supported the tremendous growth in Philadelphia's tourism, cultural, historical, dining, shopping, outdoor, music and nightlife scenes" (Greater Philadelphia Tourism Marketing Corporation, n.d.). In the commercial in which Winfrey articulates her undying love for the First City, she says, in part, "I confess I fell in love when I was making a movie. It happened in Philadelphia. When I fell, I fell hard." After listing the aspects of the city with which she grew especially enamored—including one of the zoo's bears, a suburban museum (Brandywine), and "all my new jogging buddies from Fairmount"—she concludes by insisting that she has offered viewers "my Philadelphia," which tourists will "love . . . honey, and it'll love you back."

7. Clearly, Winfrey's perspectives are infinitely closer to King's than to those of Black Power advocates.

8. See, for example, the essays by Trudier Harris and Houston A. Baker, Jr. in Kinnamon 1990.

9. For a more extensive exploration of the textual controversies about issues over which Winfrey glibly skims, see Awkward 1990, 1–28.

10. Henry Louis Gates, Jr. discusses the novel's Standard and black American vernacular English registers in Gates 1988, 170–216. Nanny's discussion of her experiences as a slave and their impact on her rearing of Janie appears on pages 16–20 in the novel.

For an astute exploration of the "coupling convention" with regard to Hurston's novel, see duCille 1993, 115–123. For an analysis of the relationship between Janie and Tea Cake, see Awkward 1989, 30–53.

11. Kelley Penfield Lewis provides an astute reading of Winfrey's emphasis on satisfyingly upbeat conclusions, insisting that "selected books [on her book club list] contend with the Oprah narrative [of personal, Algeresque triumph]; readers must read through the template proposed by Oprah in order to access the text. Oprah's personal narrative overlays the Book Club Selection, creating a kind of palimpsest that potentially obscures reader response" (2008, 211).

12. In August 2012, despite the struggles of the Oprah Winfrey Network, Winfrey returned to acting. She will be appearing in the movie *The Butler*, starring Forest Whitaker, which documents the career of a black White House butler who served eight American presidents.

References

Abt, Vicki, and Leonard Mustazza. 1997. *Coming after Oprah: Cultural Fallout in the Age of the TV Talk Show.* Madison, WI: Popular Press.

Abt, Vicki, and Mel Seesholtz. 1994. "The Shameless World of Phil, Sally, and Oprah: Television Talk Shows and the Deconstruction of Society." *Journal of Popular Culture* 28 (1): 171–191.

Adams, Carolyn, David Bartelt, David Elesh, Ira Goldstein, Nancy Kleniewski, and William Yancey. 1991. *Philadelphia: Neighborhoods, Division, and Conflict in a Postindustrial City.* Philadelphia: Temple University Press.

Anderson, John, and Hilary Hevenor. 1990. *Burning Down the House: MOVE and the Tragedy of Philadelphia.* New York: Norton.

Arblaster, Anthony. 1984. *The Rise and Decline of Western Liberalism.* Oxford: Blackwell.

Awkward, Michael. 1989. *Inspiriting Influences: Tradition, Revision, and Afro-American Women's Novels.* New York: Columbia University Press.

———, ed. 1990. *New Essays on "Their Eyes Were Watching God."* New York: Cambridge University Press.

———. 2000. *Scenes of Instruction: A Memoir.* Durham, NC: Duke University Press.

———. 2009. *Burying Don Imus: Anatomy of a Scapegoat.* Minneapolis: University of Minnesota Press.

Baker, Houston A. 1984. *Blues, Ideology, and Afro-American Literature: A Vernacular Theory.* Chicago: University of Chicago Press.

———. 1990. "Richard Wright and the Dynamics of Place." In *New Essays on "Native Son,"* edited by Keneth Kinnamon, 85–116. New York: Cambridge University Press.

———. 2006. "My First Acquaintance with Black Studies: A Yale Story." In *A Companion to African-American Studies,* edited by Lewis R. Gordon and Jane Anna Gordon, 3–19. Malden, MA: Blackwell.

Bal, Mieke. 1999. "Introduction." In *Acts of Memory: Cultural Recall in the Present*, edited by Mieke Bal, Jonathan V. Crewe, and Leo Spitzer, vii–xvii. Hanover, NH: University Press of New England.

Baldwin, James. 1953. *Go Tell It on the Mountain.* New York: Dell.

Bass, Amy. 2002. *Not the Triumph but the Struggle: The 1968 Olympics and the Making of the Black Athlete.* Minneapolis: University of Minnesota Press.

Bayles, Martha. 1994. *Hole in Our Soul: The Loss of Beauty and Meaning in American Popular Music.* New York: Free Press.

Beja, Morris. *Film and Literature.* 1979. Upper Saddle River, NJ: Prentice Hall.

Bennett, Andy. 2000. *Popular Music and Youth Culture: Music, Identity and Place.* Basingstoke, UK: Palgrave Macmillan.

Bjerga, Alan, and Jennifer Oldham. 2012. "Gingrich Calling Obama 'Food-Stamp President' Draws Critics." *Bloomberg Businessweek*, January 25. Available at http://www.businessweek.com/news/2012-01-25/gingrich-calling-obama-food-stamp-president-draws-critics.html.

Boyd, Todd. 1997. *Am I Black Enough For You? Popular Culture from the 'Hood and Beyond.* Bloomington: Indiana University Press.

Boym, Svetlana. 2001. *The Future of Nostalgia.* New York: Basic Books.

Boyz n the Hood. 1991. Directed by John Singleton. Columbia Pictures.

Brackett, David. 2000. *Interpreting Popular Music.* Berkeley: University of California Press.

Brooks, Roy. 2004. *Atonement and Forgiveness: A New Model for Black Reparations.* Berkeley: University of California Press.

Brown, James, and Marc Eliot. 2005. *I Feel Good: A Memoir of a Life of Soul.* New York: New American Library.

Brown, James, and Bruce Tucker. 1986. *James Brown: The Godfather of Soul.* New York: Da Capo Press.

Bruton, Mike. 1986. "The Sixers of '66–67: A Team for All Time." *Philadelphia Inquirer*, October 26, p. D1.

Burlein, Ann. 1999. "Countermemory on the Right: The Case of Focus on the Family." In *Acts of Memory: Cultural Recall in the Present*, edited by Mieke Bal, Jonathan V. Crewe, and Leo Spitzer, 208–217. Hanover, NH: University Press of New England.

Burns, Rebecca. 2011. *Burial for a King: Martin Luther King Jr.'s Funeral and the Week That Transformed Atlanta and Rocked the Nation.* New York: Scribner.

Caruth, Cathy. 1995. "Preface." In *Trauma: Explorations in Memory*, edited by Cathy Caruth, vii–ix. Baltimore: Johns Hopkins University Press.

———. 1996. *Unclaimed Experience: Trauma, Narrative, and History.* Baltimore: Johns Hopkins University Press.

Cleaver, Eldridge. 1968. *Soul on Ice.* New York: Dell.

Cole, Johnetta B. 2004. "Black Studies in Liberal Arts Education." In *The Black Studies Reader*, edited by Jacqueline Bobo, Cynthia Hudley, and Claudine Michel, 21–34. New York: Routledge.

Collins, Jim. 1989. *Uncommon Cultures: Popular Culture and Post-Modernism.* New York: Routledge.

Connery, R. H. 1968. *Urban Riots: Violence and Social Change.* New York: Vintage Books.

Cooley High. 1975. Directed by Michael Schultz. American International Pictures.

Cose, Ellis. 1993. *The Rage of a Privileged Class*. New York: HarperCollins.

Countryman, Matthew. 2007. *Up South: Civil Rights and Black Power in Philadelphia*. Philadelphia: University of Pennsylvania Press.

Cresswell, Tim. 1996. *In Place/Out of Place: Geography, Ideology, and Transgression*. Minneapolis: University of Minnesota Press.

Dahl, Bill. 1993. "The South: Tennessee, Alabama, Georgia, Virginia, the Carolinas." In *The Blackwell Guide to Soul Recordings*, edited by Robert Pruter, 230–263. Oxford: Blackwell.

David, Javier. 2012. "A League of Her OWN? Why Oprah's Cable Channel Is on the Brink." The Grio, May 9. Available at http://thegrio.com/2012/05/09/a-league-of -her-own-why-oprahs-cable-channel-is-on-the-blink.

Davis, Ossie. 1965. "On Malcolm X." In *The Autobiography of Malcolm X*, by Malcolm X and Alex Haley, 524–527. New York: Ballantine.

Dawson, Michael C. 1994. *Behind the Mule: Race and Class in African-American Politics*. Princeton, NJ: Princeton University Press.

Deford, Frank. 1968. "Push Comes to Shove." *Sports Illustrated*, April 15, pp. 34–39.

Denby, David. 1998. "Haunted by the Past." *New Yorker*, October 26–November 2, pp. 248–253.

Dickson, Johanna Saleh. 2002. *MOVE: Sites of Trauma*. New York: Princeton Architectural Press.

Digby, Joan. 1993. "From Walker to Spielberg: Transformations of 'The Color Purple.'" In *Novel Images: Literature in Performance*, edited by Peter Reynolds, 157–174. New York: Routledge.

Doane, Janice L., and Devon L. Hodges. 1987. *Nostalgia and Sexual Difference: The Resistance to Contemporary Feminism*. New York: Methuen.

Douglass, Frederick. (1845) 1997. *Narrative of the Life of Frederick Douglass*. New York: Signet Classics.

Du Bois, W.E.B. 1989. *The Souls of Black Folk*. New York: Bantam Books.

duCille, Anne. 1993. *The Coupling Convention: Sex, Text, and Tradition in Black Women's Fiction*. New York: Oxford University Press.

Dudley, David. 1991. *My Father's Shadow: Intergenerational Conflict in African American Men's Autobiography*. Philadelphia: University of Pennsylvania Press.

"East Final Fri. or Sun. if 76ers Win." 1968. *Philadelphia Daily News*, April 1, p. 54.

Easthope, Antony. 1990. *What a Man's Gotta Do: The Masculine Myth in Popular Culture*. Boston: Unwin Hyman.

Edwards, Harry. 1968. "Why Negroes Should Boycott Whitey's Olympics." *Saturday Evening Post*, March 9, pp. 6–10.

Ellison, Ralph. (1952) 1995. *Invisible Man*, 2nd ed. New York: Vintage International.

———. 1964. *Shadow and Act*. New York: Vintage.

Erikson, Kai T. 1994. *A New Species of Trouble: Explorations in Disaster, Trauma, and Community*. New York: Norton.

Eyerman, Ron. 2001. *Cultural Trauma: Slavery and the Formation of African American Identity*. Cambridge: Cambridge University Press.

Fanon, Frantz. 1966. *The Wretched of the Earth*. New York: Grove Press.

Farr, Cecilia Konchar. 2004. *Reading Oprah: How Oprah's Book Club Changed the Way America Reads*. Albany: State University of New York Press.

Farrell, Warren. 1979. *The Liberated Man*. New York: Bantam Books.

Fears, Darryl. 2008. "House Issues an Apology for Slavery." *Washington Post*, July 30. Available at http://articles.washingtonpost.com/2008-07-30/politics/36791322_1 _slavery-jim-crow-caucus-members.

Fiske, John. 1989. *Reading the Popular*. Boston: Unwin Hyman.

Frost, Robert. 1969. "The Death of the Hired Man." in *The Poetry of Robert Frost: The Collected Poems, Complete and Unabridged*, edited by Edward Connery Lathem, 34–39. Boston: Holt.

Garber, Marjorie B. 1992. *Vested Interests: Cross-Dressing and Cultural Anxiety*. New York: Routledge.

Gardiner, Judith Kegan. 2002. "Introduction." In *Masculinity Studies and Feminist Theory: New Directions*, edited by Judith Kegan Gardiner, 1–30. New York: Columbia University Press.

Gates, Henry Louis, Jr. 1984. "Criticism in the Jungle." In *Black Literature and Literary Theory*, edited by Henry Louis Gates, Jr., 1–26. New York: Methuen.

———. 1988. *The Signifying Monkey: A Theory of Afro-American Literary Criticism*. New York: Oxford University Press.

George, Nelson. 1988. *The Death of Rhythm and Blues*. New York: Pantheon Books.

Giddings, Robert, Keith Selby, and Chris Wensley. 1990. *Screening the Novel: The Theory and Practice of Literary Dramatization*. Basingstoke, UK: Palgrave Macmillan.

Gilgoff, Dan. 2007. *The Jesus Machine: How James Dobson, Focus on the Family, and Evangelical America Are Winning the Culture War*. New York: St. Martin's Press.

Gilroy, Paul. 1993. "Living Memory: A Meeting with Toni Morrison." In *Small Acts: Thoughts on the Politics of Black Cultures*, 175–182. London: Serpent's Tail.

Gleiberman, Owen. 1998. "Ghost Bluster." *Entertainment Weekly*, October 23, pp. 45–46.

Goode, W. Wilson, and Joann Stevens. 1992. *In Goode Faith*. Valley Forge, PA: Judson Press.

Gooding-Williams, Robert, ed. 1993. *Reading Rodney King/Reading Urban Uprising*. New York: Routledge.

Greater Philadelphia Film Office. n.d. "Welcome to GPFO." Available at http://www .film.org (accessed February 13, 2013).

Greater Philadelphia Tourism Marketing Corporation. n.d. "GPTMC's 15th Anniversary." Available at http://www.visitphilly.com/gptmc-15-years/ (accessed February 13, 2013).

Halbwachs, Maurice. 1992. *On Collective Memory*. Translated by Lewis A. Coser. Chicago: University of Chicago Press.

Haley, Alex. 1965. "Epilogue." In *The Autobiography of Malcolm X*, by Malcolm X and Alex Haley, 441–523. New York: Ballantine.

Harris, Trudier. 1990. "Native Sons and Foreign Daughters." In *New Essays on "Native Son,"* edited by Keneth Kinnamon, 63–84. New York: Cambridge University Press.

Harry, Margot. 1987. *"Attention, MOVE! This Is America."* Chicago: Banner Press.

Heller, Karen. 1998. "A Glitzy Gala for 'Beloved' Icon." *Philadelphia Inquirer*, October 10, p. A1.

Hemenway, Robert. 1980. *Zora Neale Hurston: A Literary Biography*. Urbana: University of Illinois Press.

Herman, Judith Lewis. 1992. *Trauma and Recovery*. New York: Basic Books.

Hirsch, Marianne. 1999. "Projected Memory: Holocaust Photographs in Personal and Public Fantasy." In *Acts of Memory: Cultural Recall in the Present*, edited by Mieke Bal, Jonathan V. Crewe, and Leo Spitzer, 3–23. Hanover, NH: University Press of New England.

Hogue, W. Lawrence. 1994. "The Limits of Modernity: Andrea Lee's *Sarah Phillips*." *MELUS* 19 (4): 75–90.

Hurston, Zora Neale. (1937) 1998. *Their Eyes Were Watching God*. New York: Harper-Collins.

———. (1942) 2010. *Dust Tracks on a Road: An Autobiography*. New York: HarperCollins.

Jackson, John A. 2004. *A House on Fire: The Rise and Fall of Philadelphia Soul*. New York: Oxford University Press.

Janofsky, Michael. 1994. "Mock Auction of Slaves: Education or Outrage?" *New York Times*, October 8. Available at http://www.nytimes.com/1994/10/08/us/mock-auction-of-slaves-education-or-outrage.html.

Johnson, James Weldon. (1912) 1989. *The Autobiography of an Ex-Colored Man*. New York: Vintage Books.

Johnson, William. 1968. "A Heavy Blow in a Windy City." *Sports Illustrated*, April 1, pp. 20–21.

Joyner, Will. 1998. "Staying Stubbornly True to a Writer's Vision." *New York Times*, October 18, sec. AR, p. 13.

Kaiser, Charles. 1988. *1968 in America: Music, Politics, Chaos, Counterculture, and the Shaping of a Generation*. New York: Weidenfeld and Nicolson.

Kapp, Isa. 1984. "The First Time Around: A Review of *Sarah Phillips*." *New Leader*, December 10, pp. 5–8.

King, Martin Luther, Jr. 1986a. "An Experiment in Love." In *A Testament of Hope: The Essential Writings of Martin Luther King, Jr.*, edited by James Melvin Washington, 16–20. San Francisco: Harper and Row.

———. 1986b. "I Have a Dream." In *A Testament of Hope: The Essential Writings of Martin Luther King, Jr.*, edited by James Melvin Washington, 217–220. San Francisco: Harper and Row.

———. 1986c. "Next Stop: The North." In *A Testament of Hope: The Essential Writings of Martin Luther King, Jr.*, edited by James Melvin Washington, 189–195. San Francisco: Harper and Row.

———. 1986d. "The Power of Nonviolence." In *A Testament of Hope: The Essential Writings of Martin Luther King, Jr.*, edited by James Melvin Washington, 12–16. San Francisco: Harper and Row.

———. 1986e. "Showdown for Nonviolence." In *A Testament of Hope: The Essential Writings of Martin Luther King, Jr.*, edited by James Melvin Washington, 64–74. San Francisco: Harper and Row.

———. 1986f. "Where Do We Go from Here?" In *A Testament of Hope: The Essential Writings of Martin Luther King, Jr.*, edited by James Melvin Washington, 245–252. San Francisco: Harper and Row.

———. 1986g. "Where Do We Go from Here: Chaos or Community?" In *A Testament of Hope: The Essential Writings of Martin Luther King, Jr.*, edited by James Melvin Washington, 555–633. San Francisco: Harper and Row.

Kinnamon, Keneth, ed. 1990. *New Essays on "Native Son."* New York: Cambridge University Press.

Kiser, Jack. 1968a. "Celtics Win . . . but Who Could Play Game at Time Like This?" *Philadelphia Daily News*, April 6, p. 30.

———. 1968b. "76er 'Corpse' Is Alive!" *Philadelphia Daily News*, April 2, p. 61.

LaCapra, Dominick. 1994. *Representing the Holocaust: History, Theory, Trauma.* Ithaca, NY: Cornell University Press.

———. 2001. *Writing History, Writing Trauma.* Baltimore: Johns Hopkins University Press.

Lady Sings the Blues. 1972. Directed by Sidney Furie. Paramount.

Larsen, Nella. (1928) 1986. *"Quicksand" and "Passing."* Edited by Deborah McDowell. New Brunswick, NJ: Rutgers University Press.

Lawler, Edward. 2002. "The President's House in Philadelphia: The Rediscovery of a Lost Landmark." *Pennsylvania Magazine of History and Biography* 106:5–95.

Lawrence, Ken. 2005. *The World According to Oprah: An Unauthorized Portrait in Her Own Words.* Kansas City, MO: Andrews McMeel.

Lazenby, Roland. 1996. *The NBA Finals: A Fifty Year Celebration.* Indianapolis, IN: Masters Press.

Lee, Andrea. (1984) 1993. *Sarah Phillips.* Boston: Northeastern University Press.

Lewis, Allen. 1968. "Dodgers Agree to Postponement." *Philadelphia Inquirer*, April 9, p. 26.

Lewis, David L. 1981. *When Harlem Was in Vogue.* New York: Knopf.

Lewis, Kelley Penfield. 2008. "The Trouble with Happy Endings: Conflicting Narratives in Oprah's Book Club." In *The Oprah Affect: Critical Essays on Oprah's Book Club*, edited by Cecilia Konchar Farr and Jaime Harker, 211–234. Albany: State University of New York Press.

Lippard, Lucy R. 1997. *The Lure of the Local: Senses of Place in a Multicentered Society.* New York: New Press.

Lu, Michael, Loretta Jones, Melton Bond, Kynna Wright, Maiteeny Pumpuang, Molly Maidenberg, Drew Jones, Craig Garfield, and Diane Rowley. 2010. "Where Is the F in MCH? Father Involvement in African-American Families." *Ethnicity and Disease* 20 (Winter): S2 49–S2 61.

Lynch, Wayne. 2002. *Season of the 76ers: The Story of Wilt Chamberlain and the 1967 NBA Champion Philadelphia 76ers.* Philadelphia: Dunne Books.

Lyotard, Jean-François. 1982. "Presenting the Unpresentable: The Sublime." *Artforum*, April, pp. 64–69.

MacClancy, Jeremy. 1996. *Sport, Identity and Ethnicity.* Oxford: Berg.

MacGregor, Jeff. 1998. "Inner Peace, Empowerment and Host Worship." *New York Times*, October 25, sec. AR, p. 30.

The Manchurian Candidate. 2004. Directed by Jonathan Demme. Paramount Pictures.

Manso, Peter. 1998. "Chronicle of a Tragedy Foretold." *New York Times*, July 19, sec. 6, pp. 32–37.

Marsh, Dave. 1989. *The Heart of Rock and Soul: The 1001 Greatest Singles Ever Made.* New York: Plume.

Marshall, P. David. 1997. *Celebrity and Power: Fame in Contemporary Culture.* Minneapolis: University of Minnesota Press.

Marshall, Paule. 1983. *Praisesong for the Widow.* New York: Penguin.

Massey, Doreen B. 1994. *Space, Place and Gender.* Cambridge: Polity Press.

McCormick, Adrienne. 2004. "Is This Resistance? African American Postmodernism in *Sarah Phillips*." *Callaloo* 27 (4): 808–828.

McFarlane, Brian. 1996. *Novel to Film: An Introduction to the Theory of Adaptation.* Oxford: Oxford University Press.

Meier, August. 1992. "On the Role of Martin Luther King." In *A White Scholar and the Black Community, 1945–1965: Essays and Reflections*, 212–222. Amherst: University of Massachusetts Press.

Menace II Society. 1993. Directed by Albert and Allen Hughes. New Line Cinema.

Metress, Christopher, ed. 2002. *The Lynching of Emmett Till: A Documentary Narrative.* Charlottesville: University of Virginia Press.

Morrison, Toni. (1970) 1994. *The Bluest Eye.* New York: Plume.

———. 1973. *Sula.* New York: Plume.

———. 1977. *Song of Solomon.* New York: Plume.

———. 1984. "Rootedness: The Ancestor as Foundation." In *Black Women Writers (1950–1980): A Critical Evaluation*, edited by Mari Evans, 339–345. New York: Doubleday.

———. 1987. *Beloved.* New York: Knopf.

———. 1990. "The Site of Memory." In *Out There: Marginalization and Contemporary Cultures*, edited by Russell Ferguson, Martha Gever, Trinh T. Minh-ha, and Cornel West, 299–305. Cambridge, MA: MIT Press.

Moynihan, Daniel Patrick. 1965. *The Negro Family: The Case for National Action.* Westport, CT: Greenwood Press.

Murphy, Meagan. 2011. "OWN Staffers Worried Cable Net Is Oprah Winfrey's Next 'Beloved'-Like Flop, Source Says." FoxNews.com, October 7. Available at http://www.foxnews.com/entertainment/2011/10/07/own-staffers-worried-cable-network-could-be-oprah-winfreys-next-beloved-source/.

Nash, Gary B. 2002. *First City: Philadelphia and the Forging of Historical Memory.* Philadelphia: University of Pennsylvania Press.

National Park Service. 2002. "Independence: National Historical Park." Available at http://www.cr.nps.gov/history/online_books/hh/17/hh17a.htm.

Naylor, Gloria. 1982. *The Women of Brewster Place.* New York: Penguin.

"NBA to Play Game as King Memorial." 1968. *Philadelphia Inquirer*, April 6, p. 30.

The Night James Brown Saved Boston. 2009. Directed by David Leaf. Shout Factory.

Obama, Barack. 2009. "A More Perfect Union." In *The Speech: Race and Barack Obama's "A More Perfect Union,"* edited by T. Denean Sharpley-Whiting, 237–251. New York: Bloomsbury Press.

O'Connor, Thomas H. 2001. *The Hub: Boston Past and Present.* Boston: Northeastern University Press.

Ogbu, John. 2008. "Multiple Sources of Peer Pressure among African American Students." In *Minority Status, Oppositional Culture and Schooling*, edited by John Ogbu, 89–111. New York: Routledge.

Oldenburg, Ann, and Kevin V. Johnson. 1998. "Oprah's Optimism Seems More Like Opportunism and Is Growing Oppressive, Opposition Says." *USA Today*, October 23, sec. Life, p. 4E.

Oprah Winfrey Presents: Their Eyes Were Watching God. 2005. Directed by Darnell Martin. Originally aired on ABC, March 6.

Orr, Christopher. 1984. "The Discourse on Adaptation." *Wide Angle* 6 (2): 72–76.

Otter, Samuel. 2010. *Philadelphia Stories: America's Literature of Race and Freedom.* New York: Oxford University Press.

Paolantonio, S. A. 1993. *Frank Rizzo: The Last Big Man in Big City America.* Philadelphia: Camino Books.

Paynter, Robert. 1994. "Afro-Americans in the Massachusetts Historical Landscape." In *The Politics of the Past,* edited by Peter Gathercote and David Lowenthal, 49–62. New York: Routledge.

Peacock, John. 1994. "Adapting *The Color Purple*: When Folk Goes Pop." In *Take Two: Adapting the Contemporary American Novel to Film,* edited by Barbara Tepa Lupack, 112–130. Bowling Green, KY: Bowling Green State University Popular Press.

Pendleton, Tonya. 1998. "Lights, Camera, Oprah! Winfrey Wows $250-a-Seat Crowd at Philly Premiere of Her 'Beloved.'" *Philadelphia Daily News,* October 10, p. 5.

Pereira, Malin. 2007. "Oprah's Book Club and the American Dream." In *The Oprah Phenomenon,* edited by Jennifer Harris and Elwood Watson, 191–206. Lexington: University Press of Kentucky.

Philadelphia. 1993. Directed by Jonathan Demme. Tristar Pictures.

Pluto, Terry. 1991. *Loose Balls: The Short, Wild Life of the American Basketball Association.* New York: Simon and Schuster.

Pomerantz, Gary M. 1993. *Wilt, 1962: The Night of 100 Points and the Dawn of a New Era.* New York: Three Rivers Press.

Radin, Margaret Jane. 1993. *Reinterpreting Property.* Chicago: University of Chicago Press.

Rampersad, Arnold. 1998. *Jackie Robinson: A Biography.* New York: Ballantine Books.

Reinhold, Meyer. 1971. "The Naming of Pygmalion's Animated Statue." *Classical Journal* 66 (4): 316–319.

Rickey, Carrie. 1998a. "Reality Check." *Philadelphia Inquirer,* November 23, sec. Lifestyle and Entertainment, pp. D5, D9.

———. 1998b. "Role Reversal." *Philadelphia Inquirer,* October 11, sec. Arts, p. F1.

Rojas, Fabio. 2007. *From Black Power to Black Studies: How a Radical Social Movement Became an Academic Discipline.* Baltimore: Johns Hopkins University Press.

Roots. 1977. Directed by David Greene, Marvin Chomsky, Gilbert Moses, and John Erman. ABC Television Network.

Rosenberg, Amy S. 2010. "Ex-Mayor Goode Says Tragic Day Was an 'Aberration' in His Life." *Philadelphia Inquirer,* May 12. Available at http://articles.philly.com/2010-05-12/news/24960352_1_move-tragedy-move-assault-wilson-goode.

Rubenstein, Roberta. 2001. *Home Matters: Longing and Belonging, Nostalgia and Mourning in Women's Fiction.* New York: Palgrave.

Rushdy, Ashraf. 1999. *Neo-Slave Narratives: Studies in the Social Logic of a Literary Form.* Oxford: Oxford University Press.

Russell, Bill, and William McSweeny. 1966. *Go Up for Glory.* New York: Coward-McCann.

Sachare, Alex. 1997. *100 Greatest Basketball Players of All Time.* New York: Preiss.

Salisbury, Stephan. 2002. "Discussing Slavery at Liberty Bell Site." *Philadelphia Inquirer,* April 25, p. 1.

Salisbury, Stephan, and Inga Saffon. 2002. "Echoes of Slavery at Liberty Bell Site." *Philadelphia Inquirer,* March 24, p. 1.

Schlesinger, Arthur M. 1992. *The Disuniting of America*. New York: Norton.

Schulman, Bruce. 2002. *The Seventies: The Great Shift in American Culture, Society, and Politics*. New York: Da Capo Press.

Schwarzbaum, Lisa. 1998. "Journey to Beloved." *Entertainment Weekly*, October 23. Available at http://www.ew.com/ew/article/0,,285345,00.html.

The Silence of the Lambs. 1991. Directed by Jonathan Demme. Orion Pictures.

Smith, Anna Deavere. 2002. *Twilight: Los Angeles, 1992*. New York: Dramatists Play Service.

Smith, Arthur L. 1970. "Editor's Message." *Journal of Black Studies* 1 (1): 3–4.

Smith, Valerie. 1989. "Black Feminist Theory and the Representation of the 'Other.'" In *Changing Our Own Words: Essays on Criticism, Theory, and Writing by Black Women*, edited by Cheryl A. Wall, 38–57. New Brunswick, NJ: Rutgers University Press.

Sontag, Susan. 2004. *Regarding the Pain of Others*. New York: Picador.

Sounder. 1972. Directed by Martin Ritt. Twentieth Century Fox.

Spillers, Hortense. 2000. "Mama's Baby, Papa's Maybe: An American Grammar Book." In *The Black Feminist Reader*, edited by Joy James and T. Denean Sharpley-Whiting, 57–87. Malden, MA: Blackwell.

Spitzer, Leo. 1999. "Back through the Future: Nostalgic Memory and Critical Memory in a Refuge from Nazism." In *Acts of Memory: Cultural Recall in the Present*, edited by Mieke Bal, Jonathan V. Crewe, and Leo Spitzer, 87–104. Hanover, NH: University Press of New England.

Steigerwald, David. 1995. *The Sixties and the End of Modern America*. New York: St. Martin's Press.

Stepto, Robert. 1979. *From behind the Veil*. Urbana: University of Illinois Press.

Sturken, Marita. 1997. *Tangled Memories: The Vietnam War, the AIDS Epidemic, and the Politics of Remembering*. Berkeley: University of California Press.

Sullivan, James. 2009. *The Hardest Working Man: How James Brown Saved the Soul of America*. New York: Gotham.

Taylor, John. 2005. *The Rivalry: Bill Russell, Wilt Chamberlain, and the Golden Age of Basketball*. New York: Random House.

Teaford, Jon C. 1993. *The Twentieth-Century American City*. Baltimore: Johns Hopkins University Press.

Their Eyes Were Watching God. 2005. Directed by Darnell Martin. Harpo Productions. DVD.

Thomas, Evan. 2008. "Alienated in the U.S.A." *Daily Beast*, March 12. Available at http://www.thedailybeast.com/newsweek/2008/03/12/alienated-in-the-u-s-a.html.

Thompson, Lisa. 2009. "Sex, Travel, and the Single African American Girl." In *Beyond the Black Lady: Sexuality and the New African American Middle Class*, 118–136. Urbana: University of Illinois Press.

"'Tragic' Death of Dr. King." 1968. *Philadelphia Daily News*, April 5, p. 4.

Tuan, Yi-Fu. 1977. *Space and Place: The Perspective of Experience*. Minneapolis: University of Minnesota Press.

Tucker, Ken. 2006. "Frey, Frey Again." *Entertainment Weekly*, February 3. Available at http://www.ew.com/ew/article/0,,1155909,00.html.

United States National Advisory Committee on Civil Disorders. 1968. *Report of the National Advisory Committee on Civil Disorders*. New York: Dutton.

Van Deburg, William L. 1997. *Black Camelot: African-American Culture Heroes in Their Times, 1960–1980.* Chicago: University of Chicago Press.

van der Kolk, Bessel A., and Onno van der Hart. 1995. "The Intrusive Past: The Flexibility of Memory and the Engraving of Trauma." In *Trauma: Explorations in Memory,* edited by Cathy Caruth, 158–182. Baltimore: Johns Hopkins University Press.

Vigderman, Patricia. 1985. "Review of *Sarah Phillips.*" *Boston Review,* February, p. 23.

Vincent, Rickey. 1996. *Funk: The Music, the People, and the Rhythm of the One.* New York: St. Martin's Griffin.

Von Bergen, Jane M. 1998. "In TV Spot, Oprah Loves Phila. Back." *Philadelphia Inquirer,* April 16. Available at http://articles.philly.com/1998-04-16/business/25765964_1 _commercial-campaign-tv-spot-rittenhouse-square.

Walker, Alice. 1992. *The Color Purple.* 10th anniversary ed. New York: Harcourt Brace Jovanovich.

Walker, Chet, and Chris Messenger. 1995. *Long Time Coming: A Black Athlete's Coming-of-Age in America.* New York: Grove Press.

Wallace, Michele. 1992. "Towards a Black Feminist Cultural Criticism." In *Cultural Studies,* edited by Lawrence Grossberg, Cary Nelson, and Paula A. Treichler, 654–663. New York: Routledge.

Ward, Brian. 1998. *Just My Soul Responding: Rhythm and Blues, Black Consciousness, and Race Relations.* Berkeley: University of California Press.

Washington, Mary Helen. 1985. "Young, Gifted and Black." *Women's Review of Books* 2 (6): 3–4.

———. 1998. "Foreword." In *Their Eyes Were Watching God,* ix–xvii. New York: HarperCollins.

Weigley, Russell Frank, Nicholas B. Wainwright, and Edwin Wolf, eds. 1982. *Philadelphia: A 300 Year History.* New York: Norton.

Werner, Craig Hansen. 1999. *A Change Is Gonna Come: Music, Race and the Soul of America.* New York: Plume.

Whalen, Thomas J. 2004. *Dynasty's End: Bill Russell and the 1968–69 World Champion Boston Celtics.* Boston: Northeastern University Press.

"What Is the Best Work of American Fiction of the Last 25 Years?" 2006. *New York Times Book Review,* May 21. Available at http://www.nytimes.com/2006/05/21/ books/fiction-25-years.html.

Wheat, Alynda. 2005. "Oprah Winfrey Presents: Their Eyes Were Watching God." *Entertainment Weekly,* March 2. Available at http://www.ew.com/ew/article/0,,1031439, 00.html.

Wiggins, David Kenneth. 1997. *Glory Bound: Black Athletes in a White America.* Syracuse, NY: Syracuse University Press.

Williams, Bernard. 1996. "The Politics of Trust." In *The Geography of Identity,* edited by Patricia Yaeger, 361–381. Ann Arbor: University of Michigan Press.

Williams, Otis, and Patricia Romanowski. 1989. *Temptations.* New York: Simon and Schuster.

Williams, Sherley Anne. 1985. "Sarah Phillips." *Ms. Magazine,* June, pp. 70–73.

Willis, Susan. 1989. *Specifying: Black Women Writing the American Experience.* Madison: University of Wisconsin Press.

Wilson, August. 1986. *Fences.* New York: New American Library.

Wilson, William J. 1978. *The Declining Significance of Race: Blacks and Changing American Institutions*. Chicago: University of Chicago Press.

Winfrey, Oprah, and Ken Regan. 1998. *Journey to Beloved*. New York: Hyperion.

Winter, Sylvia. 2006. "On How We Mistook the Map for the Territory . . . Black Studies toward the Human Project." In *A Companion to African-American Studies*, edited by Lewis R. Gordon and Jane Anna Gordon, 107–118. Malden, MA: Blackwell.

Witcover, Jules. 1997. *The Year the Dream Died: Revisiting 1968 in America*. New York: Warner Books.

The Women of Brewster Place. (1989) 2001. Directed by Donna Deitch. Xenon. DVD.

Wu, Yung-Hsing. 2008. "The Romance of Reading Like Oprah." In *The Oprah Affect: Critical Essays on Oprah's Book Club*, edited by Cecilia Konchar Farr and Jaime Harker, 73–88. Albany: State University of New York Press.

Yaeger, Patricia. 1996. "Introduction: Narrating Space." In *The Geography of Identity*, edited by Patricia Yaeger, 1–38. Ann Arbor: University of Michigan Press.

Young, Hershini Bhana. 2005. *Haunting Capital: Memory, Text, and the Black Diasporic Body*. Hanover, NH: Dartmouth University Press.

Young, James E. 2000. "Against Redemption: The Arts of Countermemory in Germany Today." In *Symbolic Loss: The Ambiguity of Mourning and Memory at Century's End*, edited by Peter Homans, 126–146. Charlottesville: University of Virginia Press.

Zweigenhalf, Richard, and G. William Domhoff. 1991. *Black in the White Establishment? A Study of Race and Class in America*. New Haven, CT: Yale University Press.

Index

ABC (network), 172, 178

Abt, Vicki, 164

affluent blacks, 116–117, 154

Afro-American literature, 125, 127, 156, 161; and black American literary tradition, 126, 158; and intertextuality, 140; and literary-critical circles, 157; narrative, 142–144

Afro-American studies, 2–4, 8, 18

Afrocentric tradition, 150

AIDS, 196, 200, 202; discrimination against people with, 201; hysteria over, 200

Aid to Dependent Children, 62

Ali, Muhammad, and decision to resist military induction, 31, 54

American Basketball Association (ABA), 35

American Dream, 6, 176–178

American exceptionalism, 181

American family, 83; post-1960s, 97

American materialism, 177

American racial uncanny, 216, 219

Angelou, Maya, 208

Ann Arbor, viii, 112–113

Arblaster, Anthony, 119–120

Asante, Molefi, 20; and *Journal of Black Studies*, 20

Atkins, Thomas, 59, 61

Atlantic Records, 88

Auerbach, Red, 37

Baker, Houston, 126, 142, 161; and *Blues, Ideology, and Afro-American Literature*, 126, 142

Bal, Mieke, 102

Baldwin, James, 135, 144; and *Go Tell It on the Mountain*, 135

Banderas, Antonio, 200

Bass, Amy, 27–28, 31, 33; and *Not the Triumph but the Struggle*, 27

Beamon, Bob, 30

Beloved (film), 21; commercial failure of, 164–167, 173–175, 177–178, 181–182, 194–196, 205, 212; compared to other Demme films, 196–205; and *Journey to Beloved*, 160, 163, 164, 165, 167, 169–170, 205, 208–210; and Morrison's views on historical truth, 167–169, 184; as record of events "too terrible to relate" versus narrative of "strength and courage," 171–172; and Winfrey as interpreter of black feminist literature, 176–194; Winfrey on her role in, 169–170, 172, 208–209; and Winfrey's worldview, 177, 182–184, 205–212

Beloved (Morrison): critical success of, 160, 175, 183; Winfrey's request to make film adaptation of, 160

Bennett, Andy, 98; and *Popular Music and Youth Culture*, 98

Berlin, 214

Berry, Halle, 179
A Better Chance (ABC), 69, 72
black American authenticity, 118, 156
black American condition, 139
black American heroism, 175
black American history, 173, 180
black American narrative thematic compulsions, 143
black American self-determination, 137, 184
black American suffering, 6, 22, 26, 173; exclusion and lack of freedom, 216; inferiority, 30, 154; oppression, 32; pain, 7, 8, 212
black American tradition, 128, 150
black American women's writing, 157; novels, 162, 176, 178, 182, 190–191
black athletes, 20, 30–32, 38–39, 43, 49, 50, 53–54, 66; male track and field stars, 30; professional basketball players, 51
black behavior and its representation, 175
black church, 115
black cinema, 174
black community, 3, 7, 12, 32, 38, 50, 52, 55–56, 77, 86, 88, 103, 119–121, 125, 146, 219; black families, 21, 26, 62, 74–77, 85–86, 103–105, 154, 177, 188
black cultural performance, 64, 150; and black expressivity, 64–65, 157
Black Entertainment Television, 174
black fatherhood, 21, 76, 79, 84, 87, 96–97
black female representation, 155
black female self-deception, 193
black feminists, 21, 163; black feminist literature, 176
Black Filmmakers Foundation, 174
black identity, 4–6, 9–10, 14–17, 22, 26, 40, 100, 104, 120–122, 126, 130, 158, 216, 218; jazz as representing, 150; post–civil rights, 9–10, 19, 25, 103, 109; and subjectivity, 19, 145
black male marginalization, 107
black masculinity, 21, 43, 60, 62, 80, 84–85, 87–90, 92, 95–97; and impoverished black male, 86, 97; and manhood, 60, 62–63, 85, 88; and manliness, 66. See also masculinity
black middle class, 101, 112, 115, 117–118, 120–123, 125, 145, 153–154, 157
black mothers, 85
black music, 102
Black Power movement, 3–4, 29, 41–42, 50, 61, 96, 105, 140; and black militancy, 3, 53–54, 85; and Black Panthers, 29, 42, 80; and Black Power salute, 30, 51, 53
Black Revolution, 87
black scholar community, 175
black sisterhood, 191
black social advancement, 30, 66, 104; activists for, 32; equality, 32, 145; freedom struggle, 51; resistance to, 50, 65; socioeconomic progress, 179
black studies, 2–4, 8, 18
black-themed space, 118
black utility heuristic, 115, 118–119, 121
black victimization, 174
black working class, 116–119, 154, 157
Boston, 50, 55–56, 58–59; Bean Town, 58; Boston Garden, 50, 58–59, 63–64; Roxbury, 56, 59; school system in, 53
Boym, Svetlana, 80–81, 83–84, 97, 99–100, 102
Brackett, David, 74; and Interpreting Popular Music, 74
Brinkley, David, 24
Brooks, Roy, 219; and Atonement and Forgiveness: A New Model for Black Reparations, 219
Brown, James, 21, 32, 50, 52, 58, 63–67, 75, 101; and concert in the Boston Garden, 32, 52, 65, 67; and "I Don't Want Nobody to Give Me Nothing," 52; and "Papa Don't Take No Mess," 75; and "Say It Loud—I'm Black and I'm Proud," 52
Brown, Rap, 52
Brown, William Wells, 57, 59, 61
Bulls, 41–42, 45
Burlein, Ann, 105–106
Butler, Jerry, 78; and "Only the Strong Survive," 78

Cane (Toomer), 140
Carlos, John, 31, 48–49, 51, 53
Carmichael, Stokely, 52, 65
Carter, Clarence, 86–88, 91–92, 95–96; and "Patches," 86–89, 91–93, 95–97
Caruth, Cathy, 19–20, 42
CBS Records, 102
Celtics, 32, 35–38, 43–45, 47, 50, 54, 58, 67
Chamberlain, Wilt, 28, 30, 35, 37–38, 43, 55, 66
chauvinism, racial and sexual, 101
Chicago, 179, 189–190
Chi-Lites, 75; and "The Man My Daddy Was," 75

Christianity, 129, 131–133, 151, 188; and the Bible, 128, 130, 150; and Christ, 129–132, 135; and Judeo-Christian traditions, 151
civil rights movement, 2, 14, 18–19, 27, 41, 44, 46, 60, 67, 76, 96, 101, 112, 122, 154, 157, 201, 214; and black American freedom struggle, 3, 201; and black American integration, 5, 157
Civil War, 141
Cleaver, Eldridge, 85; and Soul on Ice, 85
Clinton, George, 123
Cohen, Keith, 186–187, 191
Coleman, Christy S., 170–171, 173
collective memory, 11, 203; black American, vii, x
Colonial Williamsburg's African-American Interpretation and Presentations unit, 170–171
Connor, Bull, 24
Cooke, Sam, 51; and "A Change Is Gonna Come," 51
Cornelius Brothers and Sister Rose, 78; and "Too Late to Turn Back Now," 78
Cornelius, Don, 73; and Soul Train, 73
Cose, Ellis, 118
Cowley, Malcolm, 136
Cresswell, Tim, 19
Cunningham, Billy, 35

Dahl, Bill, 88; and Blackwell Guide to Soul Recordings, 88
Daily Pennsylvanian, viii
David, Javier, 212
Davis, Ossie, 62, 65–66
Dawson, Michael, 114–115, 118–120, 122, 146; and Behind the Mule, 114
Declaration of Independence, 26, 28, 57, 166
Deford, Frank, 37
Demme, Jonathan, 21, 163–166, 172, 177, 180, 194–196, 200, 203–205; and The Manchurian Candidate, 196, 203–204; and Philadelphia, 165, 196, 200–203; and Silence of the Lambs, 196, 197–200, 204
Denby, David, 194–196, 199, 204
Detroit, 77, 100
Dickens, Charles, 187, and Oliver Twist, 187
Dickson, Johanna, 109–110
Digby, Joan, 185–186
discrimination: against blacks, 17, 25–26, 30, 53, 75, 217; against people with AIDS, 200–201

Doane, Janice, 83–85
Dobson, James, 105–107
Douglass, Frederick, 16–17, 57, 140, 141; and Narrative, 141
Du Bois, W.E.B., 5, 15, 17, 31, 76, 150; and The Philadelphia Negro, 76; and The Souls of Black Folk, 5
Dudley, David, 86

Easthope, Antony, 88–90, 93; and "masculine myth," 88, 90–92, 94; and What a Man's Gotta Do, 88
Ebony, 66
Edwards, Harry, 28, 30–32, 66; and the Olympic Project for Human Rights (OPHR), 28, 31–32; and "Why Negroes Should Boycott Whitey's Olympics," 28
Elise, Kimberly, 165
Ellison, Ralph, 160, 219
Entertainment Weekly, 177
Erikson, Kai, 10–11, 119
Evans, Lee, 30, 32
Eyerman, Ron, 10; and Cultural Trauma: Slavery and the Formation of African American Identity, 10

family. See nuclear family
Fanon, Frantz, 4, 140, 154; and The Wretched of the Earth, 4
Farr, Cecilia, 176
Farrell, Warren, 93
fatherhood. See black fatherhood
father songs, 77, 89, 91–107
Faulkner, William, 219
feminism, 81–83, 98, 104, 106
Fifteenth Amendment, 16
Fiske, John, 114; and Reading the Popular, 114
Focus on the Family, 105–106
formulations of blackness, 114, 126, 144, 148, 155, 158
Foster, Jodie, 197, 199
Founding Fathers, ix, 201, 211
Franklin, Aretha, 70; and "Till You Come Back to Me," 70
Franklin, Benjamin, 69, 166
Freedom Riders, 50
Freud, Sigmund, 84, 86, 214

Gamble, Kenny, 73–74, 77–78, 97–99, 101–102, 104, 107; and notion of family, 105–107

Gandhi, Mohandas K., 36
Garber, Marjorie, 92
Gardiner, Judith Kegan, 84; and *Masculinity Studies and Feminist Theory*, 84
Garrity, W. Arthur, Jr., 53
Gates, Henry Louis, Jr., 17, 126, 218; and *The Signifying Monkey*, 126–127
Gaye, Marvin, 46–47, 49–50, 52, 76; and "Save the Children," 49; and *What's Going On*, 49
gender roles, 86–87, 99, 103–107
George, Nelson, 58, 65, 98, 101; and *The Death of Rhythm and Blues*, 98
Giddings, Robert, 192
Gladys Knight and the Pips, 75; and "Daddy Could Swear, I Declare," 75
Gleiberman, Owen, 195–196, 205
Glenn, Scott, 197
Glover, Danny, 165, 172, 195
Goode, W. Wilson, 109–111, 113–114; and *In Goode Faith*, 113; as Philadelphia's first black mayor, 109, 113–114
Goode, W. Wilson, Jr., 112
Gordy, Berry, 77
Governor Dummer Academy (GDA), 69, 71–72
Graham, Billy, 36
Greater Philadelphia Film Office, 165
Great Society, 2, 80, 96–97
Green, Bill, 110
Greer, Hal, 35, 43, 46

Halbwachs, Maurice, 11–14, 17
Hamilton, Lisa Gay, 195
Hanks, Tom, 200
The Hardest Working Man: How James Brown Saved the Soul of America (Sullivan), 50
Harlem Renaissance, 124, 140
Harvard University Graduate School of Business report on the music business, 101–102
Havlicek, John, 35
Hayes, Bob, 29
Heller, Karen, 166
Hemenway, Robert, 179
Herman, Judith, 6, 8–9, 44
Hines, Jim, 53
hip-hop culture, 6
Hirsch, Marianne, 12
Hodges, Devon, 83–85
Hopkins, Anthony, 197

Howell, Bailey, 35, 47
Hudlin, Warrington, 174–175
Huff, Leon, 77–78, 98, 102
Hughes, Langston, 138, 157, 194; and "A Dream Deferred," 194
Humphrey, Hubert, 49, 52, 65
Huntley, Chet, 24
Hurston, Zora Neale, 124, 134–135, 167, 178–182, 191, 193; and *Dust Tracks on a Road*, 179; and *Their Eyes Were Watching God*, 134–135, 141, 162, 178–184, 189, 193–194, 212

Impressions, 51; and "This Is My Country," 51
Imus, Don, x
intertextuality, 126, 129–151, 155–158; hyperintertextuality, 135, 140
Intruders, 76, 79, 82, 104; and "I'll Always Love My Mama," 76–81, 104; and *Save the Children*, 76–77

Jackson 5, 78; and "I Found That Girl," 78
Jacobs, Harriet, 141
Jefferson, Thomas, 57, 166
Jim Crow, 6, 9–10, 13, 15, 24, 39, 44, 120, 142, 211, 219
John, Elton, 72–74; and "Philadelphia Freedom," 72–74
Johnson, James Weldon, 125; and *Autobiography of an Ex-Colored Man*, 125
Johnson, Kevin V., 189–190
Johnson, Lyndon, 33, 36
Johnson, Rafer, 29
Johnson, Robert L., 174–175
Jones, Gayl, 161
Jones, Sam, 35
Jones, Wally, 37–38
Joyner, Will, 203

Kaiser, Charles, 37; and *1968 in America*, 37
Kapp, Isa, 124
Karenga, Ron, 87
Kennedy, John F., assassination of, 24, 33–34, 36–37
Kennedy, Robert, 58
Kerner Commission Report, 56
King, Billie Jean, 72
King, Martin Luther, Jr., vii, x, 2–6, 12, 15–17, 24–27, 29, 32–33, 36, 38, 43, 45–48, 52, 55, 57–63, 65, 67, 73, 85, 105–106, 114,

144, 171, 201; assassination of, 2, 6, 9, 20, 24–25, 27, 29–30, 32–38, 41, 43–46, 49–50, 52–56, 59–61, 63, 66–67, 76, 100, 103–104, 115, 119, 140; and "I Have a Dream" speech, 24, 144–145; as integrationist, 2; and Montgomery bus boycott, 201; and 1963 March on Washington, 55, 144–145; nonviolent philosophy of, 59–62; and "The Power of Nonviolence," 60; and "Showdown for Nonviolence," 61

King, Rodney, 6, 12, 14

Kiser, Jack, 35, 37–38

Koppett, Leonard, 50

Kristeva, Julia, 135

LaCapra, Dominick, 7–10, 12; on "retraumatization," 10; and *Writing History, Writing Trauma*, 7

Larsen, Nella, 125, 134, 136–138, 154–156; and *Quicksand*, 125, 134–136, 155, 157

Lawler, Edward, Jr., 214; and "The President's House in Philadelphia: The Rediscovery of a Lost Landmark," 214

Lazenby, Roland, 37

Led Zeppelin, 70–73; and "Stairway to Heaven," 70, 73

Lee, Andrea, 17, 21, 112, 121–122, 124–126, 128–129, 131–132, 135–136, 139–140, 142–147, 149–150, 152–158. *See also Sarah Phillips* (Lee)

Lester, Julius, 2, 6

Levert, Eddie, 104, 106–107

Levert, Gerald, 104

Lewis, David Levering, 136; and *When Harlem Was in Vogue*, 136

liberal individualism, 120

Lincoln, Abraham, 24, 57, 209; and Emancipation Proclamation, 209

Linden, George, 193

Lippard, Lucy, 18

Lipsyte, Robert, 32

Lombard, Kenneth, 173

Louis, Joe, 32

Lynch, Wayne, 37, 53

Lyotard, Jean-François, 151–152, 155; and "Presenting the Unpresentable: The Sublime," 151

MacClancy, Jeremy, 33

MacGregor, Jeff, 206–207; and "Inner Peace, Empowerment and Host Worship," 206

Macherey, Pierre, 135

Magic Johnson Theaters, 173

Major League Baseball, 35

Malcolm X, 49, 62, 65

Mansour, George, 173

Marsh, Dave, 88

Marshall, Paule, 138–141, 147, 149–150, 210; and *Praisesong for the Widow*, 138, 145, 147

Marshall, P. David, 210–212; and *Celebrity and Power: Fame in Contemporary Culture*, 210

Martin, Trayvon, 12

masculinity: and masculine biases, 101; and masculine formulations of themed space, 152; and "masculine myth," 84, 88, 90–92, 94; and masculine privilege, 82; and nostalgia for traditional patriarchy, 62, 76, 80, 82–107, 190–191; and phallus as symbol of male power, 89–90

Massey, Doreen, 18

matriarchy: as detrimental to the family, 62, 75, 104; myth of, 101

Mayfield, Curtis, 52

McFarlane, Brian, 164, 180, 193; and *Novel to Film*, 164

Meier, August, 2

Memphis, 100

Miller, Randall, 215

monumentality, 99–101; black discursive, 100–101

Morrison, Toni, 87, 89–90, 122–124, 134, 143–144, 150, 156, 160–161, 163–164, 167–169, 171, 173, 175, 177, 182–184, 196, 205, 208–209, 211, 216; and *The Bluest Eye*, 87, 89, 94, 123, 134–135, 144, 161–162; and *Jazz*, 161; and "The Site of Memory," 167, 169, 196; and *Song of Solomon*, 177; and *Sula*, 144. *See also Beloved* (film); *Beloved* (Morrison)

Mother Father Sister Brother (MFSB), 73, 77, 97

Motown, 72, 76, 78, 88, 100

MOVE, 109–113; bombing of residence of, 109–111; and *MOVE: Sites of Trauma*, 109

Moynihan, Daniel Patrick, 62, 75–76, 85–86, 107

Moynihan Report, 21, 62, 75, 77, 85–86, 89

Murphy, Meagan, 212

NAACP, 166, 170

Nash, Gary, 15

National Basketball Association (NBA), 34–36, 38–39, 42–44, 54; and threatened All-Star boycott, 39, 46
National Collegiate Athletic Association (NCAA), 33
National Football League, 34–35
National Guard, 59
National Park Service, 214–215
Nation of Islam, 42
Naylor, Gloria, 162, 167, 185, 192–194; and *Daughters of the Dust*, 162; and *Mama Day*, 167; and *The Women of Brewster Place*, 162, 167, 185, 191–193
Newton, Thandie, 165
New Yorker, 122, 157
New York Times Book Review, 160, 175
The Night James Brown Saved Boston (film), 50
1960s: revolutions of, 106; riots of, 38, 55–57, 61–62, 64, 67
Nixon, Richard, 33, 49, 52
nostalgia, 80–84, 86–87, 103; racial, 101; restorative, 102–103; for traditional patriarchy, 62, 76, 80, 82–107, 190–191
nuclear family, 71, 74, 80, 86–87, 106; as heterosexual family, 86, 91; as ideal American family, 71–72
Nutter, Michael, 220

Obama, Barack, 22, 216–220; and "A More Perfect Union," 22, 216–220
Obama, Michelle, 218
O'Connor, Thomas, 56
Ogbu, John, 119
O'Jays, 21, 51, 70–72, 74, 84, 86–87, 97, 103; and "Family Reunion," 21, 51, 71–72, 84, 86–87, 97, 102, 104, 106–107; and "I Love Music," 97; and "Stairway to Heaven," 71, 97; and "Unity," 97
Oldenburg, Ann, 189–190
Olympics, 30–31, 51, 53, 66; and Black Power salute, 48, 53, 80; 1968 boycott of, 20, 28–31, 33, 49, 51, 53–54, 66
oppression, 103, 148, 187
Orr, Christopher, 182, 191
Osage Avenue, 109, 111, 113
Otter, Samuel, 19; and *Philadelphia Stories*, 19
Owens, Jesse, 29, 32

paternal abandonment, 71–72, 76, 78, 80, 86, 87, 104, 129

patriarchy, 21, 76, 87–88, 96, 98–99, 101, 104; black, 87, 100, 116; conservative patriarchal reformation, 106; patriarchal family, 72, 76, 80, 86, 100, 105, 116
Paynter, Robert, 74; and "Afro-Americans in the Massachusetts Historical Landscape," 74
Peacock, John, 185–186
Pendleton, Tonya, 183
Penn, William, 57
Pennsylvania Utilities Commission, 110
Pereira, Malin, 176–178
phallic weakness/lack, 87, 89, 90–91
Philadelphia, vii–xi, 219–220; Art Museum in, 215; and *Beloved* film, 162–163, 164–166, 182, 205–206; black Philadelphians, 15–17, 112, 149; Boston-Philadelphia rivalry, 28; Center City, ix; City Hall in, 201; as City of Brotherly Love, vii, 18, 22, 56, 165, 201–203, 214, 220; and conflict with MOVE, 109–114; Constitution Center in, 22, 113, 216; and the Eagles, 49; as First City, x, 15, 17–19, 21–22, 69, 73, 114, 116, 162, 201, 214; Independence Hall in, 56–57, 166, 214; Independence Mall, 215; Independence Park, ix; Independence Square, 57, 67; Liberty Bell in, 28, 57, 67, 69, 214–215; Logan Square, 214; Main Line, 21, 112, 124, 145; migration of blacks to, 55–56; migration of whites from, 117; North, 131; Obama's reference to, 216–217; Old City, 166; in *Philadelphia* film, 200–202; and the Phillies, 34; President's House in, 214, 215–216; as represented in *Sarah Phillips*, 21, 112, 124, 135, 137, 143, 145, 149, 153; Riverview Cineplex in, 163, 165–166; and the 76ers, 29, 32–33, 35–38, 40–47, 50, 53, 55, 58, 67; and SNCC raid, 42; and the Sound of Philadelphia, 71, 77, 83; South, viii–ix, 18, 55, 69; Spectrum in, 33, 38, 46, 49, 54, 57; as symbolic site, 15–16, 18–20, 22, 26–27, 29
Philadelphia (film), 196, 200–203, 204
Philadelphia (magazine), 165
Philadelphia Daily News, 183
Philadelphia Inquirer, 110, 166, 172, 215
Philadelphia International Records (PIR), 21, 73, 76–78, 98–102, 104, 107
Philadelphia: Neighborhoods, Division, and Conflict in a Postindustrial City (Adams et al.), 116
Philly Soul, 73

Pickett, Wilson, 101
Pinkenson, Sharon, 165–166
Players' Association, 47
politics of identity, 114
Pope Paul VI, 36
post–civil rights era: black identity in, 5–6,
    9–11, 12–17, 19–20, 27; class division of,
    118–119; conceptions of manhood in, 66,
    88; family in, 73, 106; integration in, 21
Powelton Village, 109
Princeton, 161
Pro-slavery riot of 1834, 38
"psychic needs," 174–175

Quakers, 69

race relations: American, 4, 137; and inte-
    gration, 2–3, 5, 21, 34, 40, 43, 50, 80, 102,
    104–105, 109, 124, 143, 157; after King
    assassination, 26–27, 29–65, 66–67; Oba-
    ma's view on, 22, 216–220; shift in, 115–
    119
racial discourse, 49, 88, 99–100, 132–133, 142
racial identity, 4, 5–11, 14–20, 22, 33–34,
    218, 225n3; collective, 114–115, 119, 120–
    122, 124, 130, 156–157; and Founding
    Fathers, 216; and gender, 86–87, 90, 92,
    95, 104, 107; after King assassination, 25–
    26, 40, 43, 52, 100, 103; and MOVE bomb-
    ing, 109; and Olympic boycott, 31; in Sarah
    Phillips, 121–122, 124, 126, 130, 156–157;
    and self-hatred, 123
racism, 25, 29, 31–32, 39–41, 53–54, 61–62,
    65, 74, 85, 88, 90, 103, 105, 170, 179, 191;
    and emasculation of black men, 89–91,
    179; impact of, on black family, 75–76,
    87–99, 104–107; and racial oppression,
    7–10, 13, 19, 20, 41, 80, 99, 126, 142, 176;
    as segregation, 24–26, 29, 65; as stereotyp-
    ing, 138, 186; as systemic black American
    degradation, 13, 101; and violence, 59–65,
    67; white view of black criminality and
    inferiority, 118
Radin, Margaret Jane, 44
Ramsay, Jack, 28, 48, 53
R&B, 73, 161; as black American expressiv-
    ity, 64–65, 99; and capacity for profound-
    ness, 70–71; and emphasis on family, 74,
    75–76, 80, 83–84, 87, 92–93, 96, 99; explo-
    rations of social issues in, 75, 87; male
    pain in, 87, 101–102, 104

Reconstruction, 141
Regan, Ken, 165
Rendell, Ed, 166, 201
Report of the National Advisory Committee
    on Civil Disorders, 27
Reserve Officers' Training Corps (ROTC),
    53
Richards, Beah, 165
Richards, Dean, 189
Rickey, Carrie, 172–174, 176
Rizzo, Frank, 28, 35, 42, 56, 112, 220
Robinson, Jackie, 34
Roeper, Richard, 190
Rojas, Fabio, 2, 5; and From Black Power to
    Black Studies, 2
Rosenberg, Amy, 110, 112
Rubenstein, Roberta, 75, 81–82; and Home
    Matters, 75
Rushdy, Ashraf, 100
Russell, Bill, 28, 30, 37–38, 54–55

Salisbury, Stephan, 215
Sarah Phillips (Lee), 17, 21, 112; cover art
    of, 127–129, 131, 151; critical unpopular-
    ity of, 123–127, 157–158; and cultural
    "rootedness," 156; and intertextuality, 129,
    134–151; and resistance to collective black
    American identity, 121–127, 129–134,
    137–151, 152, 155–158; role of religion in,
    128–135, 139–140, 149–151
Scenes of Instruction (Awkward), viii
Schlesinger, Arthur, 14, 17; and The Disunit-
    ing of America, 14
school integration, 21, 25, 40, 143, 154, 157
Schulman, Bruce, 93
Schutzer, Linda, 166
Schwarzbaum, Lisa, 209–210
Scott-Heron, Gil, 77
Seesholtz, Mel, 164
segregation, 24–26, 29, 65
Selby, Keith, 192
sexism, 62, 75–76, 83–84, 101, 104, 134, 155,
    191
Shakespeare, William, 194; and A Midsum-
    mer Night's Dream, 194
"The Shameless World of Phil, Sally, and
    Oprah: Television Talk Shows and the
    Deconstruction of Society" (Abt and
    Seesholtz), 164
Shay, Jonathan, 110
Sigma Studios, 77

Simon, Paul, 77; and "Mother and Child Reunion," 77
Simone, Nina, 51; and "Young, Gifted, and Black," 51
slavery: and black American trauma, 6–7, 9–10, 13–15, 20, 24, 26, 120–121, 141–142, 145, 156, 184, 194–196, 219; and black athletes as property, 44–45; Christian doctrines to rationalize, 128, 151; as depicted in *Beloved* film, 21–22, 173–176, 177–178, 181–182, 196, 205, 207–208, 212; and George Washington, 214–216, 220; impact of, on black family, 75–76; and Michelle Obama, 218; neo-slave narratives, 101; as opposed to American ideals, 13–16, 18–20, 101; and reenactment of slave auctions, 170–171, 172; slave heroism, 173–175; slave narrators, 196; Winfrey's views on, 169–170, 171–173, 189, 191, 205, 211
Smith, Arthur L., 20; and *Journal of Black Studies*, 20
Smith, Tommie, 28, 30–32, 48–49, 51, 53
Smith, Valerie, 122–123, 128; and *Changing Our Own Words*, 122
Smokey Robinson and the Miracles, 93; and "The Tears of a Clown," 93; and "Tracks of My Tears," 93
Sontag, Susan, 181
Southern Christian Leadership Conference (SCLC), 29, 36, 61
Spartacus (film), 174
Spielberg, Steven, 163, 174, 176, 185–190; and *Amistad*, 174, 176
Spillers, Hortense, 85–86
Spinners, 75; and "Sadie," 75
Spitzer, Leo, 103
Sports Illustrated, 37
Springsteen, Bruce, 202; and "The Streets of Philadelphia," 202
Stax, 72, 100
Steigerwald, David, 4, 38
Stepto, Robert, 126; and *From Behind the Veil*, 126
Street, John, 215
Stuart, Andrea, 186
Student Nonviolent Coordinating Committee (SNCC), 29, 42
Sullivan, James, 50; and *The Hardest Working Man*, 50

Tate, James, 35, 56, 58
Taylor, John, 28; and *The Rivalry*, 28
Temple University Family Reunion Institute, 71
Temptations, 52, 65–67, 70, 86–88, 93, 95–97, 149; and "I Wish It Would Rain," 93; and "Masterpiece," 96–97, 149; and "Papa Was a Rolling Stone," 86–89, 95–97
terrorist attacks of September 11, 2001, 33
Till, Emmett, 13
trauma, racial, 6–11, 214, 218–219; and black athletes, 42–44, 66–67; as depicted in *Beloved* film, 21–22, 173, 176, 196, 204–205, 212; hesitation to address, 7–8; and King assassination, 9–10, 20–21, 26, 43, 66–67, 119; and memory, 9, 11–17; and MOVE bombing, 109–112; as reflected in R&B music, 21, 80; and *Sarah Phillips*, 21, 145, 156; scholars of, 7, 183; studies of, 6–8, 20; traumatized black subjectivity, 11, 18–19, 122, 126, 156–158; violence as manifestation of, 6–7
Tuan, Yi-Fu, 19
Tubman, Harriet, 13
Tucker, Ken, 177
Turner, Nat, 174–175

Uncle Tom, 65–66
Underground Railroad, 181
University of Michigan, 162, 167
University of Pennsylvania, viii, 111, 162

Van Deburg, William, 54, 64
van der Hart, Onno, 44–45, 183
van der Kolk, Bessel, 44–45, 183
Vigderman, Patricia, 124
Vincent, Rickey, 123

Walker, Alice, 163, 176, 185–188, 190–191; and *The Color Purple*, 162–164, 177, 184–186, 188, 190–191, 208–209
Walker, Chet, 20, 28, 38–50, 52–55, 58, 63, 65–67, 76; and *Long Time Coming: A Black Athlete's Coming-of-Age in America*, 28, 38
Wallace, George, 24
Wallace, Michele, 162–163, 175–176; and "Towards a Black Feminist Cultural Criticism," 175
Ward, Brian, 77, 88, 101–102; and *Just My Soul Responding*, 101

Washington, Denzel, 200–201, 203
Washington, George, 22, 166, 214–216, 220
Washington, Mary Helen, 122, 125–126, 155, 178–179
Wensley, Chris, 192
Werner, Craig, 98–99; and *A Change Is Gonna Come*, 98
West, Dorothy, 176
Whalen, Thomas, 55; and *Dynasty's End*, 55
Wheat, Alynda, 180–181
White, Kevin, 52, 55–56, 58–59, 63, 67
white hegemony, 145
white police, 38, 55, 64
Whitfield, Norman, 96
Wiggins, David, 30
Williams, Bernard, 114, 120; and "The Politics of Trust," 114, 120
Williams, Otis, 65–66
Williams, Sherley Anne, 122–123, 124, 158
Willis, Susan, 122–123
Wilson, August, 91; and *Fences*, 91
Wilson, William Julius, 21, 115–118; and *The Declining Significance of Race*, 21
Winfrey, Oprah, 21, 160–163, 165–185, 189–193, 195–196, 203–210; and Harpo Studios, 162, 167, 172, 179, 209; and *Journey to Beloved*, 160, 163–165, 167, 169, 205, 208–212; and *O* magazine, 211; and Oprah's Book Club, 164, 177, 182; and Oprah Winfrey Network (OWN), 206, 212; and *Oprah Winfrey Presents: Their Eyes Were Watching God*, 178, 180, 182; and *Oprah Winfrey Show*, 176, 193, 205, 208; as "Queen of Trash," 160, 165, 190
Wirtz, Arthur, 41, 45
Witcover, Jules, 34; and *The Year the Dream Died: Revisiting 1968 in America*, 34
women's liberation, 21, 85, 99
Woodward, Joanne, 200–201
World War II, 116, 223n9
Wright, Jeffrey, 203
Wright, Jeremiah, 22, 217–219
Wright, Richard, 125, 144, 176; and *Black Boy*, 125, 140; and *Native Son*, 140, 144, 176

X, Malcolm, 49, 62, 65

Yaeger, Patricia, 117, 121–122, 131
Yarborough, Richard, 122
Young, Hershini Bhana, 114; and *Haunting Capital*, 114
Young, James E., 214

Michael Awkward, Gayl A. Jones Professor of Afro-American Literature and Culture at the University of Michigan, is the author, most recently, of *Burying Don Imus: Anatomy of a Scapegoat* and *Soul Covers: Rhythm and Blues Remakes and the Struggle for Artistic Identity.*